Y0-CKP-774

ACTA UNIVERSITATIS UPSALIENSIS
Studia Oeconomiae Negotiorum
35

Lars Engwall and Elving Gunnarsson

editors

MANAGEMENT STUDIES IN AN ACADEMIC CONTEXT

Uppsala 1994

ACTA UNIVERSITATIS UPSALIENSIS
Studia Oeconomiae Negotiorum
35

Lars Engwall and Elving Gunnarsson

editors

MANAGEMENT STUDIES IN AN ACADEMIC CONTEXT

McK
HD
30.4
.M3
1994

Uppsala 1994

Abstract

Engwall, L. and Gunnarsson, E. (eds.), Management Studies in an Academic Context. Acta Universitatis Upsaliensis. *Studia Oeconomiae Negotiorum* 35. 208 pp. Uppsala. ISBN 91-554-3238-7.

The purpose of this volume is to place academic management studies in an international and historical context. The book presents empirical evidence from Germany, Japan, the Netherlands, Norway, Sweden and the United States. An introductory chapter looks at management studies in a number of different perspectives, while a concluding chapter examines the role of formal knowledge in management education.

Lars Engwall and Elving Gunnarsson, Department of Business Studies, Box 513, Uppsala University, S-751 20 Uppsala, Sweden.

Published with support from the Swedish Council for Research in the Humanities and Social Sciences.

ISSN 0586-884X
ISBN 91-554-3238-7

© The authors

Printed in Sweden by
Motala Grafiska AB, 1994

Distributor: Almqvist & Wiksell International, Stockholm, Sweden

Table of Contents

List of Figures	9
List of Tables	10
The Authors	11

Chapter 1 Perspectives on Management Studies   13
Lars Engwall and Elving Gunnarsson, Uppsala University, Sweden

1.1 Eight Portraits of Academic Management Studies	13
1.2 Comparing the Development of Academic Management Education in Different Contexts—Some Problems	18
1.3 Composition of the Programmes	20
1.4 Attitudes in the Academic Community	23
1.5 Attitudes in the Business Community	24
1.6 Concluding Remarks	26

Chapter 2 Anders Berch: A Frontrunner   33
Sven-Eric Liedman, Gothenburg University, Sweden

2.1 Anders Berch—His First Thirty Years	33
2.2 Economic Science at the Universities	34
2.3 Anders Berch after his Dissertation	36
2.3.1 The Professorship	36
2.3.2 Anders Berch's Scientific Production	38
2.3.3 Anders Berch's Academic Teaching	40
2.3.4 Ploughs	41
2.4 The Decline of Economic Science at the University	43

Chapter 3 Anders Berch's Followers. The Development of Modern Academic Business Studies in Sweden   45
Lars Engwall, Uppsala University, Sweden

3.1 Introduction	45
3.2 Institutions	45
3.3 Curricula	51
3.4 Research	54
3.4.1 Evaluations of Professorial Candidates	55
3.4.2 Doctoral Dissertations	57
3.4.3 Conclusion	59
3.5 Graduate Diffusion	59
3.6 Conclusions	62

Chapter 4 Business Administration in Norway 1936-1990   66
Rolv Petter Amdam, Norwegian Scool of Management, Sandvika, Norway,
Carl Julius Norstrøm, Norwegian School of Economics and Business Administration, Bergen, Norway

  4.1 Introduction   66
  4.2 The First Academic Business School in Norway   67
      4.2.1 The Institution   67
      4.2.2 A Survey of the First Ten Years   67
      4.2.3 A Sketch of the Development since the
            Second World War   72
  4.3 The Second Norwegian Business School   73
      4.3.1 A Follower?   73
      4.3.2 Two Business Schools During the 1960s   75
  4.4 The Formation of a New System of Business Education   76
      4.4.1 A New Strategy   76
      4.4.2 Education Abroad   77
      4.4.3 Changes in Business Education   79
      4.4.4 Recent Developments   80
  4.5 Conclusion   81

Chapter 5 Academic Management Education in the Netherlands   84
Huibert de Man, Open University of the Netherlands,
Heerlen and Luchien Karsten, State University Groningen

  5.1 Introduction   84
  5.2 The Rise of the Management Professions (1890-1940)   85
      5.2.1 Up to the First World War (1890-1918)   85
          5.2.1.1 Background   85
          5.2.1.2 Accountants   86
          5.2.1.3 Engineers   87
      5.2.2 First World War   88
      5.2.3 The Interwar Years (1918-1940)   89
          5.2.3.1 Management Consultants   89
          5.2.3.2 The Academization of Accounting: Business
               Economics   90
          5.2.3.3 Psychotechnics   92
      5.2.4 Interpretation: The Dutch Heritage   93
  5.3 New Management Ideas and the Reconstruction of the
      Economy (1945-1960)   94
      5.3.1 Economic Recovery and North American Influences   94
      5.3.2 Industrial Engineering and Human Relations   96
      5.3.3 Business Economics   98
      5.3.4 Pressures on the Dutch Academic System   99
      5.3.5 Moves towards the Business School   100

5.4 The Founding of Business Schools (1960-1977)   101
   5.4.1 Business Economics and the Social Sciences   101
   5.4.2 The Birth of Business Schools   103
5.5 The Growth of Academic Business Schools (1977-1992)   105
   5.5.1 Evolution of the School   105
   5.5.2 Government Policy: the Two-phase Structure and
          the Financing of Research   107
   5.5.3 The Labour Market for Graduates   109
   5.5.4 Business Studies as a Science and as a Profession 110
5.6 Conclusion   111

**Chapter 6 Division and Unification of German Business
Administration and Management Education**   116
Rüdiger Pieper, Paul-Löbe-Institut, Berlin, Germany

6.1 Introduction   116
6.2 A Brief Review of the Period Before the 1950s   116
   6.2.1 Business Administration in pre-war Germany   116
   6.2.2 The Post-war Years (1945-49): Continuity and
          Restoration   119
6.3 The 1950s, a Period of Dominating Theories: Gutenberg in
     the West and Political Economy in the East   120
   6.3.1 West Germany   120
   6.3.2 East Germany   121
6.4 The 1960s: Advance of Management Science and Systems
     Theory   123
   6.4.1 West Germany   123
   6.4.2 East Germany   123
6.5 The 1970s: New Approaches in the West and the East   126
   6.5.1 West Germany   126
   6.5.2 East Germany   127
6.6 After the 1970s   129
   6.6.1 The 1980s: Various Schools of Thought and the
          Growing Importance of the Human Factor   129
   6.6.2 The 1990s: Reunification of the two Germanies and
          of German Business Administration   130
6.7 Concluding Remarks   132

**Chapter 7 The Japanese System of Academic Management
Education**   138
Katsuyuki Nagaoka, Tokyo Keizai University, Tokyo, Japan

7.1 Introduction   138
7.2 Main Features of Academic Management Education in
     Japan   138

7.2.1	Predominance of Private Universities	138
7.2.2	Teacher–Students Ratio	140
7.2.3	Curriculum	141
7.2.4	Teaching Methods and Level of Achievement Required of Students	142
7.2.5	Graduate Courses and Business Schools	144
7.3	Employment and Personnel Management in Japanese Firms and Academic Management Education	144
7.3.1	Recruitment and its Timing	144
7.3.2	Employment not for Specified Jobs	145
7.3.3	Education and Training in a Lifetime Employment System	146
7.3.4	Personnel Management in a Lifetime Employment System	147
7.3.5	Employment of Students from Postgraduate Courses	148
7.4	Problems connected with the Reform of Academic Management Education	149
7.5	Conclusions	153

Chapter 8 Management Education and Higher Education since 1940 — 155
Robert Locke, University of Hawaii, Manoa, USA

8.1	Introduction	155
8.2	American Business Education	156
8.3	Management Knowledge	159
8.4	Managerial Motivation	163

Chapter 9 Formal Knowledge and Management Education — 167
Richard Whitley, Manchester Business School, Manchester, England

9.1	Introduction	167
9.2	Relations Between Formal Knowledge, Practical Skills and Work Practices	170
9.3	Formal Knowledge, Managerial Skills and Problem Solving Practices	178
9.4	Knowledge Production and Skills Development in Management Research	182
9.5	Conclusions	187

Bibliography — 191

List of Figures

3.1 Swedish Departments and Chairs in Business Administration, 1909-85   50
3.2 Destinations for Study Tours Made by Stockholm School of Economics Graduates, 1910-85   52
3.3 Theses Areas in Sweden by Period   54
3.4 Business, Law and Engineering Degrees Awarded in Sweden, 1911-85 (per cent)   60
9.1 Connections between contextual factors, reputational control and the organisation of research   184

List of Tables

3.1	Some Predecessors of the Stockholm School of Economics	46
3.2	Business Schools Mentioned in Three Swedish Business Journals at the Turn of the Century	47
3.3	Dissertation Problem Field in Sweden by Institution (%)	58
3.4	Top References Mentioned by Swedish Doctors of Business Administration	59
3.5	Functions of Business and Engineering Graduates in Swedish Industry in 1966, 1970 and 1974	61
4.1	Robert Kristenson's Lectures for First Year Students in 1936/37 and Second Year Students in 1937/38	70
4.2	Articles in *Bedriftsøkonomen* 1939-1945 by Different Topic	71
4.3	300 Norwegian Business Managers in 1939: Education or Work Experience from Countries other than Norway	78
5.1	Numbers of First-year Students (Entrants) and Numbers of Graduates in Dutch Business Studies, 1966/67-1986/87	107
5.2	Number of Graduates at Dutch Universities: General, Business Economics and Business Studies	108
7.1	Number of Applicants for Admission and New Students (in Thousands) in Japan	139
7.2	Number of Students in State, Regional (including Municipal) and Private Universities in Japan	139
7.3	Minimum Number of Teachers Required for a Japanese Department in the Field of Social Sciences	140
7.4	Number of University Teachers and Undergraduate Students in Japan (April 1990–March 1991)	141
7.5	Standard Model for the Course Programme for the Establishment of a Business Management Department in Japan (since 1986)	143
8.1	Key Qualifications	161
9.1	Types of High-Level Practical Skills	173

THE AUTHORS

Rolv Petter Amdam is Associate Professor at the Institute for Business History at the Norwegian School of Management. He has published books and articles on business history and the history of education. His latest book is *For egen regning. BI og den økonomisk-administrative utdanningen 1943-1993* (The History of the Norwegian School of Management; Oslo, 1993).

Lars Engwall has been Professor of Business Administration at Uppsala University since 1981. He has a Ph.D. from Stockholm University, has held research posts at Carnegie-Mellon University, University of California at Berkeley and the European Institute of Advanced Studies in Management, Brussels, and is a member of the Royal Swedish Academy of Sciences. His research, which has focused on general management problems, has been presented in a number of journal articles and books. The latter include *Models of Industrial Structure* (Lexington, MA: Lexington Books, 1973), *Newspapers as Organizations* (Farnborough: Saxon House, 1978) and *Mercury Meets Minerva* (Oxford: Pergamon Press, 1992).

Elving Gunnarsson is a lecturer (*universitetslektor*) in the Department of Business Studies at Uppsala University. He gained a Ph.D. from the same Department for a thesis on the development of business education in Sweden before the foundation of the Stockholm School of Economics (*Från Hansa till Handelshögskola*, From the Hanseatic League to a School of Economics, 1988). His present research interests focus on management education as an academic discipline.

Luchien Karsten obtained a degree in economics and philosophy at the University of Groningen and studied history at the École des Hautes Études in Paris 1977-78. From 1977 to 1983 he worked as an assistant at the Faculty of Social Sciences of the University of Groningen. Since 1983 he has been on the staff of the Faculty of Management and Organization of the same university. In 1989 after his Ph.D. on the eight-hour day he became associate professor of the history of management thinking. He is project manager for the collaboration between the Faculty of Economics of Ougadougou (Burkina Faso) and the Faculty of Management and Organisation.

Sven-Eric Liedman is Professor of the History of Ideas and Science at the University of Gothenburg. His publications include *The Organic Life in German Debate, 1795-1845* (Swedish, Diss., 1966), *The Interplay of Antitheses: The Philosophy of Friedrich Engels and the Sciences of the Nineteenth Century* (Swedish, 2 volumes, 1977, with an abridged German edition in 1986), and 'Institutions and Ideas: Mandarins and Non-Mandarins in the German Academic Intelligentsia' (1986). On Anders Berch and his time, he has published the monograph *The Visible Hand: Anders Berch and the Study of Economics at the Swedish Universities in the 18th Century* (1986).

Robert R. Locke holds a Ph.D. in History from UCLA and has been Professor of Economic and Social History, University of Hawaii at Manoa, since 1974. He has held a number of visiting appointments in Europe. His publications include *The End of the Practical Man: Entrepreneurship and Higher Education in Germany, France and Great Britain, 1880-1940* (Greenwich, CT, 1984), and *Management and Higher Education since 1940* (Cambridge, 1989).

Huibert de Man obtained a degree in sociology at Leyden State University in 1976. From 1977 to 1988 he worked in the field of organization studies at Groningen State University, in the Faculty of Management and Organization. His research was mainly concerned with participation in decision-making in the framework of a series of field experiments in Dutch enterprises. On the basis of this research he wrote his Ph.D. dissertation on organizational change (1988). Since 1988 until now, de Man has been employed as a senior course co-ordinator at the Open University of the Netherlands. He is responsible for the field of organization studies. His main research interest concerns the development of organization and management theory.

Katsuyuki Nagaoka holds a Ph. D. from Kobe University and teaches Business Management and History of Management Thought at Tokyo Keizai University. His main book is *Business Enterprise and Its Organization* (in Japanese, 1st ed. 1984; 2nd ed. 1990). Besides his many other publications in Japanese, he has published two papers in German: "Brauchen wir eine neue Betriebswirtshaftslehre?—Eine Situationsanalyse der deutschsprachigen Unternehmenstheorien aus der Sicht der japanischen kritischen Betriebswirtschaftslehre" (In: Koubeck, N. *et al.* (eds.), *Betriebswirtshaftliche Probleme der Mitbestimmung*, Cologne: Bund-Verlag, 1980) and "Auf der Suche nach dem Oekonomischen in der Unternehmung und der Betriebswirtschaftslehre" (In: Kappler, E. (ed.), *Rekonstruktion der Betriebswirtshaftslehre als oekonomishe Theorie*, Spardorf: Verlag Rene F. Wilfer, 1983). His recent research interests are the operation mechanism of organizational systems and the relations between management, self-organization, and reification.

Carl Julius Norstrøm obtained his Ph.D. in Economics from the Norwegian School of Economics and Business Administration. He became an assistant professor at the school in 1967 and is at present professor and prorector. Norstrøm has benefited from studies and research visits at MIT, Harvard Business School, University of Michigan, Carnegie Mellon University, Rice University and the Ruhr University in Bochum. His main research interests are in capital budgeting and accounting theory.

Rüdiger Pieper, who to our great regret died in March 1993, was president of the Paul-Löbe-Institut Berlin (the research and educational centre for East-West issues). He had been assistant professor at Freie University Berlin (Institut für Management) 1985-1989, visiting professor at Pepperdine University, Malibu, CA in 1988, visiting professor at the Technical University of Karl-Marx-Stadt (GDR) from 1990. His scientific production included various publications on organization development, human resource management and comparative management research.

Richard Whitley is Professor of Organizational Sociology at the Manchester Business School, University of Manchester. Recent publications include *Business Systems in East Asia: Firms, Markets and Societies* (Sage, 1992) and (edited) *European Business Systems: Firms and Markets in their National Contexts* (Sage, 1992). He is presently directing an ESRC-funded study of Firms and Markets in Hungary and the ESF research programme "European Management and Organisations in Transition".

Chapter 1
Perspectives on Management Studies

Lars Engwall and Elving Gunnarsson
Uppsala University, Sweden

1.1 Eight Portraits of Academic Management Studies

On 16 September 1741 Anders Berch, a Swedish civil servant, was appointed at the age of 30 to a chair of *jurisprudentiæ, economiæ et commerciorum* at Uppsala University. This was the fourth chair of its kind in the world, preceded only by similar appointments in Halle (1727), Frankfurt an der Oder (1727) and Rinteln (1730). Needless to say it was quite natural for Berch's modern successors in Uppsala to celebrate the two hundred and fiftieth anniversary of his appointment in September 1991 in a symposium on the theme of "Management Studies in an Academic Context". The purpose of the present volume, based on this symposium, is to provide a basis for a comparative analysis of management studies. Of the eight chapters that follow six thus treat academic management studies in different contexts. They deal with Sweden (Chapters 2 and 3), Norway (Chapter 4), the Netherlands (Chapter 5), the two Germanies (Chapter 6) and Japan (Chapter 7). These accounts of national experiences are followed by two chapters which elaborate on the general development since 1940 (Chapter 8) and on the relationship between formal knowledge and management education (Chapter 9).

As regards Sweden the story begins in Chapter 2 with Sven-Eric Liedman's presentation of Anders Berch and his professorship. By way of introduction the author summarizes Berch's early years up to 1731 when he presented his dissertation *De felicitate patriæ per oeconomicam promovenda* (On Promoting the Country's Felicity by Means of the Economy). To provide a little more background to the founding of the professorship and Berch's appointment at Uppsala university in 1741, he also looks at the earlier development of the ideas of economic science at the universities from Aristotle onwards. Turning then to Berch's life after the dissertation and the creation of the chair, Liedman presents some of his subject's research contributions as *Professor Jurisprudentiæ, Oeconomiæ et Commerciorum*. These were in the realms of political arithmetic (statistics) and economic science, his main work being *Inledning till Allmänna Hushållningen* (Introduction to General Economic Science) and his particular scientific field the classification and modelling of ploughs. His work resulted in models which were exhibited in the *Theatrum Oeconomico-Mechanicum*, where he also provided practical commercial courses. After Anders Berch's resignation in

1768 the economic sciences disappeared from the university for a considerable time.

Swedish developments since Anders Berch's day are treated in Chapter 3 by Lars Engwall, who deals with the institutions, their activities in terms of curricula and research, and the diffusion of business graduates. More than a century passed after Berch's resignation before any new attempts were made to establish academic education in the economic sciences. These first efforts met with a certain hostility among university professors and it was through the intervention of prominent business people that a business school was created in Stockholm in 1909. After years of struggling for recognition and many recruitment problems, this is now an institution of great prestige. It was followed by a similar business school in Gothenburg in 1923 and four business administration departments were established at the universities from the late 1950s onwards. These six institutions and some fifteen local colleges have given business administration a prominent position in Swedish higher education. An analysis of the curricula shows a pronounced German influence in the early years, followed by a corresponding American dominance later on. It is also evident that the early flagship of Swedish business education, economics, has gradually been pushed aside in the curriculum by business administration, and that the behavioural aspects have increased. Moreover, an expansion of the discipline has caused a time budget problem, which has been solved by prolonging the period of study and increasing specialization. At the same time the emphasis on scientific rather than practical qualifications has successively increased in the assessment of candidates for chairs. Like the tendency in doctoral dissertations, this also suggests a growing emphasis on behavioural rather than financial themes in research. These trends have evidently been appreciated on the market, since Swedish business education has been successful on three fronts: in the market for students, in employment and in management positions.

Another Scandinavian example is discussed in Chapter 4, where Rolv Petter Amdam and Carl Julius Norstrøm describe some characteristics of the development of academic management education in Norway. They present the pioneers at the Norwegian School of Economics and Business Administration in Bergen, which opened in 1936. The strong early influence of Germany, to some extent mediated by Sweden and Denmark, is discussed, as well as the shift towards the United States after the Second World War. The two authors also point to one feature specific to Norway among the Scandinavian countries, namely the large number of business students educated at business schools abroad and at the private Norwegian School of Management. They describe the way this private school developed from its beginnings in 1943 without any government support or legitimization, to become an institution supported by the state in 1969, with the official right from 1985 to award the *siviløkonom* degree.

In Chapter 5 Huibert de Man and Luchien Karsten report developments in the Netherlands. They refer to three significant professional groups in management studies in the period 1890–1940: engineers, accountants and psychologists. The two authors show how engineers and accountants, both with firm roots in practice, were gradually integrated into the academic system, and how industrial psychology developed as a counterweight to the economic and technical management approaches. During the reconstruction period after the Second World War the American inspiration increased dramatically, with a focus on productivity problems. This in turn provided fertile soil for Human Relations ideas among practitioners, particularly consultants. Less successful were attempts to introduce management as a subject in the economics faculties. However, in the 1950s efforts were made to establish a Dutch business studies discipline, an initiative that bore fruit in the late 1960s and the 1970s in Eindhoven (1966), Twente (1968), Delft (1969) and Groningen (1976). In the 1980s business studies became very successful in attracting students: the number of new students exceeded 1,000 in the early 1980s and in 1986/87 the number of graduates exceeded 500. At the same time business studies became increasingly integrated into the traditional academic system. All in all graduates have been successful in the labour market, although employers have started to become more cautious in the last few years. Then, as so many times before and in other places, the hesitancy about business graduates was based on the classical conflict between practice and theoretical knowledge.

This account of developments in the Netherlands is followed by a discussion in Chapter 6 by Rüdiger Pieper of the implications of the separation and later unification of the two Germanies for academic management studies. In an introductory section Pieper discusses the period before the 1950s describing the problems faced by the new discipline in gaining acceptance, the limited behavioural aspects in the business schools, the discourse on value orientation, and the adjustments just after the Second World War. He then shows how the two Germanies went different ways in the 1950s. In West Germany the work of Gutenberg was the dominating theory, while in the East a political economy approach prevailed. Then in the 1960s management science and systems theory took over, albeit with a highly political orientation in the East. The 1970s brought growing American influence on West German business administration, which in turn lead to a pluralization of the discipline within a system of enrolment expansion. At the same time in the East a more practical orientation was being called for, and the discipline of *Leitungswissenschaft* was established. In the 1980s some specialization occurred in the discipline in both West and East, while at the same time the behavioural aspects were attracting more attention. Now, in the 1990s, an integration of the management schools in the two Germanies is under way.

While the earlier chapters address the European experience, Katsuyuki

Nagaoka turns our attention to Asia in Chapter 7, providing an overview of management education at Japanese universities. He argues that Japanese management education is in a poor way, mainly because of a combination of indifference in the business world and certain features built into the educational system in Japan as a whole. The attitude of the business community is explained by the traditional recruitment procedures and career paths in Japanese firms, whereby people are employed immediately after or even some time before getting their university degree. They are then expected to spend their entire working life in the firm, and all the vocational training they need is taken care of there. What they learnt at the university is regarded as a matter of little interest. Nagaoka also points out that the Japanese educational system is characterized by very severe competition and hard work up to the university level. It is essential to get into one of the most prestigious universities, or at least to receive some kind of university education. The huge demand for university places has been exploited by a great many private universities depending on student fees. In order to make profit the number of students per teacher is high, and in order to keep costs down even more part-time teachers with low qualifications are engaged. For the same reason the predominant method of instruction consists of one-way teaching, so that one teacher can lecture to a large group of students at the same time.

If it is true that getting into a Japanese university is a very difficult task, once you are in things change, and student life is altogether easier. Almost everyone who starts the courses also passes. The standard is further reduced by the structure of the course, whereby a great deal of time is devoted to general education and not enough to more profound studies of the core subjects. However, Katsuyuki Nagaoka sees signs of changes for the better in Japanese management education. International business firms are contacting foreign education systems and are even sending some of their employees to schools outside Japan. The number of Japanese of university age will also be falling in the years to come, which will mean more competition between the universities and perhaps attempts to improve the content of the courses and the teaching methods. But if things are really to get better, some obstacles must be overcome.

The Japanese experience is also touched upon by Robert R. Locke in Chapter 8, in a broad outline of the development of management education since 1940. Although concentrating mainly on American business schools and German business education, Locke also comments on Japanese educational practices. He starts by citing an article that criticizes business schools and the education they provide and points out that most successful businessmen never attended any place of higher education. In order to investigate the critics Locke looks at the development of American business studies. The modern approach is described in terms of a transition to what he denotes "the new paradigm", i.e. the application of mathematics and scientific methods to management problems. This paradigm is the result of the needs of succesful large corporations and the widespread interaction between different elite groups in the United States, above all between managers and the military. The paradigm emerged after the Second World War and spread all over the United States and across to Europe. The training at business schools, however, is an education for management as opposed to the business education typical of Germany and to some extent Japan. As the most successful firms in the world since 1970 are from these two countries and not from the United States, Locke argues that their business education should be explored more thoroughly. The German tradition, according to Locke, is to concentrate on "key qualifications" (*Schlüsselqualifikationen*) in higher education. The most important thing is to make a person capable of doing a job (*berufsfähig*), i.e. of knowing how to learn and to relearn when conditions change, and not as in the American system to aim at being ready to do a job (*berufsfertig*).

Something of what he says about the German approach can also be applied to the Japanese system. The Japanese way adds a very important ingredient to the making of managers. The incentive system for motivating managers in Japan promotes "organization people", people who fit into group work and who are more concerned about the overall result of the firm than about their own contribution. The impressive managers of the United States—the high-flying competitive leaders who maximize their own income—are less well suited to be executives in the business world of today. Thus, according to Locke, American business schools should promote collectivist management and key qualifications in order to meet the demands of the future business world.

Finally, the role of academic management studies is further explored by Richard Whitley in Chapter 9, where the relationship between formal knowledge and management studies is discussed. Whitley refers to Locke and his concept of "the new paradigm", and suggests that the evidence showing high-level management education to be a general prerequisite for economic success is not strong. Consequently he stresses the need "to understand how and why relations between formal knowledge, management education and labour markets vary between market economies and what sort of connections between different types of knowledge and types of managerial problems are likely to develop in which circumstances". In his analysis he thus looks at different types of high-level practical skills in relation to (1) dependence on formal research-based knowledge, (2) degree of control over skill definition and certification, and (3) extent of control over work jurisdictions by academically certified skills. This analysis leads him to the conclusion that the influence and control of universities, practitioner elites, employers and the state are very important when it comes to incorporating research-based knowledge into high-level practical skills. Since this analysis is applied to academic managerial education, Whitley points out that both the varied character of management problems and the high level of employer control tend to limit the usefulness and attractiveness of research-based knowledge in management. In a subsequent section he shows that this tendency may be counteracted by a relatively loose reputational control in many subfields of management studies.

1.2 Comparing the Development of Academic Management Education in Different Contexts—Some Problems

A central issue in this volume is thus the development of academic management studies in different contexts. The separate chapters cover a relatively wide range of evidence, although there has been no attempt at producing a systematic sample. Thus it might have been tempting to try to produce a global picture from the contributions to the book. However, anyone familiar with the difficulties involved in comparing even short courses in academic programmes belonging to different educational systems will recognize the difficulties of such a task. Several fundamental circumstances will bedevil any attempt to make historical comparisons of academic studies across countries. These include:

- the simultaneous existence of several educational paths even within the same country
- differences in educational systems between countries
- differences in socioeconomic and cultural environments between countries in different parts of the world and even between neighbouring countries
- the dynamic differences that are always inherent in any study of historical development.

A thorough investigation of all the problems connected with comparing academic studies in different countries might well make us dismiss our task as an impossible one, even though in this case the comparisons are restricted to a few countries in the industrialized world. And yet the mere fact that the symposium on management studies in an academic context was held and that the participants could exchange and discuss the papers presented there seems to suggest that it is possible to trace at least some common traits and ideas, although the problems should be borne in mind. And the big differences as well as the similarities that emerge from comparisons between countries and schools can also help to highlight some of the fundamentals of university education in general (Clark, 1987).

One problem of which we should be particularly aware concerns *variations and ambiguities in terminology*. We need only consider the expression "management education". Robert Locke in Chapter 8 makes a distinction between business education and management education, the latter being reserved for the education associated with what he calls "the new paradigm". In everyday American English, however, the word "management" seems to refer to a much wider group of people. In the 1980 census, for instance, 11.5 million or 11.5 per cent of the workforce in the United States described themselves as "managers or administrators" (National Economic Development Office, 1987, p. 27). The corresponding number in the United Kingdom in 1985 was 3.3 million or over 10 per cent (*ibid.*, p. 11; Constable & McCormack, 1987 p. 6). However, in the present volume "management education" will refer as a rule to education which claims to provide an appropriate basic training for executives in large corporations. This was also clearly the aspiration of the founding fathers of the Wharton School (Wharton), Cologne (Mevissen) and Stockholm (Wallenberg), i.e. the founders of the business schools that started before or soon after the turn of the century (Redlich, 1957; Gunnarsson, 1988). Commercial and business education or studies will be used as synonyms of management education, unless some distinction is specially indicated.

A much greater problem arises when it comes to translating terminology between different languages and countries with different educational systems. The overall national educational systems vary considerably. This is as true of the higher educational systems as it is for the lower levels (Clark, 1983). Translation difficulties arise as soon as we turn to the names of the schools engaged in management education. The German *Handelshochschule* could be translated as business school, but the Scandinavian *handelshögskola* or *handelshøyskole*, names which were created as a direct translation of the German, are translated into English by the schools themselves in a variety of ways: "School of Economics" (Stockholm), "School of Economics and Business Administration" (Bergen), "Business School" (Copenhagen) and "School of Economics and Commercial Law" (Gothenburg). But despite the variety in their names the schools seem to be close enough to the American business schools to give an idea of the orientation of their educational programmes.

Another translation problem concerns the designations of the degrees awarded and the question of the relative status of different educational levels. A Bachelor of Business Administration (BBA) should take four years after high school, and a Master of Business Administration (MBA) another two years after the BBA. The Scandinavian *civilekonom* or *siviløkonom* should only take about four years after the higher school certificate level, and could consequently be translated as a BBA. But in Scandinavia the high school certificate is normally passed at the age of 19 at least, while American high school graduates are about two years younger. Furthermore, in the view of the American Assembly of Collegiate Schools of Business a substantial part of the BBA studies should be devoted to subjects outside the business field (Porter & McKibbin, 1988). It could be claimed that such subjects are taught at the Scandinavian secondary schools (ter Vehn, 1959). The

Scandinavian degree, also before the recent changes in Sweden, should then be regarded as almost the eqvivalent of an MBA. The same can be said with greater confidence about the longer German Kaufmann/Diplom-Ökonom and the traditional Dutch academic degree (National Economic Development Office, 1987, p. 45; Chapter 5 below), and about the French *maîtrise* (*ibid.*, p. 62). After business schools started in Great Britain, an equivalent to the MBA was awarded there as well, although the British situation has been traditionally different, with great emphasis on practical work experience (Whitley, Thomas, Marceau, 1981; Constable & McCormack, 1987; National Economic Development Office, 1987). The only one of the industrialized countries studied here where the existence of higher management academic studies at roughly the MBA level can be questioned, is that economically successful country, Japan (*ibid.*, p. 86; Chapters 7 and 8 below). Here intense initial academic training seems to have been replaced by on-the-job and off-the-job training after joining a firm (National Economic Development Office, 1987, pp. 88–92). But even in Japan 88.5 per cent of the top managers of large firms in Japan in 1961 were university graduates of some kind (*ibid.*, p. 86). An introductory academic education thus seems to be the rule for top managers in the industrialized countries all over the world. And, even if the schools in one part of the world such as Western Europe for instance, are organized in different ways—"professional" schools of a private, religious or state character, or studies within the traditional university system in countries with different cultural, educational, language and socioeconomic conditions—there seem to be some themes that they all share (Schieb, 1990).

Bearing the above complications in mind we will now try to identify certain patterns in the development of management education. These concern the programme content (Section 1.3), and attitudes in the academic and business communities (Sections 1.4–1.5).

1.3 Composition of the Programmes

Early attempts to establish commercial education at an academic level clearly owed much to the German influence (Redlich, 1957). The same can be said of the founding of Berch's chair in 1741 in Sweden (Liedman, 1986, and Chapter 2 below). After the 18th century professorships in the economic sciences had disappeared, new moves began towards the end of the 19th century and at the beginning of the twentieth, still mainly under the influence of German ideas on academic management education. Although there were some schools in other European countries and in the United States, the German schools were still making the greatest impact internationally (Engwall, 1992, and Chapter 3 below). This was particularly noticeable in the neighbouring Scandinavian countries. Although study tours were made from Sweden to several European countries and even to the

United States before the Stockholm School of Economics was started it was nonetheless the schools in Cologne and Berlin which were chosen as the models (Gunnarsson, 1988, pp. 226–268). The schools in Copenhagen, Gothenburg and Bergen were all influenced by Germany, either directly or indirectly via the other Scandinavian schools (Engwall, 1992, and Chapter 4 below).

But the German *Wissenschaft* influence was also evident in the early stages in the development of universities and especially at the professional schools in the United States (Light, 1983). And later, in the twenties, when Japan followed its usual habit of imitating and adapting Western organizations, this time by starting academic management studies Germany was the most influential country (Westney, 1987; Nagaoka, 1987). By this time, however, another country was also about to make its first contributions on this special export market. In growing numbers Europeans were undertaking study trips to the United States (Engwall, 1992, Chapter 7). And, after the Second World War, the earlier German influence was to be replaced by an American impact which seems to have been even stronger and to have operated worldwide (Chapters 3, 4, 5, 7 and 8 below). Countries which had previously appeared to be unwilling to admit ideas from outside their borders, such as France and the United Kingdom, have now started MBA programmes similar to those provided in the United States (Whitley, Thomas & Marceau, 1981).

The academic management programmes in some countries, like France with its analytical and intellectual training in the *Grandes Écoles*, have developed their own special profiles, but in the more internationally influential German and American schools and among their followers, the composition of the syllabus shows some common trends. When the schools started, the dominating academic subject was economics. Wharton, Cologne and Stockholm all relied heavily on the academic prestige of economics, and although schools such as Berlin and Harvard placed more emphasis on business studies, economics was very strong in all schools (Redlich, 1957, and Chapter 3 below).

History and historians were also influential in the first period. In fact it has been said of the Wharton School that it "was in the light of modern educational practice largely a device to give students at the University of Pennsylvania a major in history and the social sciences" (Kirkland, 1956, p. 98). Carl Hallendorff, first director of the Stockholm School of Economics, and Ignaz Jastrow, first director in Berlin, were both historians (Lendin, 1946; Redlich, 1957). Frank Taussig at Harvard, although he was an economist, wrote a classic work on the tariff history of the United States, while Eli Heckscher, the first professor of economics in Stockholm, later became the founder of economic history as an academic subject in Sweden (Taussig, 1967; Söderlund, 1946).

But even if there was a substantial element of historical studies, as there still is in the Japanese universities (Chapter 7 below), economics dominated most of the earlier programmes. This remained true, at least in Scandinavia, even after business administration had acquired easily the strongest position in terms of time spent by students. Even though new fields were added to the original accounting and finance courses, such as marketing (rather than simply descriptions of trade institutions), time-and-motion study, managerial economics and personnel recruitment in the scientific management tradition, business administration could still be regarded for some time to come as grounded in microeconomic theory (Engwall, 1980, 1992 and Chapter 3 below).

The obviously practical orientation of traditional business administration studies was the main target of the critics, as reported by two committees which reviewed the state of the art in the United States in the late 1950s (Gordon & Howell, 1959; Pierson *et al.*, 1959). The main conclusion of these reviews was that the education as a whole was of low academic quality, compared with what should be demanded of it. This criticism was particularly disturbing, since after the Second World War the United States had put itself indisputably in the lead in the world in this field. The definite victory of what has been dubbed "the new paradigm" in management education should be viewed in light of various changes proposed by these reviews and by other critics at the time (Porter & McKibbin, 1988). The main features in the new paradigm were operations research and other quantitative studies, complemented by behavioural aspects to create an education which could be accepted as "academic".

As several contributions to this volume (cf. e.g. Chapters 3 and 5) will show, the behavioural aspects have become extraordinarily important in modern management studies. In a sense they can be seen as the prime segmentation device between economics and business studies, the former basing its arguments on rationality and the idea of "Economic Man", and the latter on bounded rationality and the concept of "Social Man".[1] This difference between the two disciplines has arisen primarily as a result of empirical studies undertaken by management scholars. Initially adopting a neoclassical view of the firm, they have gradually developed alternative theories (cf. particularly Chapter 3 below). These have not been grounded solely on the above-mentioned empirical studies, however, but have also found inspiration in psychological and sociological research, which particularly in the North American business schools was introduced by the hiring of professors with such backgrounds. An interesting effect of all this has been that the ideas of earlier immigrant Europeans in America, such as Kurt Lewin, have later been re-imported to Europe from the United States (cf. e.g. Chapter 6 below).

---

[1] The pathbreaking work here was Simon (1947) with important followers like Cyert & March (1963). For an account of the development of these concepts, see Simon (1991).

Overall we have thus found an early tendency to stress economics and, to a certain extent, history. Over the years business administration has become more important than economics in the business school curricula. However, the emergence of operations research during the war and the criticism of the scientific content of business school courses have led to the introduction into business studies of certain elements previously treated by economists. At the same time an increasing awareness of the need to consider behavioural constraints has emerged among management researchers.

1.4 Attitudes in the Academic Community

Academic organizations safeguard their existence on the principle of barriers to entry, screening and rites of incorporation (Engwall, 1992). It is not therefore surprising that we find evidence also in the contributions to this volume (cf. e.g. Chapters 2–4) of opposition among those inside the system towards any potential new entrant such as management studies. Even in the United States, where society as a whole had a very positive view of businessmen, Thorstein Veblen wrote in 1918:

> The work of the College of Commerce, accordingly, is a peculiarly futile line of endeavour for any public institution, in that it serves neither the intellectual advancement nor material welfare of the community. (Veblen, 1918, pp. 208–209)
>
> A college of commerce is designed to serve an emulative purpose only—individual gain regardless of, or at the cost of, the community at large—and it is, therefore, peculiarly incompatible with the collective cultural purpose of the university. It belongs in the corporation of learning no more than a department of athletics. (*Ibid.*, pp. 209–210.)

In a footnote to this passage Veblen even suggested that there was more justification for associating athletics with the universities than commerce (*Ibid.*, p. 210). This kind of criticism from the academic world could still be heard in the 1950s. In 1955 the following appeared in an article in *The Daily Pennsylvanian*:

> The first and most destructive influence at Pennsylvania of the atmosphere important for the nourishment of the human arts is the Wharton School of Finance and Commerce. [...] An undergraduate body where half the members have definite educational interests of a material, nonacademic nature is bound to create an atmosphere that reflects something less than enthusiasm for the theoretical sciences and the liberal arts. (Griffin, 1955, p. 3.)

This hostility to the introduction of management education into academia is quite natural, since academic education represents a product whose chief value lies in its reputation, and this in turn is largely determined in a social interaction process of the kind discussed by sociologists in the Berger & Luckmann (1966) tradition. We can therefore expect insiders to try to maintain their exclusiveness and their reputation, and outsiders to strive to acquire just these qualities. The success of their efforts will then have a negative effect on exclusiveness and reputation, with the result that successful intruders are soon likely to behave like real insiders.

Those who succeed in breaking into the academic system may also come under criticism for not meeting the standards of this community. The main visible evidence which we have of this is provided by the reports of the Carnegie and Ford Foundation Committees set up in the mid-1950s (Gordon & Howell, 1959; Pierson *et al.*, 1959; cf. also Cheit, 1975, pp. 99–101; Schlossman, Sedlak & Wechsler, 1987). Their comments also had an impact on the design of the management studies curricula, and ultimately led to the advent of the above-mentioned "new paradigm". This has probably helped to raise the scientific status of management studies.[2] But the huge demand for this kind of education has probably been at least as important.

The efforts that have been made to raise the academic status of business schools in the United States provide us with an illustrative example of the difficulties involved in supplying a management education in an academic context. As the research and education at the business schools attained an accepted scientific standard, a new kind of criticism was heard. This criticism, like the earlier version, was launched mainly by academic teachers who began to doubt the usefulness to business managers of the kind of research now being done.[3]

Another very powerful obstacle facing a new discipline (or new schools for that matter) is the initial lack of competent scholars. This has been amply confirmed by the Scandinavian (Chapters 3 and 4), the Dutch (Chapter 5) and the Japanese experience (Chapter 7). The problem of attracting teachers was also felt in the United States, where the conditions in the business world were found to be far more lucrative and challenging at the time of the Ford foundation initiatives. The "new revolution" had to start by improving the conditions for researchers in order to attract more doctoral students to the business schools (Schlossman, Sedlak & Wechsler, 1987). Differences in the ability to attract doctors as teachers and researchers also led to differences in reputation between schools in the university system. This differentiation between academic institutions is most advanced in the United States, where information on faculty performance is widely used in promotion decisions and in the students' choice of school (see e.g. Fishgrund, 1990; Miller, 1990; Stuart, 1990).

1.5 Attitudes in the Business Community

A particularly awkward fact for practice-oriented fields like management studies is that they are likely to come under criticism not only from the

---

[2] According to Halpern (1985, p. 17) these two studies could be regarded as the starting-point for the professionalization of management.

[3] For an overview of earlier and more recent criticism of management education as not providing adequate training for the business world, see Cheit (1975).

academic world but also from the business community, where traditionally the focus has been on the idea of the practical man (cf. e.g. Kirkland, 1956, pp. 86–87), i.e. that ability in business is acquired from practical experience and not from academic studies. The nineteenth century saw the development of a number of non-academic commercial schools, whose graduates with the passage of time found their way into business firms. Neither they nor the "practical men" would have been very likely to appreciate academic education, which after all could still be attacked in the middle of the twentieth century by representatives of the business world for not being vocational enough (Whyte, 1956, pp. 107–108). Likewise, in many countries degrees in engineering and law were traditionally regarded as an adequate training for administrative posts, while elsewhere, as in England, degrees in the humanities were preferred. These traditions naturally created barriers to entry to top positions for the graduates of the newly created business schools. With the passage of time, however, these graduates have succeeded in overcoming such barriers and their numbers have quickly increased in the business community. Academic management studies have thus achieved an overwhelming success. Most schools have enjoyed a seller's market, i.e. they have an excess of applicants to choose from. This also means that companies have the chance to choose from among the elite of the academically-minded if they employ business graduates. As this elite comes largely from the same socioeconomic group as the executives and owners of business firms, candidates with prestigious academic degrees may be preferred in the selection.[4]

The vague relationship between formal education and skill requirements that this last implies, may certainly lead some people to question the need for an academic education in management. The inconclusive evidence of any connection between academic management studies and economic success point in the same direction. Also, since universities as organizations are themselves characterized by ambiguity, this connection is even less susceptible to proof (March & Olsen, 1976). Many, like Robert Locke in Chapter 8, have thus asked themselves why Japan with a fairly modest management education system, has achieved such an impressive economic performance (cf. e.g. Cheit, 1985, pp. 50–51 and Subocz, 1984). But as Richard Whitley will be pointing out in Chapter 9, this may be a result of differences between countries regarding influence and the control of universities, practitioner elites, employers and the state. Needless to say the complications mentioned in Section 1.3 may also play an important part in such comparisons.

Finally it is important to repeat that the efforts described here to make management studies credible in the eyes of the scientific community have had countereffects in the business world. As business schools became more

---

[4] According to Collins (1971) this reason for selection accounts for much more of the educational stratification in society than the increasing complexity of the skills required for the job.

research-oriented in the United States, a new wave of criticism appeared, claiming that management studies were now losing touch with reality.[5] So, like Odysseus between Scylla and Charybdis, management studies face the difficult task of striking a balance between academia and the world of practice.

1.6 Concluding Remarks

Although details in the patterns of development in academic management education differ between the countries studied, some general features occur in them all. Some form of academic education has become an almost indispensable requirement for top executives in large and medium-sized corporations. The number of executives with such an education has been growing steadily. Consequently we can perhaps partly explain the success of academic management studies by looking at them from the perspective of the business world.

It is widely held today that the most valuable attributes of a top executive lie not in any formal research-based analytical knowledge but in other more general human capacities such as an ability to communicate and to handle interpersonal cooperation and conflict (Hales, 1986; Gordon & Howell, 1959; Pierson *et al.*, 1959; Porter & McKibbin, 1988, and Chapter 9 below). From this standpoint the traditional training of top business people in England—a gentlemanly education in the humanities—might seem to have been quite adequate. But this traditional approach had several serious weaknesses compared with other educational paths and particularly with the American business school system.

The gentleman's route into business depended on the inheritance of a place in a family business—a type of recruitment that is lumbered with several disadvantages. In terms of *democratic* ideals, the inheritance principle can be questioned as unfair. If selection is made on the basis of some kind of evaluation of personal qualifications such as the level of education attained, this is regarded as more acceptable than claims of family alone.[6] As meritocratic recruitment proves to give a relatively high proportion of top executive posts to the children of business leaders, the method can still be acceptable from a personal perspective.[7] But if the education system suc-

---

[5] Critical comments came from business people (cf. Cheit, 1985 for an overview) and from business school professors (cf. e.g. Hayes & Abernathy, 1980, and Behrman & Levin, 1984). The criticism was later followed by a more systematic study of the whole issue (Porter & McKibbin, 1988).

[6] That the consequences of an efficient meritocratic recruitment system can be disastrous was shown by Young (1958).

[7] Family background was found to explain about 48 percent of the variance in mature men's occupational status in the studies undertaken by Jenks *et. al.* (1979), the second main explanatory factor being years of education. (Corcoran, 1979) Occupational status was measured by Duncan's Socio-Economic Index. (Duncan, 1961).

ceeds in attracting many more students than there are business leaders' children, as management studies have done, then there will be a bigger, and hopefully a better, population to choose from. This means that to a great extent business can select from an elite group of people disposed to academic success and endowed with a certain practical orientation. As much of this elite comes from the same social group as the executives and owners of business firms, the personal interests of these executives can enhance the selection process, which may be one reason for the success of academic business studies.

Another advantage of the German and American academic business education systems compared with the "gentlemanly" way concerns their reliance on the prestigious and successful scientific approach to the production of knowledge. During the last century many spectacular innovations were the result of scientific research. English university education at the time provided little acquaintance with science and thus no means of communicating with the increasingly influential scientists in the business world. In Germany the *Wissenschaft* tradition remained very strong even in the *Fachhochschulen*. In the United States the *scientific management* movement linked management with a *scientific* approach as early as the beginning of the century, albeit science at the time meant little more than time-and-motion studies for blue collar workers and, a little later, aptitude tests for vocational recruitment. However, it was not until the late 1950s, as part of the "revolution" in the American business schools, that the need for a more widespread adoption of a scientific approach, and one with a more modern thrust, was really stressed. "Scientific" then came to mean the rigorous application of mathematical and analytical methods, mainly in economics and business administration.

Another major disadvantage of the old British lay in the actual subjects studied. In the eyes of subordinates a knowledge of history and Latin does not justify a person's entry into the business hierarchy at a top level, as readily as the study of some aspects of the business world might do. A purely "learned" education can also obstruct communication with employees trained in a more practical mode.

On quite another tack, scientific research of the kind conducted in Germany and the United States also helps to raise the prestige of a field like business in society at large.

In several respects modern academic education in management has thus been providing the business world with a highly satisfactory product. The schools are attracting many more applicants than they can admit, which means they can select the "best" candidates for management studies. In the selection process a fair proportion of the heirs to business leaders and entrepreneurs tend to be accepted, but together with a sufficient number of "outsiders" to show that merit, not money, counts. The training provides familiarity with established scientific quantitative techniques. The application of these methods to problems related to the business world confirms that management can exploit advanced mathematical techniques to advantage, and that it is a field worthy of scientific investigation. The graduates of the business schools can then enter the business world with self-confidence, in the knowledge that they have been selected from a great many applicants and that they have learnt to handle the established scientific tools. The self-confidence and legitimacy provided by their training for a high position in the hierarchy can give them a very good start for a career in business. The "screening" of students and their legitimization through the "credentials" provided by prestigious degrees, can thus be regarded as an important function of management education (cf. Stiglitz, 1975; Blaug, 1976).

From this discussion, however, very little has emerged about what the content of an education in management *should* be. Given that it can be linked in some way to business, and that it can endow the student with some kind of scientific reputation, almost any subject could be studied. And this does seem to be very much the case in academic management studies. Apart from the acquisition of some basic skills such as an understanding of balance sheets, profit-and-loss statements and management accounting—knowledge that at the required minimum level can hardly be regarded as academic—there is very little in an academic management education which can be said to be compulsory.

Though the business world has many grounds for appreciating the management education provided today, there are also some grounds for dissatisfaction. Teachers in the field have been particularly vociferous here. Three of the main points raised seem to be (Porter & McKibbin, 1988, 64–66): 1. The student should receive more training in the general human capacities for social communication and handling people which are needed in management work, and less in rigorous analytical and mathematical methods that are hardly ever used in business. 2. The research produced at business schools should have more relevance to "real" business problems, and not so much to academic reputation. 3. Management education should do more to promote creativity and entrepreneurism and be less concerned with the reproduction of knowledge.[8]

Although substantial changes have been made, the hope expressed by the philosopher Alfred North Whitehead at Harvard in the late twenties that "the justification for a university is that it preserves the connection between knowledge and the zest of life" (Whitehead, 1929, p. 139) and that the business school in particular should "produce men with a greater zest for business" (*ibid.*, p. 140) has not yet been fulfilled. Some doubt can be expressed about whether the "scientification" of management education has been the

---

[8] Objections have been raised to the length of time spent in education and the influence of academic training on the equality between socioeconomic groups in society has been criticised (Berg, 1970; Thurow, 1972).

right way to yield a "zest for business". If even the "scientific" approach to inventive product development in new technological fields has been questioned (Karnøe, 1992), how much more can it not be doubted in business.

There is no doubt that many questions remain to be answered about the development and role of academic management studies. For instance we need to know more about how and why various ideas are diffused. It is also important to note in this context that management cannot be regarded as a profession in quite the same way as medicine, dentistry, the law, etc., which apply strict authorization system and sanctions for breach of professional norms.[9] And although there have been occasional proposals for mandatory formal training for entrepreneurs, management seems to have little chance of ever claiming "true" professional status. However, it may very well develop into a kind of semi-profession as a result of the networks created in the business schools. This also seems to be one of the ideas behind recent efforts on the part of the Commission on Admission to Graduate Management Education to improve American graduate schools of management (*Graduate Management Admission Council*, 1990). If the Commission's recommendation to concentrate less on "the building of elegant, abstract models that seek to unify the world economic system"(*Ibid.*, p. 7) and more "on the development of frameworks to help students understand the messy, concrete reality of international business" (*Loc. cit.*) are seriously taken up, we could be witnessing an even greater revolution than the changes in the 1950s.

For the future it would be of considerable interest to make more systematic cross-cultural comparative studies of the diffusion of management ideas by academic education, management consultants, popular management books, etc.[10] Such studies will become even more important as the former socialist countries become market economies and former public-sector organizations such as day-care centres, hospitals, universities and so on are transformed into commercial operations. Thus the agenda for research must be regarded as challenging, to say the least. A scientific investigation addressing the education of top executives could provide a good start to producing a "zest for business". This volume is just a beginning . . .

References

Behrman, J. N. & Levin, R. I., 1984, "Are Business Schools Doing their Job?", *Harvard Business Review*, 62, January/February, pp. 140–147.

Berg, I, 1970, *Education and Jobs: The Great Training Robbery*, New York: Praeger Publishers.

---

[9] For a discussion of such "closure mechanisms", see e.g. Larson (1977). The students of business who come closest to professional status seem to be the chartered accountants.

[10] For a current study along these lines, see Furusten (1992).

Berger, P. L. & Luckmann, T., 1966, *The Social Construction of Reality: A Treatise in the Sociology of Knowledge*, Garden City, NY: Doubleday.
Blaug, M., 1976, "The Empirical Status of Human Capital Theory: A Slightly Jaundiced Survey", *Journal of Economic Literature*, 14, No. 3, pp. 827–855.
Cheit, E. F., 1975, *The Useful Arts and the Liberal Tradition*, New York: McGraw-Hill.
— 1985, "Business School and their Critics", *California Management Review*, 27, Spring, pp. 43–62.
Clark, B. R., 1983, *The Higher Education System*, Berkeley, CA: University of California Press.
— 1987, "Introduction" and "9. Conclusions", In: Clark, B. R. (ed.), *The Academic Profession*, Berkeley and Los Angeles, CA: University of California Press, pp. 1–9 and pp. 371–399.
Collins, R., 1971, "Functional and Conflict Theories of Educational Stratification", *American Sociological Review*, 36, December, pp. 1002–1019.
Constable, J. & McCormack, R., 1987, *The Making of British Managers*, Northants: British Institute of Management.
Corcoran, M., 1979, "Who Gets Ahead: A Summary", In: Jenks, C., et. al., *Who Gets Ahead? The Determinants of Economic Success in America*, New York: Basic Books Inc, pp. 213–230.
Cyert, R. M. & March, J. G., 1963, *A Behavioral Theory of the Firm*, Englewood Cliffs, NJ: Prentice-Hall.
Duncan, O. D., 1961, "A Socioeconomic Index for All Occupations", In: Reiss, A. J. Jr, *Occupations and Social Status*, New York: The Free Press of Glencoe Inc.
Engwall, L. (ed.), 1980, *Företagsekonomins rötter. Några bidrag till en företagsekonomisk doktrinhistoria* (The Roots of Business Administration. Some Contributions to a History of the Business Administration Doctrine), Lund: Studentlitteratur.
— 1992, *Mercury Meets Minerva*, Oxford: Pergamon Press.
Fishgrund, T. (ed.), 1990, *The Insider's Guide to the Top Ten Business Schools*, 4th ed., Boston, MA: Little, Brown.
Furusten, S., 1992, *Management Books—Guardians of the Myth of Leadership*, Licentiate thesis, Department of Business Studies, Uppsala University.
Gordon, R. A. & Howell, J. E., 1959, *Higher Education for Business*, New York: Columbia University Press.
Gordon, R. A. & Howell, J. E., *Higher Education for Business*, New York: Columbia University Press.
Graduate Management Admission Council, 1990, *Leadership for a Changing World. The Future Role of Graduate Management Education*, Los Angeles, CA: Graduate Management Admission Council.
Griffin, M., 1955, "Problems of Liberal Arts Magnified By Disunifying Campus Influences", *The Daily Pennsylvanian*, January 14, p. 3, 7.
Gunnarsson, E., 1988, *Från Hansa till Handelshögskola. Svensk ekonomundervisning fram till 1909* (From the Hanseatic League to a School of Economics. Swedish Business Education up to 1909), Acta Universitatis Upsaliensis. Studia Oeconomiae Negotiorum 29, Uppsala: Almqvist & Wiksell International (diss.).
Hales, C. P., 1986, "What Do Managers Do? A Critical Review of the Evidence", *Journal of Management Studies*, 23, January, pp. 88–115.
Halpern, S. A., 1985, "Professional Schools in the American University", *Working Paper # 6*, Comparative Higher Education Group, University of California, Los Angeles, CA (mimeo).
Hayes, R. H. & Abernathy, W. J., 1980, "Managing our Way to Decline", *Harvard Business Review*, 58, July/August, pp. 67–77.

Jenks, C., et. al., 1979, *Who Gets Ahead? The Determinants of Economic Success in America*, New York: Basic Books Inc.

Johnson H. T. & Kaplan, R. S., 1987, *Relevance Lost: the Rise and Fall of Management Accounting*, Boston, MA: Harvard Business School Press.

Jönsson, S., 1992, "Editorial: Applying for Research Grants", *Scandinavian Journal of Management*, 8, No. 4, pp. 281–282.

Karnøe, P., "Approaches to Innovation in Modern Wind Energy Technology: Technological Policies, Science, Engineers and Craft Traditions in United States and Denmark 1974–1990", *Center for Economic Policy Research Publication No. xx, Stanford University*, Stanford, CA.

Kirkland, E. C., 1956, *Dream and Thought in the Business Community, 1860–1900*, New York: Cornell University Press.

Larson, M. S., 1977, *The Rise of Professionalism*, Berkeley, CA: University of California Press.

Lendin, W., 1946, "Hallendorff, Carl", In: *Svenska män och kvinnor 3* (Swedish men and women 3), Stockholm: Albert Bonniers förlag, pp. 256–257.

Liedman, S.-E., 1986, *Den synliga handen* (The Visible Hand), Stockholm: Arbetarkultur.

Light, D. W., 1983, "The Development of Professional Schools in America", In: Jarausch, K. H. (ed.), *The Transformation of Higher Learning 1860–1930*, Stuttgart: Klett-Cotta, pp. 345–365.

Locke, R. R., 1989, *Management and Higher Education since 1940*, Cambridge: Cambridge University Press.

March, J. G. & Olsen, J. P., 1976, *Ambiguity and Choice in Organizations*, Bergen: Universitetsforlaget.

Miller, E., 1990, *Barron's Guide to Graduate Business Schools*, 7th ed., New York: Barron's Educational Series.

Nagaoka, K., 1987, "Business Management Study in Japan. Its Development under the Influence of Germany and the USA", *Paper presented at the Symposium on the Relationship between Academic Business Education and Industrial Performance in Europe and Japan*, Brussels, 21–22 May 1987.

National Economic Development Council, 1987, *The Making of Managers. A Report on Management Education, Training and Development in the USA, West Germany, France, Japan and UK*, London: National Economic Development Office.

Pierson, F. C. et. al., 1959, *The Education of American Businessmen*, New York: McGraw-Hill Book Company.

Porter, J. L., Muller, H. J. & Rehder, R. R., 1989, "The Making of Managers: An American Perspective", *Journal of General Management*, 14, No. 4, pp. 62–76.

Porter, L. W. & McKibbin, L. E., 1988, *Management Education and Development: Drift or Thrust into the 21st Century?*, New York: McGraw-Hill.

Redlich, F., 1957, "Academic Education for Business: Its Development and the Contribution of Ignaz Jastrow (1856–1937). In Commemoration of the Hundredth Anniversary of Jastrow's Birth", *Business History Review*, 31, Spring, pp. 35–91.

Schieb, P.-A., 1990, "Des modèles nationaux ou un modèle européen?" (National Models or a European Model?), *Revue française de gestion*, 15, Mars-avril-mai, pp. 105–110.

Schlossman, S., Sedlak, M. & Wechsler, H., 1987, *The "New Look:" The Ford Foundation and the Revolution in Business Education*, Los Angeles, CA: Graduate Management Admission Council.

Simon, H. A., 1947, *Administrative Behaviour*, New York: MacMillan.

— 1991, *Models of My Life*, New York: Basic Books.

Stiglitz, J. E., 1975, "The Theory of "Screening," Education and the Distribution of Income", *The American Economic Review*, 65, June, pp. 283–300.

Stuart, B. S., 1990, *Top Business Schools: the Ultimate Guide*, New York: Arco: Prentice Hall Press.

Subocz, V., 1984, "Management Education in Japan: Extent, Directions and Problems", *Journal of Management Development*, 3, No. 4, pp. 23–46.

Söderlund, E., 1946, "Eli Heckscher", In: *Svenska män och kvinnor 3* (Swedish men and women 3), Stockholm: Albert Bonniers förlag, pp. 336–338.

Taussig, F. W., 1967, *The Tariff History of the United States. Including a Consideration of the Tariff of 1930*, New York: A. M. Kelley.

ter Vehn, A., 1959, *Kompendium. Inledning till företagsekonomien* (Compendium. Introduction to Business Administration), Gothenburg School of Economics (mimeo).

Thurow, L. T., 1972, "Education and Economic Equality", *The Public Interest*, 28, Summer pp. 66–81.

Veblen, T, 1918, *The Higher Learning in America*, New York: B. W. Huebsch.

Westney, D. E., 1987, *Imitation and Innovation. The Transfer of Western Organizational Patterns to Meiji Japan*, Cambridge, MA: Harvard University Press.

Whitehead, A. N., 1929, *The Aims of Education & other Essays*, New York: The MacMillan Company.

Whitley, R., Thomas, A. & Marceau, J., 1981, *Masters of Business. Business Schools and Business Graduates in Britain and France*, London: Tavistock.

Whyte Jr, W. H., 1956, *The Organization Man*, New York: Simon and Schuster.

Young, M. D., 1958, *The Rise of the Meritocracy 1870–2033*, London: Thames and Hudson.

Chapter 2
Anders Berch
A Frontrunner

Sven-Eric Liedman
Gothenburg University, Sweden

2.1 Anders Berch—His First Thirty Years

Anders Berch was born in 1711. His father derived a handsome income from working in Stockholm as an agent for a group of important industrialists of the Bergslagen mining district. In his early years at home the young Anders met several important people who in the 1720s, 1730s and 1740s were to reform Swedish economic and political life. They remained his patrons and allies. Anders Berch is very typical of the period in Swedish history which is called the Age of Freedom, which lasted from the death of Charles XII in 1718 and up to the bloodless *coup d'état* of Gustavus III in 1772. From his early youth he was imbued with the ideas of the mercantilist so-called Hat party, which for a long time dominated Swedish political life in competition with the Caps.

In the late 1720s, Anders Berch was a student in Uppsala, where he soon joined a group of talented young men with a common interest in economic and political issues as well as in the natural sciences. The group, whose leader was the astronomer Anders Celsius, inventor of the centigrade thermometer, held very radical utilitarian ideas and scorned traditional academic subjects such as Latin, poetry or Hebrew, propagating the dangerous ideas of the German philosopher, Christian Wolff (Ferrner, 1776; Petander, 1912, p. 5). It was under the auspices of Anders Celsius that in 1731 Anders Berch defended a dissertation entitled *De felicitate patriæ per oeconomiam promovenda* ("On promoting the country's felicity by means of the economy"; Celsius & Berch, 1731).

This 48-page booklet is a standard work in the mercantilist spirit, advocating measures to stimulate population growth, to foster manufacturing, and to improve the trade balance. It is written by a person with good knowledge of recent trends in practical economic science.

The most interesting thing in the dissertation is a suggestion in the introductory chapter which deals with economic science in general. Here the author launches the idea that the government should institute a professorship in economic science, so that young men of ability could come to the universities to be taught the skills necessary for engaging in trade and economic life. And he explicitly points out that such a professor should have a thorough knowledge of mathematics and physics.

This idea was not absolutely new, even in Sweden. Some years before it had been proposed by Anders Celsius in a somewhat different form (Schück, 1908). In Germany a whole series of radically utilitarian philosophers and reformers had suggested the creation of university chairs in economic science.

2.2 Economic Science at the Universities

In order to understand what the proposals about economic science meant to a traditional university system, we have to leave Anders Berch and look backward. In other words, it is necessary to give a hint of the history of economic theory at the universities.

Economic theory, like politics, was considered by Aristotle to be one aspect of practical philosophy, in which guise it long pursued a somewhat obscure life in the universities. It was as a professor of moral philosophy that Adam Smith revolutionized economic science at the end of the eighteenth century.

The domain of moral philosophy bordered on that of jurisprudence, and in the study of this subject, too, there was a place for economic theories. Here the emphasis was on economic jurisprudence, or the theory of the law of taxation, trade and other down-to-earth subjects.

The basic Greek meaning of the word "economy" survived until the end of the eighteenth century or longer. Economy was in other words household management in a literal sense, and "household management" covered anything that concerned the livelihood of a family, a prince, or a state. The theory of the state's business was called *oeconomia publica*, i.e. public economy or political economy (if the focus was on the sovereigns and their wellbeing, then the term was *oeconomia principum*). The rest was labelled *oeconomia privata*.

All this sturdy wisdom could hardly be accommodated under the umbrella of moral philosophy with its prudent rules of life, or of jurisprudence with its dry juridical expositions. Household managemant included the art of tilling the soil, mining the ore from the hills, hunting and fishing, keeping the books of large establishments, collecting taxes for the realm. Most economic knowledge was developed and preserved outside the universities. Economic learning, even in the formal sense, was long the concern of people in practical occupations. In England the leading economic theorists in the early eighteenth century still belonged to the East India Company or similar institutions. New ground in economic theory was broken at this time in the hectic world of commerce, with which the theories were concerned.

This was primarily the theory of an expanding middle class, whose strength was growing steadily. The movement which Adam Smith labelled mercantilism, and which dominated the thinking of the seventeenth century and much of the eighteenth, is largely a theory of trade, of the right way to conduct trade, of the importance to trade of production and consumption, etc. The economists were fond of speaking of the business of the state, but the business of the state was intertwined with private affairs. It was still hard to distinguish between state and private in general. The great trading companies augmented the wealth of the few, but officially and according to economic theory they served the interests of the whole country.

In countries with an autocratic government, such as France, the favoured few could feather their nests as employees of the state, and economic theory became the tool of civil servants. In countries where the bourgeoisie was gradually acquiring a more independent political status—such as the Netherlands or England—economic theory could develop a few steps further away from the centres of political power.

Posterity has had many harsh words to say of the doctrine of mercantilism. For a long time, however, it was intellectually and scientifically a very advanced system. It had close ties with the scientific revolution of the seventeenth century, and in some respects may be seen as a branch of it. The road from the economic doctrines of Child or Davenant, or even of the French controller-general Colbert, to the triumphant new science was not a long one. Not that their theories implied a breakthrough in the way that those of Galileo, Kepler, and Newton did. On the economic front we have to wait at least until Smith to find anything comparable. The world of which economists spoke before Smith was far too complicated and also, in a sense, far too undeveloped to be the subject of a terrestrial mechanics of household management.

It was on a more direct and often purely personal level that revolutionary science and economic theory met. The economists created theories of the balance of trade and noble metals and wealth-creating labour, but as practical men, they were also aware of the need for quite different doctrines, theories of heavenly bodies, the refraction of light, the combination and decomposition of substances. The economists were strict utilitarians; everything that favoured welfare and wealth should be utilized. Men such as Petty and Child were sufficiently perspicacious to understand the utility of the new science. If one knew how nature worked, one would be able to harness it and exploit its riches, all to the greater good of the mother country.

Not until a few decades into the eighteenth century did economic science become a subject in its own right at any university. The pioneers were in Prussia (Halle and Frankfurt an der Oder), followed by Hesse (Rinteln), and Sweden (Uppsala) (Stieda, 1906). It was not by chance that all these universities were situated in Lutheran countries. Politically, Lutheranism meant that the state had direct power over the church and, consequently, over the universities. The king of Prussia, the duke of Hesse and the four Estates of the current Swedish parliament could all decide that the universities should have chairs in economic science.

The chair in Uppsala was instituted ten years after Berch's dissertation. In

1731, however, the other three chairs were already functioning, Halle and Frankfurt since 1727 and Rinteln since 1730. These facts were not unknown to the author of the dissertation. Anders Berch had probably got interesting information at least about Halle from his elder brother, Carl Reinhold Berch, a numismatist, who travelled to Germany in 1729–30 and visited the university in Halle. We have every reason to believe that Carl Reinhold told his younger brother the latest news from the University of Halle, including the professorship in that exciting new subject, economic science.

Anders Berch did not write his dissertation *De felicitate patriæ per oeconomiam promovenda* entirely on his own. In the eighteenth century, the identity of the author was of minor importance—it was the defence that was the essential thing. In many cases the candidates wrote their dissertation themselves, but equally often the professor in charge—or even a third person—wrote it. In this case, we can be quite sure that Anders Celsius, Berch's most influential teacher, gave him at least the main lines; Berch's dissertation has in fact been extracted from another dissertation, dealing with the utility of a whole series of sciences (Celsius & Råfelt, 1732). At the same time, it is very likely that Berch had worked out the details himself. Much of what it says is quite similar to what Berch was later to say about economic science. However, the dissertation was not for a degree but was only "pro exercitio", for the sake of the exercise. Anders Berch never completed his university studies.

2.3 Anders Berch after his Dissertation

After his dissertation Anders Berch left Uppsala and was employed by the Board of Commerce (*Kommerskollegium*) in Stockholm (Ferrner, 1776). The reason is quite clear. The Board of Commerce was the nucleus of economic policy-making and theoretical discussion, and Berch's chances of learning about practical as well as theoretical economic life was certainly greater there than in Uppsala. He also had numerous opportunities for meeting the leading Hat politicians and other men of influence. It is difficult not to see the years at the Board of Commerce as another step in a career planned for the non-existent first Swedish chair in economic science.

2.3.1 The Professorship

During the parliamentary session of 1738–39, the Hat party gained a majority in the important parliamentary committees. Immediately the question of a chair in economic science at the University of Uppsala appeared on the agenda. All the four estates of which the parliament was composed—Nobles, Clergy, Burghers, and Peasantry—were in favour of establishing such a useful professorship. Moreover the burghers presented a lengthy memorandum which eloquently argued in favour of the proposal, discussing the kind of material that such a professor should teach and describing a number of personal qualifications required for the position. In retrospect we can see that all these points fit in well with Berch's views on economic science, and that the personal characteristics give a surprisingly accurate picture of him, and of his background in the natural sciences and practical economic science. It is hard to avoid the suspicion that the good burghers had received some help in writing this memorandum by an ambitious 28-year-old bureaucrat at the Board of Commerce (Staf, 1972, pp. 455–456).

The idea of the new chair met with resistance in Uppsala, where the professors were accustomed to having some say in their own business. But their grumbling was of no avail. The chair was established and several candidates immediately applied for it. Despite their considerable formal competency, they had no chance this time as the decision was taken not at the university of Uppsala at all but in Stockholm (Annerstedt, 1913, p. 101 ff.). It was up to the Delegation on Trade and Manufacturing to suggest a suitable person for the professorship during the 1740–41 parliamentary session. Berch had just been appointed secretary to the delegation—a delicate position it may seem, but certainly an advantage. The delegation suggested its own secretary, and the king appointed Berch *Professor Jurisprudentiae, Oeconomiae et Commerciorum* on 16 September, 1741.

In the first years following his appointment Berch was sometimes scorned by his colleagues in Uppsala, who regarded him as a political appointee of dubious scholarly qualifications. However, during the 1740s he acquired increasing respectability, and although his connections with the rich and mighty down in Stockholm made him a somewhat alien creature in the academic community, he seems to have been getting on well with most of the other university professors. Browsing through the the old minutes of faculty meetings from the 1740s and 1750s, I have been struck by the recurrent conflicts between Berch and the university's international superstar, Carolus Linnaeus. The latter tended to regard economic science as *his* subject, a field closely related to botany. Berch on the other hand saw economic science as a field of its own, requiring knowledge in the natural sciences, law and social institutions, with an emphasis on commerce as well as agriculture. Linnaeus and Berch had ample opportunity to develop their arguments, for example when discussing recruits for promotion to various university positions in economic science and related subjects. In 1759 Linnaeus was given his "own" chair in "Practical Economy" in Uppsala, the so-called *Borgströmianska professuren*, devoted mainly to applied botany, zoology and mineralogy (Annerstedt, 1912–14, pp. 401–402). The holders of this chair were disciples of Linnaeus but, unfortunately, rather bad scientists. In the nineteenth century, the professorship became exclusively a chair in botany.

2.3.2 Anders Berch's Scientific Production

In 1746 Berch published his first major work in economic science, *Sätt, at igenom Politisk Arithmetica utröna länders och rikens Hushållning* ("On studying the wealth of nations by political arithmetics", Berch, 1746). Political arithmetics was the term used for what we now call statistics, and Berch's book is therefore the first book on statistics to be published in Sweden. By that time it was already a well-established field abroad; the Englishmen John Graunt and William Petty (to whom Berch refers in his book) had written their studies on birth rates and mortality almost a century earlier, and in the 1730s and 1740s several works by German and Dutch statisticians appeared. One of the cornerstones of the mercantilist doctrine was that a large population was a prerequisite for the wealth of a nation, and that by possessing detailed quantitative knowledge of the population, the government could find out how to stimulate its growth, thereby enriching the country.

Berch's purpose in his *Arithmetica* was to provide an estimate of Sweden's population. At that time, this could be done in two ways. One was to start from the flow data, i.e. the fairly detailed figures on births and deaths which, although scattered, did actually exist, and use them together with assumptions about the average life expectancy and steady-state properties of the population etc. to calculate the stock variable, i.e. the size of the population. This had been the method adapted by Graunt and Petty, for example. The other was to use tax data to compute the total number of taxpayers in the country, and by assuming that a given proportion of the people pays tax, it was possible to obtain an estimate of the whole population. This route had been followed by the Englishmen Charles Davenant and Gregory King, and Berch now chose it for his work.

From the tax records he computed the number of agricultural units, assumed various family sizes and various numbers of servants, farm-hands, etc. depending on the size of the unit, and arrived at the conclusion that the population in the Swedish countryside—including Finland, then a part of Sweden—amounted to 2,708,000 persons. By similar methods, he then estimated the urban population at 342,000, which gave him a national total of 2,990,000.

At the same time another statistician, Pehr Elvius, used the alternative method and arrived at a considerably lower estimate: 2,072,000 (Hjelt, 1900). From the point of view of national security, this figure (which we now know was close to the correct one) seemed alarmingly low, and its publication was therefore suppressed by the authorities. After this bewildering exercise, the government decided to take econometrics seriously. In 1748 it therefore created a national agency whose task was to produce and process economic data (which basically meant population data). Today, thanks to this decision, Sweden and Finland possess the longest demographic time series in the world. They begin in 1749 and consist of actual as opposed to estimated figures—the population was literally counted, person by person.

A natural question for a political arithmetician believing firmly in the mercantilist doctrine that the complex and unstable economy needed the firm guidance of an enlightened planner, was whether the distribution of people among the different professions was really the optimal one. In two publications (Berch, 1749 and 1761) Berch asked the following question: is the number of students at the Swedish universities too large? Using the same approach as in his *Arithmetica*, he made a rough estimate of the number of people with an academic education needed in Sweden, and to the dismay of his fellow professors he found that at present too many were being educated. This work led him to start collecting information about the students at the university, and from 1761 onwards we therefore have an interesting data set which has not yet been systematically analysed: yearly figures on the number of students, their age distribution, their distribution among the faculties, their social background, etc.

One year after the appearance of the *Arithmetica* Berch published the book which was to become his most influential work, the *Inledning till Allmänna Hushållningen* ("Introduction to General Economic Science", Berch, 1747). It was nothing less than Sweden's first—and for almost a century only—textbook in economic science. It was used at Swedish universities until the beginning of the nineteenth century, and a German translation published in 1763 was used at several universities on the continent.

Being intended as a textbook, it did not contain anything really new. Moreover, as a scientist Berch was a collector and systematizer rather than the kind of creative and epoch-making innovator that since the romantic movement of the nineteenth century we tend to identify as "great scientists". Nonetheless, the book made an important contribution to the field; as a comprehensive and well-written exposé over current mercantilist doctrine, it acquired widespread and long-lasting influence. Compared to its immediate predecessors in the shape of books written by German cameralists in the 1720s and 1730s, Berch's book aimed at considerable generality; it does not lose itself completely in institutional detail but tries to some extent to disentangle the more fundamental economic mechanisms. It also won an international reputation for its author, and Berch was elected fellow of a few scientific societies in Germany and England.

The main thrust of the book was of course standard mercantilism: the economy cannot manage by itself, but needs the guidance of what we may call "the visible hand", i.e. the controls of an enlightened government. And the main source of national wealth is the (positive) trade balance, i.e. the stock of precious metals accumulated in the country. But in his discussion of these matters Berch shows considerable moderation.

To mercantilism in its crudest form, import duties constitute a tempting solution to the problem of improving the trade balance. Berch is sceptical;

he does not want to dismiss tariffs altogether, but he points out the risk of retaliation and trade war. With first-hand knowledge of many of the industrial enterprises of the time, he also writes that a "reasonable" degree of competition from abroad could be beneficial to society, since it invigorates the firms and precludes the emergence of monopolies.

Political arithmetics are naturally included in the textbook, and Berch advocates a large and concentrated population. He also discusses whether the choice of occupation should be left to the individuals themselves. Being a moderate, he is fully aware of the potential errors: if people are allowed to choose their profession, there may be too many workers of one type and too few of another, but if the government decides (or if, as before, everybody is forced to remain in his father's trade) there will necessarily be some misallocation of exceptional talents. Weighing the pros and cons, he finally concludes that the best system would involve a mixture of the two principles.

This issue is closely connected with the question of the division of labour. Today most people tend to associate the discovery of the value of specialization with Adam Smith, and the famous section in Book I of *The Wealth of Nations* is a standard reference in any discussion of the topic (Smith, 1776). Yet the value of the division of labour was known to economists long before Smith. In fact this is a typical example of the kind of observation which the mercantilists loved, and Berch's textbook contains an extensive discussion of it. Besides, one of the doctoral dissertations defended under his auspices and certainly written by him, is entitled *Tankeförsök om särskilda näringars särskilda idkande* ("Essay on the special cultivation of special industries") (Berch & Westbeck, 1747), and it contains a detailed analysis of the usefulness of an increasing division of labour. According to Berch, the division of labour is the real motor of an expanding economy. He found it a drawback that the normal farmer was still a Jack-of-all-trades, and hoped for future specialization in agriculture, as advanced as that prevailing in manufacturing.

2.3.3 Anders Berch's Academic Teaching

Berch's *Introduction to General Economic Science* formed the basis for most of his lectures in Uppsala. These lectures, however, were very detailed and exhaustive as we can see from the enormous amount of neatly written and carefully phrased manuscripts preserved in the University Library at Uppsala. Annotations in the margins make clear that these lecture notes—and not only the printed *Introduction* itself—were used by Berch's successors in the chair at least until the first decades of the nineteenth century. This means that Berchs' lectures could still be heard half a century after his death. Needless to say, his successors were by no means as assidiuous as he had been. His own son Christian Berch, who mainly as a result of Anders' academic manipulations held the chair for some decades, was so lazy that he even extracted dissertations for his Students from his father's lecture notes!

Anders Berch's students were not very numerous—especially compared with the hundreds listening to Linnaeus—but he normally had an audience of forty or fifty people. Most of his listeners were future rural vicars. The original bold idea that Anders Berch's professorship would help to mould a new type of more down-to-earth academic had obviously failed. The great majority of students remained unaffected by Anders Berch's teaching.

Berch did not surrender to the inertia of academic life, however. In the 1750s he succeeded in realizing the most original of his early ideas, namely an "economic theatre", the *Theatrum Oeconomico-Mechanicum*, opened in 1754. This was a museum displaying artefacts which Berch found relevant to the study of economic science: raw materials in various stages of processing, models of machines and tools, and samples of finished and semi-finished products. The house where the *Theatrum* was located is still standing—it is an old, monumental stone building in the Old Square in Uppsala, where Berch and his successors also had their lodgings. To build such a house was an expensive affair, and the university could not spend so much money on such an exclusive purpose, but Berch's wealthy and powerful friends in Stockholm now came to his aid. As he notes in an academic programme in connections with a doctoral promotion, the house could be completed only after substantial economic support had been provided by a whole series of very wealthy people, whose names he mentions with gratitude. As far as I know, this was the first private donation of any real importance, at least from trade and industry, to a Swedish university (Berch, 1763, p. 3).

Berch's *Theatrum* did have some predecessors in Germany, but the Uppsala institution was by far the most important economic museum, as visitors from abroad have also certified. One of them, the German botanist and economist Daniel Schreber, has left us a very vivid and detailed description of the collections (Schreber, 1755–62). From this and from Berch's own correspondence we know that in order to illustrate the work of the manufactories he exhibited models of the machines that were in use there, as well as specimens of raw materials and products, and even typical "weaving faults" (the equivalent of the zoologists' collections of deformities and monstrosities). But he encounted opposition from the manufactories of whom he had spoken and written so warmly—they did not want to reveal their trade secrets!

2.3.4 Ploughs

Schreber's description makes it clear that Berch burned with the same feverish desire to classify objects as Linnaeus did, with the difference that

Berch mainly classified artefacts of various kinds. Thus, for example, he grouped at least thirty different types of ploughs in use in Sweden, into four plough "families".

Berch's plough models have been and still are justly admired for their exactitude and neatness. And it is not only from the *Theatrum* that we know of the great interest which Berch—that son of big finance in Stockholm—always felt for ploughs and ploughing. It goes without saying that he was also a member of the young Royal Academy of Science in Stockholm, and his topic of discussion at the Academy was ploughs. The generally wretched quality of Swedish ploughs was well-known. The eighteenth century was the great age of agricultural reform, and the reformers in England and France found imitators in Sweden, who also borrowed ideas on new types of plough. Anders Berch—who had been taught mechanics and physics by Anders Celsius—dealt with the subject thoroughly. In a well-known essay which appeared in the Academy's Proceedings for 1759 under the title of *Anmärkningar öfver de svenske plogar* ("Notes on the Swedish ploughs", Berch, 1759), he went into great detail about the function of the plough, the different ploughs to be found in Sweden, and even the names of different parts of the plough in various Swedish dialects.

Man first got the idea for ploughs from the sight of pigs rooting around in the soil, said Berch, with an acknowledgment to Pliny the Elder. This learned allusion was not merely for the sake of ornament. In a true mercantilist spirit, the author wished to make the point that the workings of the plough could not be achieved by manual labour. In other words the plough did not contradict the essential need for an increase in the population. On the contrary, improving the plough would serve to increase prosperity, for with better ploughs more people could be supported. Berch therefore advised "our good Mechanici" to tackle the problem of improving Swedish ploughs. But they must remember that a simple machine was needed, not one as complex as the works of a clock.

As we already know, Berch possessed vast knowledge of the different types of ploughs in Sweden. But in this essay he admitted that he was not sure which one was really the best, and hence the most promising subject for technical refinement. He therefore rounded off his essay with an imaginative suggestion. Peasants from all parts of Sweden after all had to come to Stockholm to attend the parliamentary sessions. Could not the good members of the Estate of the Peasants bring ploughs and competent ploughmen with them? A ploughing contest could be arranged on Gärdet in Stockholm. Anders Berch declared: "The result would then surely show which is the best plough." As far as we know, this ploughing contest never happened.

2.4 The Decline of Economic Science at the University

In 1768 Uppsala was shaken by a great scandal: the University's financial manager, Peter Julinsköld, went bankrupt, and it was soon discovered that he had used university funds to cover his private deficits. In this situation Berch was asked by the administration to take over Julinsköld's job and to put the University's finances into order. He accepted and served as financial manager (to everybody's satisfaction, it would seem) until his death in 1774.

As professor of economic science he was followed by N. P. Christiernin, a very clever but unfortunately also very quarrelsome and cantankerous academic, who after only a year decided to exchange this chair for another one in philosophy. Christiernin, however, has won some fame in the history of economic doctrine: in 1760 he formulated the quantitative theory of money in a more general and elegant way than David Hume had done a decade before.

After Christiernin the decline was rapid. Times had changed; utilitarian ideas were losing ground. Berch's chair, which had always been attached to the faculty of law, was now occupied by jurists who gave scanty versions of Anders Berch's old lectures. Similarly the Borgström an professorship in practical economy became increasingly a seat of pure botany; the economic side was forgotten. In the early nineteenth century it would have been difficult to imagine the thriving departments of economic science at Uppsala university today. To Anders Berch, however, such a development would have seemed quite natural. In many respects, he seems to us a very modern figure, diligently working in close relation with state, trade, industry and university. He is still among us.

References

Annerstedt, C., 1912, *Upsala universitets historia, Bihang 3* (History of Uppsala University, Appendix 3), Uppsala: Almqvist & Wiksell.
— 1913, *Upsala universitets historia, Band 3:1* (History of Uppsala University, Volume 3:1), Uppsala: Almqvist & Wiksell.
— 1914, *Upsala universitets historia, Band 3:2* (History of Uppsala University, Volume 3:2), Uppsala: Almqvist & Wiksell.
Berch, A., 1746, *Sätt, at igenom politisk arithmetica utröna länders och rikens hushåldning* (Means to Ascertain the Economy of Countries and States through Political Arithmetics), Uppsala: Ferrner.
— 1747, *Inledning til almänna hushålningen, innefattande grunder til politie, oeconomie och cameral wetenskaperne [...]* (Introduction to General Administration Including the Basis for Political, Economic and Fiscal Sciences), Uppsala: Ferrner.
— 1749, *Tal om den proportion, som de studerande är fordra til de ledige beställningar i riket, hållet för den academiska ungdomen i Upsala [...] då han afträdde rectoratet D. 17 junii 1749. Öfversatt från det latinska [...] af H. L.* (Speech about the Proportion between the Number Students and Employment Openings in the Country, Made to the Academic Youth in Uppsala when he Resigned from the

Vice-Chancellorship on 17 June 1749. Translated from the Latin [...] by H. L.) Uppsala: Akad. Program.
— 1759, "Anmärkningar öfver de svenska plogar" (Remarks on Swedish Ploughs), I: *Vetenskaps-Akademiens Handlingar*, Stockholm: Kungl. Vetenskapsakademien.
— 1761, *Quod ad illustrem*, Uppsala: Akad. Program.
— 1763, *Ut florens bonarum artium*, Uppsala: Akad. Program.
— 1747, *Tankeförsök om särskilda näringars idkande* (Intellectual Efforts on the Practising of Certain Industries), Uppsala.
Celsius, A. & Berch, A. 1731, *De felicitate patriæ per oecconomiam promovenda*, Uppsala (diss.).
— 1732, *De felicitate civili per philosophiam comparanda*, Uppsala (diss.).
Ferrner, B., 1776, *Åminnelse-Tal, öfver [...] Herr Doctor Anders Berch, hållet [...] för Kongl. Vetenskaps-academien den 20 Januari 1776* (Speech in Commemoration of [...] Mr. Dr. Anders Berch, Made [...] to the Royal Academy of Sciences on 20 January 1776), Stockholm: Kungl. Vetenskapsakademien.
Hjelt, A., 1900, *Det svenska tabellverkets uppkomst, organisation och tidiga verksamhet* (The Origin of the Swedish Collection of Statistical Tables, Its Organisation and Early Activities), Stockholm: Fennia.
Petander, K., 1912, *De nationalekonomiska åskådningarna i Sverige sådana de framträda i litteraturen. Bd I, 1718–1765* (The Economics Way of Thinking in Sweden as they Appear in the Literature. Vol. I, 1718–1765), Stockholm: Norstedts.
Schreber, D. (ed.), 1755–62, *Sammlung verschiedener Schriften, welche in die Ökonomischen, Policey- und Cameral auch andere Schriften einschliessen*, Halle: Henselmann.
Schück, H., (ed.), 1918, *Bokwetts gillet*, Uppsala: Uppsala universitet.
Smith, A., 1776, *An Inquiry into the Nature and Causes of the Wealth of Nations*, London.
Staf, N. (ed.), 1972, "Borgarståndets protokoll från frihetstidens början" (The Records of the Burghers from the Beginning of the Gustavian Era), I: *Borgarståndet*, Stockholm: Almqvist & Wiksell.
Stieda, W., 1906, *Die Nationalökonomie als Univärsitätswissenschaft*, Leipzig: Königl. sächsischen Gesellschaft der Wissenschaft.

Chapter 3
Anders Berch's Followers
The Development of Modern Academic Business Studies in Sweden

Lars Engwall
Uppsala University, Sweden

3.1 Introduction

A few years ago, in 1987, a Swedish business journal published an article under the headline: "The Battle is Over—the Engineers Lost. The Business Graduates Control the Companies." It reported that 32 per cent of the top managers in the 1,000 largest Swedish firms were business graduates and 22 per cent engineering graduates. But the engineers still held the lead in manufacturing (34 vs. 31 per cent), and consulting (30 vs. 21 per cent), in the second case largely due to the preponderance of engineers in computer consultancy. But even in the traditional strongholds of engineering, business graduates had made significant breakthroughs. Of these the promotion of Percy Barnevik, a graduate of the Gothenburg School of Economics, to the top post in ASEA, traditionally a very "technology-heavy" company, is probably the most spectacular.[1]

The present chapter will explore the developments which brought business education to this position. First in Section 3.2, we will look at the development of institutions for academic business education. Section 3.3 focuses on the activities of institutions in terms of curricula, while Section 3.4 investigates research. This analysis will be followed in Section 3.5 by a discussion of the diffusion of business graduates and in Section 3.6 by some concluding remarks.[2]

3.2 Institutions

An important platform for the institution created by Anders Berch consisted of mercantilistic ideas. However, the standing of these ideas gradually declined during the 18th century, and so did the academic teaching of economic subjects. Anders Berch, who continued as professor until 1771,

---

[1] *Ledarskap* (1987).
[2] For a more extensive treatment of the subject, see Engwall (1992), Gunnarsson (1988) and Wallerstedt (1988).

Table 3.1 *Some Predecessors of the Stockholm School of Economics*

1820	Paris (École Supérieure de Commerce)
1851	University of Louisiana
1856	Wiener Handelsakademie
1869	Washington and Lee University
1881	Wharton School of Finance and Commerce at the University of Pennsylvania, Paris (École des Hautes Études Commerciales)
1898	University of California, University of Chicago, Leipzig, Vienna, Aachen, St. Gallen
1900	Budapest, Dartmouth College (Amos Tuck School)
1901	Cologne, Frankfurt am Main
1902	Milan, Birmingham (Commerce degree)
1903	Brussels
1904	Manchester (Commerce degree)
1906	Berlin
1907	Mannheim
1908	Columbia University, Harvard University

did have some successors, among them his own son Christer. But in the 1780s the chair took on a more legal orientation, and the economic sciences disappeared from the universities for quite some time.

However, at the turn of the present century a government committee recommended that bookkeeping courses should be introduced into the universities. It was a proposal which did not appeal to Carl-Axel Reuterskiöld, at the time Professor of Juridical Encyclopaedia, Roman Law and International Private Law at Uppsala. He found it inappropriate to arrange "all sorts of teaching courses useful in practical life" at the university, and therefore strongly disapproved of the committee's suggestion. Despite negative reactions like this, university courses in bookkeeping were started. But this was not the real breakthrough in the revival of academic business education. Instead, this occurred with the opening of the Stockholm School of Economics in 1909, after businessmen had taken matters into their own hands. In 1903 Marcus Wallenberg donated 100,000 Swedish Crowns for a business school in the name of his half-brother Knut, primarily with a view to improving the reputation of businessmen. According to a contemporary observer it was thus of minor importance to him what the students actually learnt at the school. In this respect his attitude was very similar to that of the sponsor of the Städtische Handels-Hochschule in Cologne, as reported by Robert Locke (1984, p. 136).[3]

---

[3] Sources for the comments in this paragraph are the Minutes of the Faculty of Law at Uppsala University, November 9, 1903 paragraph 3; also *Handelshögskolan i Stockholm 1909–1959* (1959, pp. 7–9), Key (1900), Gårdlund (1976, pp. 261–262), Munthe & Nordfelt (1907), Heckscher (1951, p. 20), and Nordfelt (1943, p. 94)

Table 3.2 *Business Schools Mentioned in Three Swedish Business Journals at the Turn of the Century*

Name of Business School	Per Cent
Leipzig	10.6
Frankfurt am Main	10.2
Cologne	7.5
Aachen	5.4
Berlin	4.3
Antwerp	3.8
Birmingham	3.2
London	3.2
46 schools mentioned less than 6 times	51.8
Total (N=186)	100.0

Source: Gunnarsson (1988, p. 237).

The Wallenberg donation opened the way for Swedes to take part in an international movement already under way in the rest of Europe and the United States (Table 3.1).

There were predecessors in France, the United States, England and Germany. A very early entrant had been the École Superieure de Commerce in Paris. But the real start is often said to have occurred in 1881, when the Wharton School at the University of Pennsylvania and the École des Hautes Études Commerciales in Paris were established. Several German universities, such as Leipzig, Cologne, Frankfurt am Main and Berlin, later followed suit, as did American universities such as the University of California, the University of Chicago, Columbia and Harvard.[4]

Inspiration in Stockholm came primarily from Germany, as can be seen from Table 3.2, which shows the distribution of mentions of different business schools in three leading Swedish business journals.

A top troika, which accounted for almost one-third of the mentions, was composed of Leipzig, Frankfurt am Main and Cologne. Cologne and Berlin, the fifth on the list, became the models adopted for the curriculum of the new school by its head Carl Hallendorff, a Doctor of History from Uppsala who was then teaching at one of the Stockholm grammar schools.

This meant concentrating on two main subjects—business administration and economics with statistics—and two subordinate subjects—jurispru-

---

[4] See Byrt (1989), Hensmann (1969, pp. 278–279), Hugstad (1983, p. 2), Redlich (1957), Ruml (1928), Seyffert (1926, c. 1213), ter Vehn (1959, Inl. 1), Wanous (1969, p. 38), and Whitley, Thomas & Marceau (1981). Needless to say, there is some uncertainty about some of the founding years.

dence and languages. Chairs were created for the two main subjects and for geography, and Hallendorff had to find occupants for them. In economics he appointed Eli Heckscher, at the time reader at Stockholm University, and in geography, Gunnar Andersson, a lecturer at the Institute of Forestry. Business administration was much more problematic, since there were no Swedes available. Discussions with the German Grand Old Man in this field, Eugen Schmalenbach, almost led to his coming to Stockholm, but he withdrew at the last minute. Instead the Stockholm School of Economics appointed one of his students, Ernst Walb.[5] Since Walb lacked the qualifications for a chair, he was taken on as reader, but at an annual salary 12 per cent higher than his two professorial colleagues.[6] This was certainly a sign of the great dependence of the Stockholm School of Economics on expertise in business administration. Even stronger evidence of this was Walb's promotion on grounds of his practical experience to the chair in 1910, after he had threatened to leave for Germany.

Walb did eventually return to Germany and was succeeded in 1912 by Oskar Sillén, a Swede who had graduated from the *Städtische Handels-Hochschule* in Cologne in 1905. At the time when he was approached by the Stockholm School of Economics he was working with the Berlin subsidiary of the Swedish company, Separator. He was hesitant about accepting the job in Stockholm, however, because of the poor pay. It was therefore arranged that he would combine his position at the business school with consultancy work for a subsidiary of the Swedish Federation of Industries. In this way academic business education and practice became closely united in one person, something which must surely have affected the flow of ideas between practice and academe. Needless to say it was also very important to the diffusion of business graduates in industry, particularly as Sillén remained at the Stockholm School of Economics for 40 years.[7] During this time he published books and articles, developed the courses in business administration, and created a research institute and a journal. He was also instrumental in founding the Authorized Public Accountants' Association. He thus became a dominant norm-setter in Sweden's largest enterprises, and enjoyed the respect of the practical world. The story goes that the Swedish publishing company SLT used to put out the flags twice a year: once on Sweden's National Day and once when Oskar Sillén came to do his final audit for the year.

For its first seventeen years the Stockholm School of Economics had to operate in temporary premises at Brunkeberg's Square.[8] In 1926 the school

---

[5] For a more extensive treatment of the search for business administration professors at Stockholm School of Economics, see Wallerstedt (1988, Ch. 2).
[6] Wallerstedt (1988, p. 41).
[7] For a fuller treatment of Sillén's background, his career at SSE and in business, see Wallerstedt (1988).
[8] Interestingly enough the site of the hotel where the school was located nowadays houses the Central Bank of Sweden.

moved to its present location on Sveavägen. In this way the existence of an academic education in business was given very concrete expression. The building was designed by the well-known Swedish architect Ivar Tengbom, and it was opened in the presence of the Swedish King Gustav V.

Three years before the Stockholm School of Economics moved into its new premises, a second business school had been founded in Gothenburg. Plans to create a school there were in fact even older than the plans for Stockholm, but for various reasons Stockholm got there first. Developments in business administration followed much the same course as in Stockholm: difficulty in recruiting a professor in business administration, the appointment of a German who returned fairly soon to his own country, and then a long-term solution. In Gothenburg it was Albert ter Vehn who featured in this role. At the age of 26 he became professor of business administration, and then stayed in office even longer than Oskar Sillén in Stockholm—for 41 years![9]

As well as the way professors were hired other features at the Gothenburg School of Economics were similar to those in Stockholm, and the sequence of events can perhaps be characterized as a "follow-my-leader" pattern of adaptation. Many of the events which occurred in Stockholm were later repeated in Gothenburg after a certain time-lag.

The two professors mentioned—Oskar Sillén and Albert ter Vehn—acquired no professorial colleagues until 1933 and 1951, when marketing chairs were created first in Stockholm and then in Gothenburg. In Stockholm a donation from industry made it possible to create a chair with a special emphasis on administration in 1946. Further donations, among them from the City of Stockholm, later provided for new chairs at the Stockholm School of Economics. In Gothenburg, however, it was not until the 1960s that any more chairs were created, and by the time this happened business administration had already been introduced at the universities of Lund and Uppsala. As early as the 1930s there were proposals to introduce business administration as part of the social science degree, but nothing materialized until 1958.

To a certain extent this delay had to do with exclusion ambitions on the part of the professors at the Stockholm School of Economics, who were very hesitant towards the proposals. And they had good reasons to be, since according to a source then active in the Ministry of Education, the government's intention was in fact to break the duopoly.

A certain continuity obtained, however, since the new professors in both departments were former professors at the Stockholm School of Economics. Nils Västhagen, who had been the first person to defend a doctoral dissertation in business administration in 1950 and was Sillén's successor, now

---

[9] For developments in Gothenburg, see Berglund (1933), Berglund & Grönfors (1977), Gunnarsson (1988, Section 6.4–6.5), and Engwall (1992, Section 2.3).

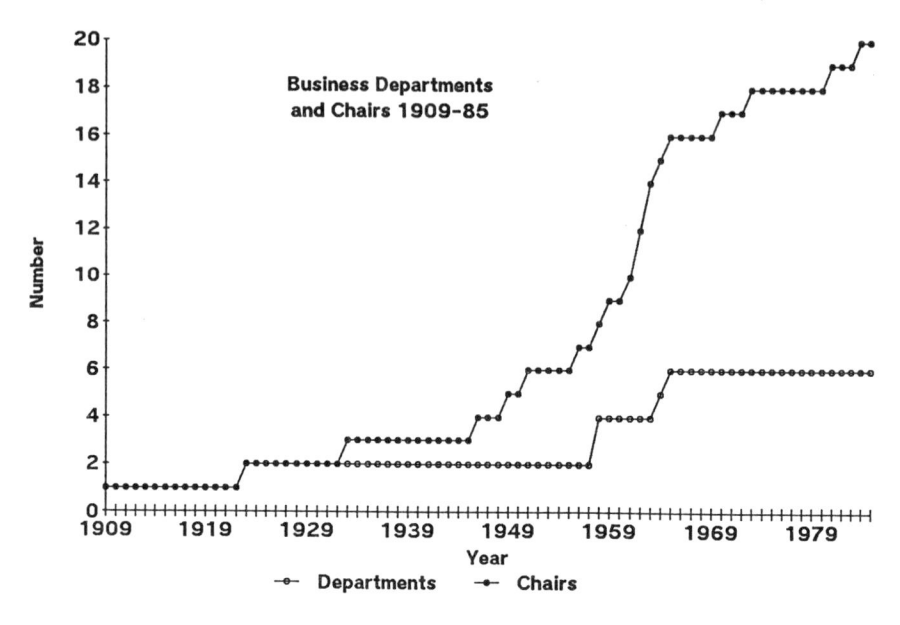

Figure 3.1 *Swedish Departments and Chairs in Business Administration, 1909-85.*

moved to Lund. In his inaugural lecture he was already calling for a third business school in Lund, and a few years later a Faculty of Economics and Business Administration was created there.[10]

Västhagen's colleague at Uppsala was Sune Carlson, whose inaugural lecture was entitled "On Apples and Snakes. Some Economic-Theoretical Aspects of Corruption"—a subject which was familiar to him after six years working for the United Nations. But Carlson's choice of lecture topic was not the only thing that distinguished him from his colleague in Lund; he also felt differently about the role of business administration in the universities. He maintained that business administration should be one subject among others in the faculties of arts, and thought that it was best combined with subjects such as art history, philosophy, history and languages.

After Lund and Uppsala, business administration was also introduced at Stockholm and Umeå, and eventually several more chairs were created. A summary of the development in terms of ordinary chairs and departments up to 1985 (Figure 3.1), reveals that the early decades were marked by rather slow growth. Then in the 1960s many new departments were opened and several new chairs created.

To-day the discipline can thus boast more than twenty ordinary chairs and in addition to them a large number of extra professorships. Simultaneously student enrolment has been increasing to such an extent that business ad-

---

[10] Engwall (1992, Section 2.4).

ministration departments are now very large, if not the largest in the Swedish universities. Furthermore, training in business administration is a major activity in most local colleges.[11]

Business administration has thus made considerable progress in Sweden. However, it has developed in face of powerful resistance. One sign of this was the declaration of the law professor quoted above. Another was the refusal of the Stockholm Association of Student Unions to accept the Student Union of the Stockholm School of Economics as one of its members, because the business students belonged to a category "whose studies and interests [did] not have an academic character"[12].

Reactions such as these are not specific to Sweden. For instance, the Harvard Business School, now regarded as offering golden passports to its graduates, was once "looked down on and even despised by many professors and students at Harvard". A Harvard professor of literature has even been quoted as demanding rhetorically when the business school was mentioned: "What? Sully the robes of Chaucer and Shakespeare with seekers of gold?"[13]

In the terminology of institutional organizational theory we can thus talk about *exclusion ambitions* on the part of insiders who wanted to protect their territory from the intrusion of outsiders. However, we can also find evidence of *adaptation*, another feature in this theory. Once institutions have been able to break down the barriers to entry, they have adopted the behaviour of the insiders. One example is the exclusion behaviour which has been adopted by former outsiders as soon as they have become insiders. Another is the pattern of "follow-my-leader" which has appeared when new institutions have been created. The Stockholm School of Economics, which first had German and later American prototypes, eventually became a prototype for its successors.

3.3 Curricula

Adaptive behaviour is also evident in the curricula. Four important features here are: (1) marked foreign inspiration, (2) declining importance of economics, (3) a gradual increase in behavourial aspects and, (4) a continuous time budget problem.

As regards the first point, *foreign inspiration*, it is irrefutable that German models came to dominate in the early years. The very first curriculum was obviously modelled closely on the one Ernst Walb had previously used in Königsberg, whereas Sillén's first syllabus was inspired by his studies in Col-

---

[11] It should also be mentioned that several chairs embracing an element of business administration have been created at the institutes of technology and at the Agricultural University.
[12] Gunnarsson (1988, p. 15).
[13] Ewing (1990, pp. 267–268).

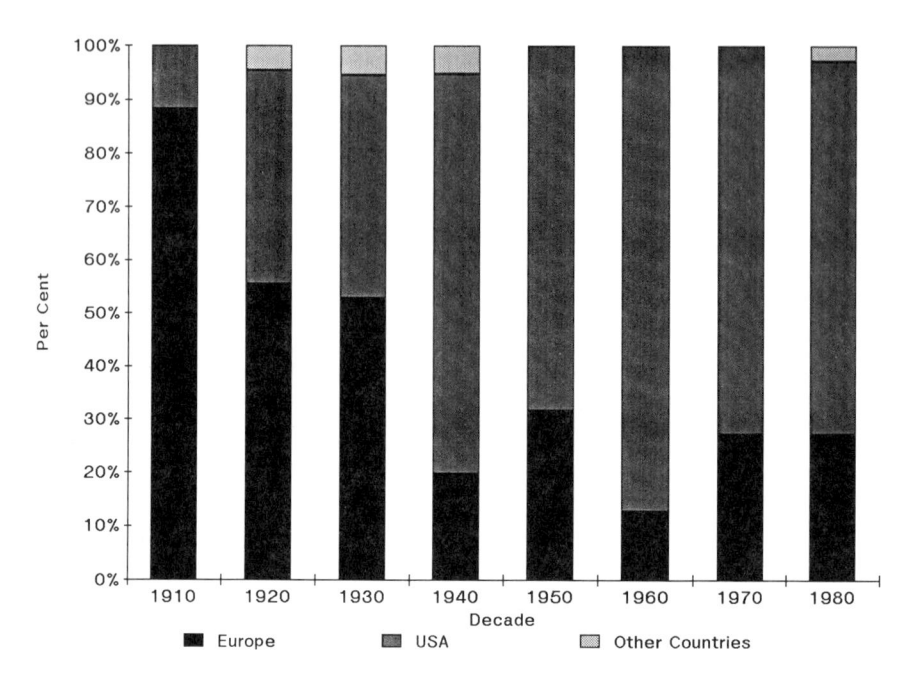

Figure 3.2 *Destinations for Study Tours Made by Stockholm School of Economics Graduates, 1910-85.*

ogne. In later revisions the United States was an important source of inspiration. Sillén himself made a study trip to the United States in 1920, and this apparently influenced his thinking. This tendency must have been reinforced when he was joined by Gerhard Törnqvist, a Columbia M.S. graduate, in 1934. Another indication of the same trend can be seen in the destinations of the study trips made by graduates of the Stockholm School of Economics (Figure 3.2).

In the early years Europe dominated, and in particular Germany, but as early as the 1920s the United States started to emerge as the country of inspiration for Swedes. A certain revival in the European influence occurred after 1969, but the predominance of the United States is still considerable.

Moving to the second point, *the position of economics*, it is clear that this subject occupied a dominant position in the early curricula. Carl Hallendorff, president of the Stockholm School of Economics, thus described it as being "at the centre of the studies at the Stockholm School of Economics".[14] And Eli Heckscher declared: "The purpose of economics in the curriculum

---

[14] Hallendorff (1909, p. 12). Further, in the application for government support in 1909 the order of the two disciplines had been reversed, so that economics came before business administration. This must have been an intentional change, since in alphabetical order the Swedish word for economics, *nationalekonomi*, comes after business administration, which at the time was called *handelsteknik*.

of SSE is to depict the general character and organization of trade and industry, and therefore also to constitute the foundation of studies in the commercial sciences over all."[15] This strong emphasis on economics also proved to be one of the main distinguishing features of the Stockholm School of Economics as compared with the commercial institutes. Two other such features were the omission of practical skills, particularly typing and shorthand, and less emphasis on languages.[16]

Later on, particularly as a result of changes in the curriculum in the 1940s and 1950s, business administration came to be the dominant discipline. This was formally confirmed in the revision of the curriculum in 1957,[17] and was also clearly underlined in 1965 by the Board of the Alumni Association in a policy document.[18]

As regards the third point, *the gradual increase in behavioural aspects*, it should first be emphasized that business administration represented the innovation in the new business schools. All other subjects could be studied academically elsewhere. It is then interesting to note that during the first thirty years the balance between financial and behavioural aspects developed as shown in Figure 3.3.

In the early years the financial aspects dominated, i.e. accounting, finance and managerial economics, constituting about 80 per cent or more of the book titles. A radical change occurred in 1929 when the behavioural elements, i.e. administration and marketing, gained in prominence. And this trend continued until the late 1930s, when the behavioural elements in the eighth syllabus were on a par with the financial side. This development can be seen as a consequence of the link between this discipline and the world of practice. The growing size of business corporations generated administrative problems, and the development of mass markets increased the need to handle marketing problems.

Fourth and finally, *a time budget problem* arose as a result of the consider-

---

[15] *Handelshögskolan i Stockholm* (1909, p. 11). Here we can see Schmalenbach's distinction between economics and business economics: "Economics and business economics handle, to a large extent, the same materials but they do not have the same spirit. Economics is a philosophical science with philosophical characteristics. Business economics is, on the other hand, an applied science. Chemistry and mechanical technology are closer in spirit to business economics than is economics. Business economics is purposeful. It must think purposefully" (Schmalenbach, 1919, p. 259, translation in Locke, 1989, p. 24).

[16] However, the introductory pamphlet indicated that, if necessary, SSE could arrange teaching in typing and shorthand. Apparently this did not materialize to any great extent. This is in contrast to the development in both Denmark (Nielsen, 1986, p. 98 and Handelshøjskolen i Århus 50 år, 1989) and Finland (Sandström, 1977, p. 22).

[17] *Handelshögskolan i Stockholm* (1957, Examination statutes, paragraph 3). This change in favour of business administration, like the tendency for specialization, was also a development simultaneously observed in the United States (Grether, 1959, p. 27).

[18] The Alumni Association was founded in 1912 as *Föreningen Diplomerade från Handelshögskolan i Stockholm* (The Association of Diplom Holders from SSE). In 1919 it changed its name to *Svenska Ekonomföreningen* and in 1954 to *Svenska Civilekonomföreningen* (Junker, 1951).

Figure 3.3 *Theses Areas in Sweden by Period.*

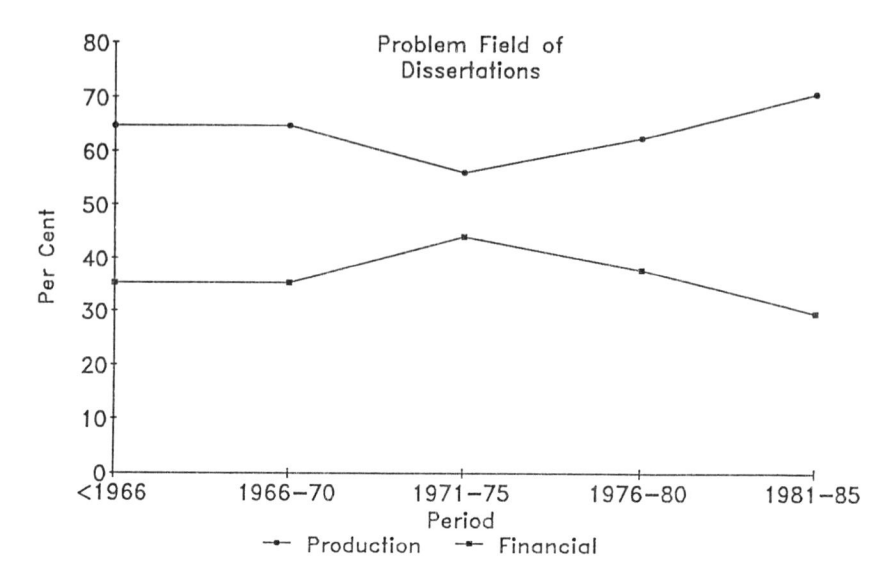

able growth in the mass of material which was considered relevant. As early as 1927 the number of book titles had more than doubled, from 28 to 71. And in the late 1930s the number rose to about 100. Two methods were chosen for solving this problem. One was to introduce a gradual extension of the period of study—from two to three years in 1939, and to three-and-a-half years in 1981. At present an extension to four years has been introduced. The second solution was to allow students to specialize after completing their basic courses. In this way it was possible to expand the curriculum as a whole, while also controlling the amount of material for each individual student.

What has been said so far has mainly concerned developments at the Stockholm School of Economics. With certain variations these patterns also apply to the other institutions. The revision of the curriculum in 1957, with its specialization in four areas, was particularly important. The Stockholm School of Economics has provided a model. Changes in later decades have been minor compared with those of the early years.

3.4 Research

The development of research, the other major activity of the institutions, can be illustrated with the help of two data sources. One consists of the evaluation reports made in the screening of professorial candidates. The other is a questionnaire survey covering the authors of 270 dissertations in business administration submitted in the period ending 1985.

3.4.1 Evaluations of Professorial Candidates

Four epochs can be identified from an examination of the evaluations of professorial candidates: 1909–32, 1933–56, 1957–68, and 1969–85. In the first period (1909–32) research was taken into consideration, but deficiencies in this respect could be compensated by practical experience. This can be seen most clearly in the case of Ernst Walb, already mentioned above; Walb was appointed despite his lack of scientific competence. In presenting his case the head of the Stockholm School of Economics, Carl Hallendorff, admitted that this lacuna was a considerable drawback, "which in any other subject would certainly be considered an obstacle to a possible appointment as professor at the School of Economics." But, according to Hallendorff, Walb possessed, another important qualification for successful teaching in his field, namely practical experience. Eli Heckscher, Walb's colleague in economics at the Stockholm School of Economics, did not share this opinion and was very hesitant about Walb's appointment to the chair. He finally agreed, after declaring that such an appointment would have been impossible "in any other subject but commercial techniques".[19] The question of practical orientation arose again a year later as the search for a second professor was made among German candidates: the one with the best formal qualifications was turned down since he was considered to be too theoretical! Another indication of the appreciation of practical experience was the arrangement we have already mentioned whereby Oskar Sillén was appointed both as professor and as head of a consultant organization. It is also worth noting that practitioners were included on the evaluation committees.

Two explanations can be given for this recognition of practical experience in the early years. First, the supporters of business administration as an academic discipline were probably thinking of the market, i.e. recognizing the importance of these graduates finding jobs. It would not do for prospective employers to consider them too theoretical. Second, a new discipline will always by definition have difficulty at first in finding scientifically qualified candidates for professorships.

Although practical experience was still appreciated in the second period (1933–56), it was now being played down in favour of scientific competence. And in this context the experts were arguing over the core of the discipline. One fundamental difference seems to have been that Albert ter Vehn in Gothenburg was much more apt to stress accounting than his colleagues in Stockholm, who were more inclined to emphasize managerial economics. In a sense this difference may be interpreted as a cultural difference. Albert ter Vehn had the German *Handelshochschule* as his prototype, whereas

---

[19] Minutes of a meeting on 27 April 1910. For a more extensive discussion of the case, see Wallerstedt (1988, pp. 40–42).

many of the professors at the Stockholm School of Economics had a more American orientation with an emphasis on statistics and economic theory. ter Vehn was, again like his German colleagues, also keen on maintaining definite boundaries between his own and other disciplines.

Gerhard Törnqvist, Oskar Sillén's marketing colleague, was the first to formulate explicit criteria for competence when he was acting as an evaluator for the third chair at the Stockholm School of Economics in 1946. For anyone to qualify for a chair he established two indispensable conditions, corresponding in a way to his own profile as a researcher: (1) proven competence regarding managerial economics, and (2) proven scientific competence and practical experience within the relevant special field.

In the third period (1957–68) practical experience was dropped completely, but instead the empirical character of the discipline was underlined. Thus in 1965 Ulf af Trolle, professor of marketing at Gothenburg, declared his regret at "the tendency I have found to construct opinions about commercial life from the depth of one's mind, instead of going out and watching what things actually look like".

Theoretically microeconomics was established as the important foundation at Lund in 1962. The criteria were:

1. a command of microeconomic theory in the field of the applicant's work,
2. an understanding of microeconomic theory in relation to the setting within which firms work,
3. demonstrated knowledge of the internal and external data available for the scientific illustration of business administration problems, and
4. a command of current methods for the treatment and analysis of such data.

Sune Carlson, in sharp contrast to what had been said in many of the earlier evaluation cases, declared: "It is not necessary that an applicant should have written anything in the field of managerial economics."[20]

In connection with two vacancies in the late 1960s a tendency appeared to supplement economic theory with organization theory as an appropriate tool for analysis. As early as 1965 Sune Carlson at Stockholm University had mentioned behavioural theories as a complement to economic theory, and at Umeå University in 1968, in connection with a chair with a special focus on marketing he substituted "organization theory" for "behavioural theories".[21]

As regards production volume, the committee for the second chair at

---

[20] Evaluation report submitted in September 1962 (Quotations from pp. 2, 58–59).
[21] Evaluation report submitted in May 1968.

Lund University in 1962 established criteria which were often used later on. They called for *docent* competence (i.e. roughly the qualifications for a readership), in one field, some valuable work in another field and some additional work in yet another, to show breadth of interest.

In the last period (1969–85) the criteria used in evaluations changed somewhat, although those established in 1962 at Lund University seem to have been applied in many subsequent appointments even after 1970. Particularly important was a stronger emphasis on organization theory as a vital foundation for qualified work in business administration.

However, the diversity of the discipline was increasingly emphasized in subsequent assessments. An expert discussing the requirements for a chair at Stockholm University in 1974, for instance, described a development from the microeconomic core of managerial economics surrounded by different subfields that prevailed in the 1930s and 1940s, via the operations research of the 1950s and the years of systems theory in the 1960s, to the then current situation with its enormous variety of model constructions in business administration. He concluded: "It is thus difficult today to point to a definitive core of 'general business administration' [and] there are thus many ways of making a significant contribution to the evolution of business administration theory."[22] The committee at Umeå University in 1976 extended this argument by pointing out that business administration no longer dealt only with the individual firm; it was also concerned with aggregates of firms or organizations. It was further emphasized that the discipline uses "a spectrum of methods and approaches", that business administration problems were often expressed as decision problems or behavioural or systems problems, and that a command of economic theory and organization theory were essential for a general chair in the field.

3.4.2 Doctoral Dissertations

Since the first doctoral dissertation in business administration was not submitted until 1950, it is not surprising to find that behavioural aspects had already gained a strong position in the earliest examples. An analysis of the distribution between financial and behavioural aspects shows a predominance of administration and marketing throughout. These two areas accounted on average for more than 50 per cent of the chosen topics, while accounting, finance and managerial economics together accounted for about one-third. However, certain differences can be observed between the six institutions (Table 3.3).

Lund and Umeå lead with respect to administrative problems, whereas

---

[22] Evaluation report submitted in November 1974. The quotation from Erik Johnsen's evaluation, p. 3.

Table 3.3 *Dissertation Problem Field in Sweden by Institution* (%)

Problem Field	GSE	LU	SSE	SU	UmU	UU	Total
Administration, Strategy, Organization, Leadership	31.1	46.2	21.3	27.4	42.1	25.0	30.9
Accounting/Finance	11.3	10.4	13.7	4.8	0.0	10.0	9.8
Managerial Economics	18.9	10.4	27.4	23.8	5.3	10.0	18.3
Marketing	31.1	16.0	17.1	21.4	5.3	40.0	22.0
Public Administration	0.0	5.7	5.5	10.7	0.0	0.0	4.3
Small Business and Industrial Organization	1.0	5.7	2.7	2.4	36.8	0.0	5.0
International Business	0.0	1.9	2.7	0.0	0.0	15.0	2.8
Economic Psychology	0.0	0.0	8.2	2.4	0.0	0.0	2.6
Others General	6.6	3.7	1.4	7.1	10.5	0.0	4.3
Number	53	53	73	42	19	30	270

Uppsala is strong in marketing and the Stockholm School of Economics and Stockholm University in managerial economics. Of the specialized fields, Umeå has focused on small business and industrial organization and Uppsala on international business.

An examination of the bibliographical references most frequently mentioned in a questionnaire by the authors of dissertations also shows the emergence of behavioural aspects (Table 3.4).

Again there is a bias towards organization theory. Outstanding as regards both frequency (F) and distribution over departments (D) were Thompson (1967), Cyert & March (1963) and March & Simon (1958). Since other works by James G. March and Herbert A. Simon were also mentioned (16 mentions, altogether), the results clearly indicate that the research tradition of the Carnegie Institute of Technology with its focus on bounded rationality, uncertainty and satisficing behaviour, has made a particularly strong impact on Swedish business research.

An examination of data-collecting methods reveals a similar behavioural orientation. Interviews and questionnaires accounted for about 50 per cent of the data-collecting work. Together with secondary sources they account for almost 80 per cent of such activities.

Table 3.4 *Top References Mentioned by Swedish Doctors of Business Administration*

F	D	Reference
14	6	Thompson, J. D., 1967, *Organizations in Action*, New York: McGraw-Hill.
11	4	Cyert, R. M. & March, J. G., 1963, *A Behavioural Theory of the Firm*, Englewood Cliffs, N.J.: Prentice-Hall.
10	5	March, J. G. & Simon, H. A., 1958, *Organizations*, New York: Wiley.
6	2	Lawrence, P. R. & Lorsch, J. W., 1967, *Organisation and Environment*, Boston, MA: Harvard University.
6	2	Silverman, D., 1970, *The Theory of Organisations*, London: Heinemann.
5	3	Glaser, B. G. & Strauss, A. L., 1967, *The Discovery of Grounded Theory*, New York: Aldine.
5	1	Håkansson, H. (ed.), 1982, *International Marketing and Purchasing —An Interaction Approach*, New York: Wiley.
5	1	Schon, D., 1971, *Beyond the Stable State*, London: Maurice Temple Smith.

We can also see that qualitative methods have been used increasingly for data processing: the trend since 1966 is clear: 12, 23, 34 and 53 per cent. It is also worth noting that the purely theoretical dissertations are few, and in the last period non-existent.

3.4.3 Conclusion

With regard to research orientation we have thus seen evidence of a gradual movement away from the first modest demands for scientific qualifications, via a focus on financial aspects towards a stress of behavioural elements. There has thus been a movement from the earlier core ingredients towards areas on the borderlines of other disciplines such as sociology and psychology. Sweden shares this development with other countries such as Norway, where our colleague Øivind Bøhren has compared business administration research to a doughnut with a little research in the middle and most of it on the edges (Norstrøm, 1991).

3.5 Graduate Diffusion

As we turn to the final aspect of Swedish business studies to be discussed in this chapter, the diffusion of graduates, we find that business education has been successful on three fronts: the markets for students, employment, and management positions. In the first case the business degree has competed mainly with engineering and law degrees. A study of five-year market shares reveals the picture shown in Figure 3.4.

The business graduates thus started out at a very low level representing about 15 per cent of the graduates in 1915, whereas engineers and law

Figure 3.4 *Business, Law and Engineering Degrees Awarded in Sweden, 1911-85 (per cent).*

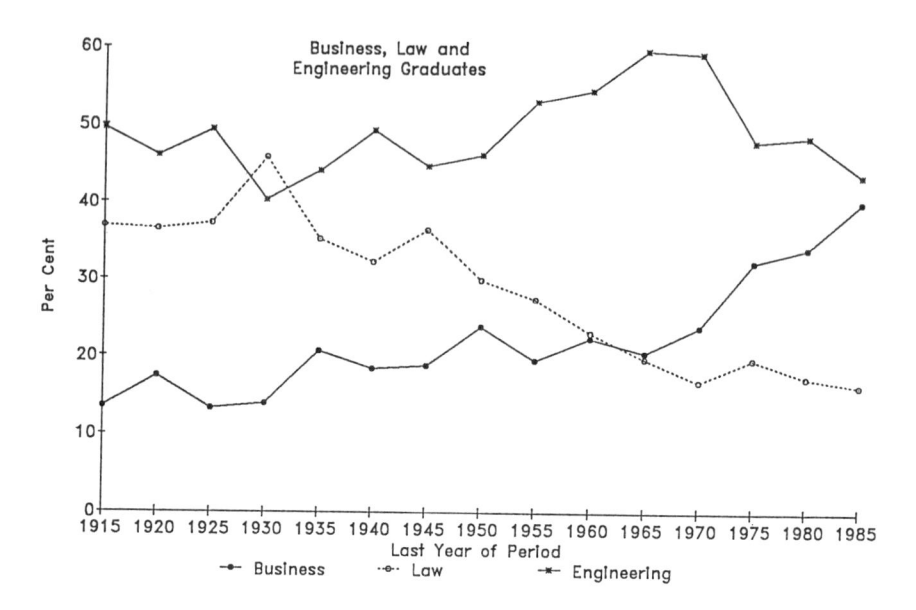

graduates represented about 50 and 35 per cent respectively. Following a peak in the 1930s the proportion of law graduates has declined continuously from 45 per cent to about 15 per cent in 1985, i.e. the same level as business graduates seventy years earlier. Engineers have been fairly stable around or even a little over 50 per cent, but their relative share has been falling since the early 1970s. At the same time the proportion of business graduates has increased from less than 20 per cent in 1965 to almost 40 per cent in 1985. Behind this development we can discern the institutional growth that we have already discussed in Section 3.2.

However, it was not enough for business students to graduate. They also had to be accepted by practitioners, in other words to find employment. It was not only university people who were sceptical about academic business education. Many businessmen felt the same, since their tradition dictated that practice was the one and only way into business. If any business employees had enjoyed a formal higher education, it would have been in engineering or law.

An important means of promoting the diffusion of business graduates was by giving them a title. This was a difficult question and it took many years of discussion before the Alumni Association decided in 1943 to adopt the title of *civilekonom*. It is apparent from this choice that the ambition of the business graduates was to achieve parity with the graduates of the institutes of technology, who were traditionally known as *civilingenjör*, to differentiate them from engineers trained under the auspices of the military. In en-

Table 3.5 *Functions of Business and Engineering Graduates in Swedish Industry in 1966, 1970 and 1974*

Function	Business Degree 1966	1970	1974	Engineering Degree 1966	1970	1974
Economic Control	42	39	42	0	0	0
Marketing	25	32	31	11	10	12
Administrative Control	22	18	15	4	4	4
Data Control	5	6	5	1	3	6
Assistance	3	2	4	1	1	1
Purchasing	2	2	2	0	0	0
Production Control	1	1	1	22	20	18
Research & Development	0	0	0	61	62	59
Number	943	1336	1863	5182	6997	9225
Average Competence Level	3.3	3.4	3.7	3.5	3.5	3.8

gineering there was thus a historical explanation of the prefix *civil*. The closest the business graduates could come to a similar analogy was the title of *civilintendent* (literally a non-military quartermaster), but this was felt too strange to introduce on the labour market. The fact that the title *civilekonom* was odd for another reason—that there were never any military economists—only worried a few, among them Eli Heckscher.[23]

Table 3.5 tells us something about the functions of the business graduates, showing that they work mainly in economic control, marketing and administrative control, whereas engineers appear mainly in production control and R & D. It is also worth noting that although the level of competence is falling, the business graduates on average have higher competence levels than their engineering colleagues—that is, their figures are lower in the last row.

Studies going further back in time shows that marketing-oriented industries have been more apt to hire business graduates. Manufacturing and auditing are important sectors, but so too is the public sector, particularly in recent decades.

If we look at the success of business graduates in the third market, i.e. in obtaining management positions, we again find that penetration has been gradual. In early studies engineering was the most common degree among Swedish top managers, but a study undertaken in the early 1970s showed

---

[23] Regnstrand (1951, pp. 53–65), Junker (1951, pp. 84–85) and interview with Albert ter Vehn.

that business had surpassed engineering as the most frequent degree in this group, with the former accounting for 35 per cent and the latter for 30 per cent of the total.[24] And as we have seen, the 1980s the predominance of the business graduates among top managers had become more pronounced.

3.6 Conclusions

Thus looking at the development of business administration in Sweden, it is no exaggeration to say that the discipline has undergone a considerable transformation during the present century. And there is little evidence of established researchers blocking change, as might be expected according to Thomas S. Kuhn's argument in his book *The Structure of Scientific Revolutions*. Instead these people seem to have been fairly open to new problems and new methods. One important reason for this seems to be that the discipline has maintained a constant connection with practice. At the same time Swedish scholars of business administration have been part of an international development, which has been greatly influenced by work in the United States. In the words of Robert Locke: "The scientific techniques, the tools used in financial analysis, in marketing, in inventorying, in production layout, and so on, are part of a common managerial science, one which the Americans largely, if not exclusively, invented, and one everybody borrowed" (Locke, 1989, p. 54). Thus, although we can see variations between countries, there is a tendency for business administration to spread worldwide. Business schools are being opened in many different countries today, regardless of religion or political system.

A natural question in conclusion is of course what will happen next. In market terms we know that demand today is higher than supply. In Sweden there are six applicants for every student place, and those accepted have to have excellent marks from school. According to one scenario this may change, as more and more business graduates find employment. At some point according to this line of argument there will be excess supply, and demand will drop.

According to an alternative view, business administration concepts have become a modern language which is employed in communications between the various actors in modern organizations. This development is not limited to the business world, but applies nowadays to public organizations as well. The business administration concepts have come to constitute a language which people have to know to be able to survive in present-day organizations. According to this hypothesis the demand for business administration knowledge will increase by a more or less self-reinforcing process: the more

---

[24] This calculation is based on Table 3:3 in Bolin & Dahlberg (1975). The figures imply that double degrees have been counted.

people who go into business studies, the greater the future demand for such studies will be.

References

Berg, G., 1979, "Anders Berch—en forskar- och lärargestalt i 1700-talets Uppsala" (Anders Berch—A Teacher and Researcher in the Eighteenth Century Uppsala), In: *Tal över blandade ämnen*, Collegium Curiosorum Novum årsbok 1977–78, Uppsala: Carmina, pp. 7–25.
Berglund, H. & Grönfors, K. (eds.), 1977, *Handelshögskolan i Göteborg 1923–1971. En minnesbok* (The Gothenburg School of Economics 1923–1971. A Memorial Publication), Göteborg: Västsvenska Akademibokhandeln.
Berglund, H., 1933, *Handelshögskolan i Göteborg. Tioårsöversikt 1923–1933* (Gothenburg School of Economics. An Overview for the Ten Years 1923–1933), Göteborg: Handelshögskolan i Göteborg.
Bohlin, E. & Dahlberg, L., 1975, *Dagens storföretagsledare* (Top Managers of Today), Stockholm: SNS.
Byrt, W. (ed.), 1989, *Management Education. An International Survey*, London: Routledge.
Carlson, S., 1983, *Studier utan slut* (Studies without an End), Stockholm: SNS.
Cyert, R. M. & March, J. G., 1963, *A Behavioral Theory of the Firm*, Englewood Cliffs, NJ: Prentice-Hall.
Engwall, L. (ed.), 1980, *Företagsekonomins rötter. Några bidrag till en företagsekonomisk doktrinhistoria* (The Roots of Business Administration. Some Contributions to a History of the Business Administration Doctrine), Lund: Studentlitteratur.
— 1992, *Mercury Meets Minerva*, Oxford: Pergamon Press.
Ewing, D, W, 1990, *Inside the Harvard Business School. Strategies and Lessons of America's Leading School of Business*, New York: Times Books.
Grether, E. T., 1959, "Handelsutbildning. American Style" (Business Education. American Style), *Ekonomen*, 35, No. 15, pp. 24–30.
Gunnarsson, E., 1988, *Från Hansa till Handelshögskola. Svensk ekonomundervisning fram till 1909* (From the Hanseatic League to a School of Economics. Swedish Business Education up to 1909), Acta Universitatis Upsaliensis. Studia Oeconomiae Negotiorum 29, Uppsala: Almqvist & Wiksell International (diss.).
Gårdlund, T., 1976, *Marcus Wallenberg 1864–1943. Hans liv och gärning* (Marcus Wallenberg 1864–1943. His Life and Work), Stockholm: Norstedts.
Hallendorff, C., 1909, "Handelshögskolerörelsen och den svenska handelshögskolan" (The Business School Movement and the Swedish School of Economics), *Föredrag vid Handelskammarföreningens årsmöte den 24 april 1909* (Speach at the Annual Meeting of the Society of the Chambers of Commerce on 24 April 1909).
Handelshøjskolen i Århus 50 år (The Århus School of Economics), 1989, Århus: Handelshøjskolen i Århus.
Handelshögskolan i Stockholm (Stockholm School of Economics), 1909, Stockholm: HHS.
— 1909–1959 (Stockholm School of Economics 1909–1959), 1959, Stockholm: HHS.
Heckscher, E., 1942, "Anders Berch och den ekonomiska vetenskapens första steg i Sverige" (Anders Berch and the First Steps of the Economic Sciences in Sweden), *Lychnos*, 7, pp. 33–64.

— 1951, "Handelshögskoleidéen och Handelshögskolans begynnelse i Sverige" (The Business School Idea and the Beginning of the Business School in Sweden), In: Forsberg, B. (ed.), 1951, *Handelshögskolorna i Sverige* (The Business Schools in Sweden), Stockholm: Forsbergs förlag, pp. 11–23.

Hensmann, J., 1969, *Die Entwicklung der Betriebswirtschaftslehre in Skandinavien unter besonderer Berücksichtigung Schwedens*, Inaugural Dissertation zur Erlangung des akademischen Grades eines Doktors der Wirtschaftswissenschaft durch die Rechts- und Staatswissenschaftliche Fakultät der Westfälischen Wilhelms-Universität zu Münster. (diss.).

Hugstad, P. S., 1983, *The Business School in the 1980s*, New York: Praeger.

Junker, B., 1951, "Svenska Ekonomföreningen 1938–1950" (The Swedish Association of Economists 1938–1950), In: Forsberg, B., *Handelshögskolorna i Sverige* (The Business Schools in Sweden), Stockholm: Forsbergs förlag, pp. 79–90.

Key, H., 1900, "Om betydelsen av handelshögskolor" (On the Importance of Business Schools), *Svensk Export*, 6, 149, pp. 73–76.

Kjaer Hanssen, M., 1927, *Almindelig bedriftsøkonomi* (General Business Administration), Copenhagen.

Ledarskap, 1987, "Ekonomerna styr företagen" (Business Graduates Control the Companies), 6, No. 11, pp. 45–46.

Liedman, S.-E., 1986, *Den synliga handen* (The Visible Hand), Stockholm: Arbetarkultur.

Locke, R. R., 1984, *The End of the Practical Man: Entrepreneurship and Higher Education in Germany, France, and Great Britain, 1880–1940*, Greenwich CT: JAI Press.

— 1989, *Management and Higher Education since 1940. The Influence of America and Japan on West Germany, Great Britain, and France*, Cambridge: Cambridge University Press

March, J. G. & Simon, H. A., 1958, *Organizations*, New York: Wiley.

Munthe, Å. W:son & Nordfeldt, A., 1907, *Handelshögskola i Stockholm. Redogörelse och förslag* (School of Business in Stockholm. Report and Proposal), Stockholm: Nordstedt & söner.

Nielsen, M. M., 1986, "Erhvervsøkonomiens udvikling i forskning och praksis" (The Development of Business Adminstration in Research and Practice), In: Andersen, H. (ed.), *Videnskabsteori & metodlaere for erhvervsøkonomer* (Theory of Science and Methodology for Business Administration Students), Fredriksberg: Samfundslitteratur, pp. 59–111.

Nordfelt, A., 1943, *Läroverksminnen. Ur Alfred Nordfelts memoarer* (Memories from the Secondary School. From the Memoirs of Alfred Nordfelt), Falun: Föreningen för svensk undervisningshistoria.

Norstrøm, C. J., 1991, "Bedriftsøkonomiens innhold" (The Content of Business Administration), Presentation at the 1991 Norwegian Conference of Business Administration, NHH, Bergen (mimeo).

Redlich, F., 1957, "Academic Education for Business: Its Development and the Contribution of Ignaz Jastrow (1856–1937). In Commemoration of the Hundredth Anniversary of Jastrow's Birth", *Business History Review*, 31, Spring, pp. 35–91.

Regnstrand, O., 1951, "Svenska Ekonomföreningen under dess första kvartssekel 1912–1937" (The Swedish Association of Business Graduates During Its First Twenty-Five Years 1912–1937), In: Forsberg, B. (red.), 1951, *Handelshögskolorna i Sverige* (The Business Schools in Sweden), Stockholm: Forsbergs förlag, pp. 53–78.

Ruml, F., 1928, "The Formative Period of Higher Commercial Education in American Universities", In: Marshall, L. C. (ed.), *The Collegiate School of Business*, Urbana: University of Illinois.

Sandström, H., 1977, *Handelshögskolan vid Åbo Akademi 1927–1977* (The Business School at Turku Academy 1927–1977), Skriftserie utgiven av Handelshögskolan vid Åbo akademi, serie A:18, Turku.

Schmalenbach, E., 1919, *Grundlagen dynamischer Bilanzlehre*, Leipzig: Gloeckner.

Seyffert, R., 1926, "Betriebswirtschaftslehre, ihre Geschichte", In: Nicklisch, H. (ed.), *Handwörterbuch der Betriebswirtschaft*, Stuttgart: Poeschel Verlag, Vol. 1, cc. 1198–1220.

ter Vehn, A., 1959, *Kompendium. Inledning till företagsekonomien* (Compendium. Introduction to Business Administration), Gothenburg School of Economics (mimeo).

Thompson, J. D., 1967, *Organizations in Action*, New York: McGraw-Hill.

Wallerstedt, E., 1988, *Oskar Sillén—Professor och praktiker. Några drag i företagsekonomiämnets tidiga utveckling vid Handelshögskolan i Stockholm* (Oskar Sillén—Professor and Practician. Some Traits in the Early Development of Business Administration at Stockholm School of Economics), Acta Universitatis Upsaliensis. Studia Oeconomiae Negotiorum 30, Uppsala: Almqvist & Wiksell International (diss.).

Wanous, S. J., 1969, "A Chronology of Business Education in the United States", *Business Education Forum*, 23, No. 7, pp. 36–43.

Whitley, R., Thomas, A. & Marceau, J., 1981, *Masters of Business. Business Schools and Business Graduates in Britain and France*, London: Tavistock.

Chapter 4
Business Administration in Norway 1936–1990

Rolv Petter Amdam and Carl Julius Norstrøm
Norwegian School of Management, Sandvika, Norway and Norwegian School of Economics and Business Administration, Bergen, Norway

4.1 Introduction

In 1936 the Norwegian School of Economics and Business Administration was founded in Bergen as the first Norwegian business school at an academic level. Even though Norway acquired its first business school 20–25 years later than the other Scandinavian countries, its school was established in the same German tradition as its Scandinavian neighbours. It soon developed a close and friendly relationship with other Scandinavian business schools, and after World War II it found a model, as they did, in the United States (Engwall, 1992; Handelshøjskolen i Århus, 1989; Vibaek & Kobbernagel, 1980).

What is peculiar to Norway, however, is the strong and monopolistic position that this business school has occupied. For many years the Norwegian School of Economics and Business Administration was the only academic business school in Norway. The school was granted the exclusive right by the government to award its graduates the degree and title of *siviløkonom*, and it retained this exclusive position until 1985. During and since the 1940s several private business schools of a non-academic kind have appeared, and after 1969 also some public regional colleges, offering shorter courses in business administration. Some of these schools subsequently extended their courses to four years, as the school in Bergen had done, and became academic business schools. But it was not until 1985 that the private Norwegian School of Management in Oslo and the regional college in Bodø acquired the right to award the *siviløkonom* degree. In 1991 the regional college in Kristiansand/Agder also acquired this right.

At the present time (1992) there are still some four-year private business schools and public regional colleges which are not allowed to grant this degree. The history of business education in Norway has thus long been—and still is—characterized by a certain tension between authorized business schools (i.e. those authorized to award the *siviløkonom* degree) and those not so authorized.

In this chapter we will focus on two main themes. We will first give a brief survey of the development of the field of business administration at the first academic business school in Bergen during the first ten years of its existence. Our purpose is to show how the school was established as a typical

Scandinavian business school inspired by German business administration education. Our second theme concerns what has been peculiar to Norway, namely the dichotomies between private and public business schools, and between certified and uncertified institutions. In particular we will look at the processes that led to the decision to extend the numbers of authorized business schools in 1985 from one to three.[1]

4.2 The First Academic Business School in Norway

4.2.1 The Institution

In 1917 the Norwegian Parliament decided to establish a business school in Bergen. Due to the economic crises of the 1920s and early 1930s, neither government nor private fund-rasing succeeded in financing the new school. The opening of Norges Handelshøyskole, as the school is called in Norwegian, was thus postponed until 1936.[2]

The new business school was strongly influenced by the German *Handelshochschulen*. The main course of study consisted of a two-year programme in which business administration and economics were the two compulsory subjects. In addition the students had to choose one language (English, German or French), and one of three options: law, commercial geography or commercial history. Although some of the other subjects, especially economics and law, are important to the study of business administration, their development will not be discussed here. In 1938 a further year was added for those graduates who wanted to become teachers in commercial colleges. This year consisted of educational theory and practice, as well as the further study on one subject, usually business administration.

4.2.2 A Survey of the First Ten Years

As the Norwegian School of Economics and Business Administration (NSEBA) was the first business school in Norway at an academic level, there was no natural supply of professors or teachers in its main field of business administration. Those who became professors or lecturers also shaped the new field. Hence it is essential to an understanding of the way the field developed, to take a look at the intellectual background of those people.

---

[1] The Norwegian *handelshøyskole* may be translated as *Handelshochschule* in German. In this chapter we use the English term "business schools", even though the names of the schools are translated in different ways in their official publications. The official English name of the school in Bergen is the Norwegian School of Economics and Business Administration. The school in Oslo was called the Oslo Institute of Business Administration until 1981, when its official English name was changed to the Norwegian School of Management.

[2] Our main source for this section has been the history of the school published for its 50th anniversary in 1986 (Jensen & Strømme Svendsen 1986). Another important source has been the journal *Bedriftsøkonomen*, first published in 1939 by some of the graduates of the school.

At the outset there were two positions to be filled in business administration, one as full professor and one as associate professor (*dosent*). The other positions were two professors of economics, one associate professor in commercial geography, one in commercial history, one in law and one lecturer in each of the foreign languages.

The evaluation committee for the first professorship in business administration found that none of the applicants fulfilled the necessary qualifications. However, a Swedish applicant, Robert Kristensson, was judged to be qualified as associate professor. Kristensson accepted the post and thus became the first teacher of business administration at the school. He became a full professor in 1937, following an evaluation of his further work.

Kristensson had graduated as an engineer from the Royal Institute of Technology in Stockholm in 1919 and as a business economist from the Stockholm School of Economics the same year. After working in industrial firms and lecturing in business administration at a lower level for some years, he lectured for two years under Oskar Sillén at the Stockholm School of Economics. He left the school in 1925, and before arriving in Bergen he had further experience both as a manager in an industrial firm and as a researcher on a project in the United States on behalf of the Swedish Department of Commerce. Kristensson left Norway after the German invasion in 1940 and later became professor in industrial economics at the Royal Institute of Technology in Stockholm. During his stay in Norway Kristensson published a textbook in cost accounting (Kristensson, 1936) as well as several articles on costing, pricing, changes in accounting legislation, and the economic education of engineers. As the first professor in business administration he exerted considerable influence, in spite of the relatively short duration of his stay.

Eilif W. Paulson graduated as an engineer from the Institute of Technology in Trondheim in 1915. After various jobs as research assistant, engineer, business manager and consultant, he became head of a new research institute of business in Bergen in 1932. This institute later became part of the NSEBA, and Paulson became associate professor in 1939 after adding to his qualifications by studying business administration for three terms in 1936–37 under professor Albert ter Vehn in Gothenburg. Paulson was asked to fill the post of acting professor when Kristensson left for Sweden and he became a full professor in 1946. He served as acting rector for brief periods during and after the war. Paulson published widely in several areas. His approach was typically empirical. Among his most important contributions were his studies of shipping firms. He also took a special interest in the economics and organization of trade, especially at the retail level. His approach to accounting problems was practical and factual. His works included an overview of the Norwegian legislation and practice in financial accounting (Paulson, 1940). The factual approach is also evident in his publications on finance and insurance.

Dag Coward studied economics at the University of Oslo. After his graduation in 1931 he became a research assistant under Professor Ingvar Wedervang, who was professor of economics at the University of Oslo. Coward and Wedervang made statistical studies of the cost structure of different industries in Norway. In 1935 Coward, like Paulson later, studied business administration under ter Vehn in Gothenburg. After passing the examination with the highest grade awarded at that date (*Norges Handelshøyskole*, 1953/54, p. 25), Coward went to Germany in the autumn of 1936 to meet some of the foremost German professors. In 1937 he went to the US on a Rockefeller scholarship and visited Harvard and the University of Chicago. Among the many prominent professors Coward met during his stay in the US, Frank H. Knight made a particularly strong impression on him (Jensen, 1980).

Coward became a researcher at the NSEBA in 1939. One reason for this choice in his career may have been that Professor Wedervang had become rector of NSEBA in 1937. Coward served as an associate professor after Kristensson left in 1940 and became a full professor in 1954. He was rector of NSEBA for nine years from 1964 to 1972. Dag Coward's publications include several articles on financial and cost accounting. Topics covered include the calculation of income under changes in the price level, and depreciation and interest calculations. He also made studies of the use of printed, standardized forms in organizations, and wrote articles on business administration as an academic discipline. His work on the standardization of the Norwegian terminology presented in his seminal textbook on cost accounting has been particularly important (Coward, 1944). His doctoral thesis on risk and uncertainty did not appear until 1953 (Coward, 1953), but his first contribution in this field came as early as 1939 in the form of mimeographed lecture notes.

These three first professors of business administration in Norway shared the same Swedish-German intellectual background. Robert Kristensson was deeply influenced by Oscar Sillén, who studied business administration in 1903–1905 in Cologne where Eugen Schmalenbach was one of his teachers (Wallerstedt, 1988). For about ten years from 1915 Sillén was the only professor of business administration in Sweden, and due to his personality and ability he remained a dominating force for much longer. Although Sillén was deeply influenced by a long trip to the United States in 1920, his intellectual roots were in Germany. Albert ter Vehn, who also influenced the new staff in Bergen, was German by birth and had studied business administration in Frankfurt under professor Fritz Schmidt. He became a professor at the business school in Gothenburg in 1926, a position he held until his retirement (Wallerstedt, 1988). Oscar Sillén, Albert ter Vehn and the German Erich Schneider, at the time professor at Aarhus in Denmark, were also members of the first evaluation committees for the chairs in business administration at NSEBA along with Professor Ingvar Wedervang.

In 1937 Tyge Filseth became the head of the Institute of Sales and Adver-

Table 4.1 *Robert Kristenson's Lectures for First Year Students in 1936/37 and Second Year Students in 1937/38*

1936 Autumn Term
  Bookkeeping and Cost Calculation (3 hours/week)
  Accounting Theory (2 hours/week)
  Office Organization (2 hours/week)
  Financial Mathematics (2 hours/week)
  Distribution and Trade (2 hours/week)

1937 Spring Term
  Bookkeeping and Calculation (2 hours/week)
  Accounting Theory (2 hours/week)
  Cost Accounting
  Finance

1937 Autumn Term
  Risk and Insurance (1 hour)
  Seminar (2 hours/week)

1938 Spring Term
  Industrial Organization and Economics (2 hours/week)
  Seminar (2 hours/week)

Source: *Norges Handelshøyskole* 1936/37–1937/38

tizing. This institute was funded by private donations until 1945, when it had to be abandoned due to lack of financing. Tyge Filseth was educated in marketing under the well-known Danish professor Max Kjær Hansen in Copenhagen. It is again possible to point to an indirect German influence, as Max Kjær Hansen had studied in Cologne.

What did the first Norwegian business school teach in its business administration courses? When the first students entered the school in 1936, Kristensson was the only teacher in business administration. His lectures for the first sixty students from 1936 to 1938 are shown in Table 4.1.

During the first year Professor ter Vehn taught practical accounting techniques as a guest lecturer. During the second year several lecture series were given by various practical specialists. Subjects included bank organization, insurance, work organization and auditing. Tyge Filseth also gave some lectures on sales and advertising.

As we have seen, Robert Kristensson left the school during 1940; Eilif W. Paulson took over the vacant chair while Dag Coward took over Paulson's position as associate professor. Gunnar Håland was appointed assistant lecturer in business administration in 1939, and was thus the first of the school's own graduates to become a teacher there. He was replaced in 1942 by Arne Fostvedt, another graduate of the school. The same year Olav Harald Jen-

Table 4.2 *Articles in Bedriftsøkonomen 1939–1945 by Topic*

General Business Administration	7
Financial and Cost Accounting	45
Sales, Distribution and Advertisement	14
Organization	33
Personnel Management	15
Finance	4
Other	13
Total	131

Source: *Bedriftsøkonomen* (1939–1945)

sen and Frøystein Wedervang became researchers in business administration. Fostvedt and Jensen had the same educational qualifications as Håland, namely an additional year of education studies and further studies in business administration on top of the two-year programme. All these three men were later to play an important part in the development of NSEBA. Olav Harald Jensen, who took his degree with one of the best grades in the history of NSEBA, became a professor in 1960 and was rector in the period 1973 to 1978. Frøystein Wedervang later became a professor of economics. Arne Fostvedt became the director of NSEBA's external programme and was for many years editor of *Bedriftsøkonomen*, a business administration journal founded in 1939 by graduates of the school.

The curriculum did not change in any substantial way during World War II. The core of the programme consisted of different aspects of accounting such as bookkeeping, charts of accounts, accounting theory, cost accounting, auditing, and various practical issues connected with accounting. Next in importance came finance, different aspects of the organization of distribution and trade, and risk and insurance. Teaching in other subjects such as sales and advertising, banking, practical insurance etc. was provided by guest lecturers. Some of these like Tyge Filseth came from institutes affiliated with the school; others occupied posts in commercial or industrial firms in Bergen.

There were several other contributors to the field of business administration during the war, in addition to Coward and Paulson who were mentioned above. In the journal *Bedriftsøkonomen* Tyge Filseth published articles on sales, advertizing and personnel management. Olav Harald Jensen published articles on cost accounting. Most of the articles in this journal, however, were written by graduates of the school. As can be seen in Table 4.2 most of the articles were on financial and cost accounting or on organization.

4.2.3 An Outline of Developments since the Second World War

Education in business administration in Norway has experienced tremendous expansion since World War II. There are now more than fifteen institutions providing courses in business administration at an academic level in programmes lasting from two to four years. In addition the size and scope of many of the institutions have increased substantially.

After the war NSEBA's position in the Norwegian academic community was strengthened, and historically the school has been predominant among Norwegian business schools. Even though it is not possible to treat the postwar period here in the same detail as the first ten years, a short survey of some of the main developments at NSEBA could be appropriate before we look at the way in which the relationship between different business schools has changed.

One important event that extended the scientific base of the school was the establishment of a chair in organization psychology and personnel management. Rolf Waaler was appointed to this chair in 1950. Waaler had originally been trained as an engineer, but later became interested in industrial psychology. Together with enthusiastic colleagues such as Rolf Jangård and Svein M. Kile he established a research group in this area. One of the most important consequences of this was the establishment in 1952 of the Administrative Research Foundation, a research and educational institute which will be described further in Section 4.4.3.

In 1959 Karl H. Borch became a researcher at NSEBA and head of the Department of Insurance, which was established the same year. Borch obtained his Ph.D. at the University of Oslo in 1962 and became professor in insurance at NSEBA in 1963. During his relatively short period as a researcher Borch made important contributions to the creation of an economic theory of insurance (Borch 1961 and 1962), work that he continued to pursue after receiving his chair. Being an actuary by training, he was well equipped to take part in the new developments in the economics of uncertainty, and his work became well known abroad (Borch, 1968), especially in the United States. What is perhaps most important in our context is the influence which he had on the recruitment of a new generation of scholars. During the late 1960s Borch took over the training of a large share of the growing number of researchers in economics and business administration; he also encouraged many others to study abroad. One of these scholars who was greatly influenced by Borch was Jan Mossin, who made an important contribution to the development of the capital asset pricing model (CAPM) with an article in Econometrica (Mossin, 1966). This was later to give William Sharpe the 1990 Nobel Prize in Economics (Hagen, 1990). The mathematical-economic approach to business administration and economics developed by Borch is still characteristic of NSEBA.

The third point that must be mentioned concerns the development of the behavioural approach to business administration which emerged from the field of marketing. Leif Holbæk-Hanssen, who like Tyge Filseth had received his basic training under Max Kjær Hansen in Copenhagen, became a researcher in marketing in 1957 and was made professor in 1960. The Department of Marketing grew in both numbers and reputation under the inspired leadership of Holbæk-Hansen. A new dimension was added when Johan Arndt joined the staff in 1972. After receiving his *siviløkonom* degree at NSEBA, Arndt had obtained a Ph.D. at Harvard with an emphasis on the behavioural approach to business problems. Not least as a result of his example and inspiration a strong behavioural research tradition gradually developed at NSEBA which is still very evident today. Arndt later became a professor at the Norwegian School of Management.

A very important factor in the development of business administration after World War II has been the American influence. Virtually all teachers and researchers at NSEBA have stayed in the US for periods of varying length. This practice has continued up to the present, since one of the privileges which most academics in Norway enjoy is paid sabbatical leave for study and research, and the United States has been the most attractive destination. Another dimension of the American influence was added at the beginning of the 1960s, when Norwegian researchers started to study for the Ph.D. degree in the United States. The result of this is that several of the best researchers in business administration in Norway belong intellectually to the American research community. Over the last five or ten years this tendency has declined slightly, as NSEBA's own doctoral programme, which is now modelled on the American Ph.D, has become more efficient. However, it is still true that the American model is the predominant foreign influence on the field of business administration in Norway.

4.3 The Second Norwegian Business School

4.3.1 A Follower?

The most important private business school, the Norwegian School of Management (NSM), was established in Oslo in 1943. It was founded by Finn Øien seven years after the new business school in Bergen, as a 100 per cent privately owned business school. However, it is difficult to interpret the first 20 or 25 years of NSM's history in terms of leader and follower, with NSEBA in Bergen as the leader and NSM in Oslo as a follower trying to attain the same status as the Bergen school.[3]

During the first years of its existence NSM, or *Bedriftsøkonomisk Institutt* (BI) as it was called in Norwegian, was more of a consulting firm than a

---

[3] This section is based on R. P. Amdam's history of the school (Amdam, 1993). For a more detailed discussion of the concept of "leaders and followers", see Engwall (1992).

school. During the war NSM worked as a consulting firm in accounting and industrial organization, as well as arranging some short courses in business administration. Education was thus only one of many tasks undertaken by the new institution.

The first course in business administration was a three-month course, and no specific entry qualification was required. But the director, Finn Øien, was genuinely interested in studying business administration and lecturing on the subject, and gradually the courses were extended. In 1946 the school had developed a two-year course in business administration, and final secondary school grades were required for acceptance. This course was provided alongside evening courses, of which a two-year evening course was the most important.

At that time the school claimed to be a business school on the same level as other business schools (*Handelshochschulen*) (*Bedriftsøkonomisk Institutt*, 1946). This claim implied that the school wanted to be compared with the business school in Bergen, which suggests that it was acting as a follower. In a way this is correct, but there is no doubt that NSM was in fact trying to create a school quite different from the business school in Bergen.

The new two-year course at NSM was announced as a "*practical* higher course in business administration" (*Bedriftsøkonomisk Institutt*, 1946). With this pronouncement NSM was seeking to profile itself as a non-academic business school, while also insinuating that the business school in Bergen was too academic and that its ties with real business life were too weak. At NSM, as at the business school in Bergen, the core of the teaching programme consisted of accounting. But less emphasis was laid on accounting theory, and more on accounting practice. Next in importance came different aspects of the organization of production and sales. Finance and economics were hardly taught at all. The school actively profiled itself as a business school without economics as a core subject, again implying that the business school in Bergen was influenced too much by academic economics, which meant that business managers found it hard to accept it (*Bedriftsøkonomisk Institutt*, 1946).

At NSM Finn Øien was the only fully employed teacher. He had a master's degree in mathematics and physics, and teaching experience from a commercial school at the secondary school level. Practically no research was undertaken, and most of the lectures were given in the evenings by people employed in different companies during the daytime.

With such a profile we can hardly say that the school acted as a follower of the more academic business school in Bergen. On the other hand only a few new students entered the school each year,[4] and most of the part-time

---

[4] During the first 15 years approximately 20 new students started the two-year programme on NSM each year compared to c. 50 on the three-year *siviløkonom* programme in Bergen.

teachers had rather peripheral jobs in Norwegian business life, which meant that this school too found it difficult to develop strong ties with the real business world.

4.3.2 Two Business Schools During the 1960s

During the 1950s and 1960s the business school in Bergen continued to develop its academic and scientific profile, as shown in Section 4.2.3. The *siviløkonom* programme was extended from two to three years. In the 1950s and 1960s the academic staff increased: the school had nine professors in 1950, 16 professors in 1960 and 21 in 1970 (Jensen & Strømme Svendsen 1986, p. 326). In 1957 Ole Myrvoll became the school's first Ph.D. From the 1950s onwards professors from the school also played an active role in developing Scandinavian cooperation in business education, and during the 1960s in particular the school's international scholarly reputation grew. Karl Henrich Borch and Jan Mossin for example, enjoyed international recognition.

The business school in Oslo, however, was still developing in a different direction. Most of its students attended the shorter evening courses, which were arranged in parallel with the above-mentioned two-year course. Most of the evening students were working during the day. In 1958 the NSM graduates organized an association of their own, quite independent of the Bergen association.

In 1968 NSM had five full-time lecturers as well as more than 20 part-time teachers, most of whom also worked in industrial or commercial firms. None of them had a doctor's degree. At the same time NSEBA in Bergen had 20 professors. And when in 1969 the Norwegian Parliament (*Stortinget*) decided to subsidize NSM and a few other private schools, it was not as a result of any initiative on the part of the school. Rather, the decision seems to have come as a surprise to its members.[5]

The tendency is clear. In general NSM in Oslo made no attempt to copy NSEBA in Bergen either in the 1950s or in the 1960s. Instead it developed its own profile. In the Norwegian system of education NSEBA was an insider financed and run by the state, with the exclusive right to award the title of *siviløkonom*. NSM on the other hand was a private outsider.[6] They represented two different models of business education, one academic and one evolving a more practical profile.

But something must have happened during the 1970s and 1980s, since in 1985 NSM was accepted as an academic business school with the same right

---

[5] Source: interviews with Finn Øien and Gerson Komissar, directors of the school in 1943–1975 and 1975–1981 respectively.
[6] For a more detailed discussion of the insider and outsider concept, see Engwall (1992).

as the business school in Bergen to award the *siviløkonom* degree. In the next section we will look at some of the factors which may explain this change in the Norwegian system of higher business education.

4.4 The Evolution of a New System of Business Education

4.4.1 A New Strategy

During the 1970s the Norwegian School of Management gradually changed its strategy. Its aim now was to be accepted as an academic business school. This change was partly inspired by Parliament's decision to subsidize NSM in 1969. This decision was a result of a general debate on private education in Norway. Even though Norway has traditionally had few private schools, a small number did exist in the 1960s, mainly at the primary and secondary levels. Some of these were also partly financed by the state, some were not. But the agreements between the state and the schools which received public money, had developed more or less arbitrarily. In order to reorganize the policy towards private schools, and to establish a more uniform pattern of financial support, a committee was set up in 1967 to prepare a reform. One of the results of their work was that NSM now had 75 per cent of its budget paid by the state, even though the school had not applied for any money. This increase from 0 to 75 per cent naturally influenced the school management's view of the relationship between the school and the rest of the educational system. One result was that the school saw a chance of becoming more generally accepted by the state authorities as a central element in higher education; a lot could be gained from improving its relationship with the state, and restraining its attempts to create a school quite different from the only business school authorized to award academic degrees.

This change in strategy was also connected with internal processes concerning the relationship between academia and the world of practice. Even though NSM had stressed the practical dimension in business education in the 1950s and 1960s, the staff had also undertaken a certain amount of research. Finn Øien, who was the founder and director of the school from 1943 to 1975, had originally studied theoretical physics and mathematics at the University of Oslo. During the first ten years of the school's history, it is hard to find any connection between these qualifications and the curriculum. But around the mid-1950s Øien became interested in ways of using new data processing techniques in business education, and he did some work which could be classified as research. From 1956 the school arranged courses in data processing and in operational research.

Compared to the research activity at NSEBA in Bergen or the other Scandinavian academic business schools, the research at NSM was obviously not on the same general level. But the focus on data processing, operational research, statistics and mathematics, brought NSM into contact with a new scientific element in international business education. According to Robert Locke the use of quantitative methods entailed by operations research represented a new paradigm in academic management education after the war (Locke, 1989). Thus, more or less by chance, NSM became a participant in this process which changed the foundations of business education.

Around 1970 NSM appointed several new teachers, some of whom had university degrees in mathematics, statistics or finance. These appointments were made possible by the new financial support from the state. Some of the new teachers found the school's focus on operations research and data processing especially attractive. Some of them were also interested in developing research at NSM. With these appointments NSM had created an internal force working for a more general change in attitudes to research. This process also affected the school's decision to move towards academic status.

But it is not enough to decide to become an insider. NSM's acceptance as an "authorized" business school was the result of a combination of a strong internal desire for acceptance and certain external processes working in favour of the school. One of these was the increasing numbers of Norwegians going abroad to study business; other processes were to be found within the business school in Bergen.

4.4.2 Education Abroad

Although NSEBA in Bergen was the only Norwegian business school with the right to award the *siviløkonom* degree, another route existed for those who did not want to study in Bergen or who were not accepted as students there. It was possible to study at foreign business schools, and even to become a *siviløkonom* on returning to Norway, provided NSEBA and the professional association accepted the foreign education as equal to the education provided in Bergen.

This foreign dimension had long traditions in Norway. Before the first business school was established, the Norwegian system of management education was characterized by a first phase of education in Norway combined with education or practical experience abroad. This well-established tradition was connected with the importance to the Norwegian economy of export industries such as shipping, and the fishery and timber trades. Ever since the eighteenth century an increasing number of Norwegian merchants had been sending their sons to foreign countries to train at commercial schools or in offices. This link with foreign countries seems to have compensated for the lack of domestic educational institutions (Amdam, 1994).

A study of a random sample of 300 business managers in 1939 can illustrate the importance of education and practice in other countries. Sixty-three per cent of the managers in industry, 60 per cent in commerce, and 36

Table 4.3 *300 Norwegian Business Managers in 1939: Education or Work Experience from Countries other than Norway*

	Industry	Commerce	Banking
Education in other Countries	43	25	16
Work Experience Abroad for More than One Year	40	41	25
Education and/or Work Experience Abroad	63	60	36

Source: Amdam (1994).
Note: Managers with an essential part, even if not the whole, of their education in countries other than Norway are included.

per cent in banking, had studied or worked abroad before they became top managers (Table 4.3).

The old tradition of travelling abroad for a business education was further developed after World War II. Since NSEBA in Bergen was not able to open its doors to all qualified applicants in the first post-war years, an agreement was made with the Danish business school in Copenhagen whereby 50 Norwegian students could study there. Agreements were also reached with the Swiss business schools in Neuchâtel and St.Gallen. In 1947 the Norwegian State Educational Loan Fund was established, and it became possible to get financial support for study in other countries. Last but not least, the association of the Bergen graduate, the Norwegian Association of Masters of Science in Business, also accepted graduates from foreign business schools as members of their association (*Norges Handelshøyskole*, Annual Reports).

Since the war the number of Norwegian business students abroad has increased at almost the same rate that domestic business education capacity has grown. In the 1950s approximately 50 Norwegians graduated from foreign business schools each year, about the same as from NSEBA in Bergen. In 1975, 225 students graduated from NSEBA and 225 from foreign business schools (Brandt, 1986). The same year about 175 graduated from NSM.

The growing numbers of Norwegian students studying abroad exercised considerable influence on the development of business education in Norway. The increase was used as an argument both for extending the educational capacity at Bergen in 1963, and for granting NSM the right to award the degree *siviløkonom* and establishing the Bodø Graduate School of Business in 1985. It was expected that these arrangements would lead to a drop in the numbers of students going abroad. The old tradition of studying business abroad was thus a creative force in changing the Norwegian educational system. As well as encouraging the increase in educational capacity, the growing number of students in different foreign business schools also helped to widen horizons in the debate on the organization of business education. It became increasingly difficult to defend a system whereby academic business education was monopolized by a single Norwegian business school.

4.4.3 Changes in Business Education

As we have seen, the first academic business school in Bergen and the Norwegian School of Management in Oslo represented two different models of business education. They represented a dichotomy between "authorized" and "non-authorized" education, and between the private and the public sectors in education. The decision in 1969 to allow NSM financial support from the state inspired the school to move closer to the model represented by NSEBA in Bergen. On the other hand, the business school in Bergen also showed a tendency to adopt some elements from what we could call a typical private organizational model.

During the 1950s there was a tendency at NSEBA to adopt private financing, not for the *siviløkonom* courses, but for research, further education and advanced management education. In 1952 the Administrative Research Foundation (ARF) was founded. It was founded by Norwegian industrial companies and its board included representatives of the business school and of Norwegian firms. The same year ARF launched an eleven-week residential course inspired by the courses at the Henly Administrative Staff College in England and the Harvard Advanced Management Course in the United States (Bakke, 1959).

These courses were financed by the students or by the companies sponsoring them, and not—like the rest of the school's teaching programme—by the state. The courses represented a pioneering effort in the European context, and were regarded as a success (*Ibid.*, pp. 9–11). The establishment of ARF had a certain impact on how business education should be organized. Although ARF was organized as an independent department of NSEBA, it helped to promote a more dynamic attitude towards private elements in the system of education.

ARF's structure was inspired by American models and had nothing to do with the fact that NSM in Oslo was a private school. But in the case of other innovations at NSEBA, the influence of NSM seems to have been stronger. In 1963 NSEBA began to arrange short courses in business administration in some Norwegian towns. Four years earlier NSM had started up a short course in business administration in Drammen, near Oslo. The course in Drammen was the prelude to a system of cooperating institutions, offering short NSM courses in several Norwegian towns. This regional system has been a distinguishing feature of NSM in the 1970s and 1980s.

The regional system has mainly provided two-year evening courses in business administration with practically no restrictions on admission. In 1971 the two-year evening course was held in seven Norwegian towns. 1,684 students attended these courses, including evening courses in Oslo. Ten years later, in 1980, the number was almost the same. But during the 1980s the number of students in the regional system increased from 1,815 in 1981 to 11,387 in 1987.

NSM's short courses were very successful in the 1980s—indeed, more successful than the course offered by NSEBA since the 1960s. The student fees from these courses have enabled the school to finance its academic expansion. The success of the regional system has also strengthened the school's general position in the Norwegian educational system.

The growth of the school's regional system came at a time when the state was also developing its own system of regional colleges. Some of these have been offering lower courses in business administration since the beginning of the 1970s. The main programme in business administration has consisted of a two-year course. In 1970 four regional colleges offered this course; in 1980 eight and in 1990 twelve. As a result of this expansion the number of new students has increased from 280 in 1970 to 700 in 1980, and to 1,200 in 1990 (Amdam & Mordt, 1992).

The success of NSM's regional system has not only inspired NSEBA to develop a new system of short courses during the 1980s, financed by student fees, but it also told the critics of private schools that private institutions can play a creative part in the Norwegian system of education. By the 1970s and 1980s it was no longer possible to ignore NSM's contribution to Norwegian business education.

4.4.4 Recent Developments

In 1985 NSM was given the right, as the first private business school, to award the *siviløkonom* degree. The same year the Bodø Graduate School of Business was established and granted the same right. NSM's route to insider status had taken a different course relative to the business school in Bergen. As a private school its expansion was financed by student fees. Thanks to the growth in student numbers and the financial support provided by the state, the school had been able to acquire a qualified academic staff. The government and NSEBA both accepted that NSM was now an *academic* business school, and that it should no longer be denied the right to award the *siviløkonom* degree.

The background of the Bodø Graduate Business School, however, was quite different. It was established by the government primarily to strengthen the system of education in northern Norway. The business school grew out of the regional college in Bodø, making it possible for students with a two-year degree in business administration from this or other regional college, to extend their education for another two years and thus to earn the title *siviløkonom*.

Since 1985 the roles of the institutions have changed. NSM's acceptance as an insider first inspired the other private business schools to stress the practical elements in their curriculum. During the 1980s NSM became an academic business school. To begin with, in reaction to this, the other private business schools tried to take over NSM's historical role as a practical business school.

Around 1990, however, two of the private business schools, the Norwegian School of Marketing and the Oslo Business School, changed their strategies and tried to transform themselves into academic institutions and to gain acceptance as insiders in the same way as NSM. But neither the government nor the academic business community accepted the schools in this guise. As a result of the failure of this strategy, and because of financial problems, both schools merged with NSM in 1992.

The transformation of the regional college in Bodø into a graduate school has inspired other colleges to apply for permission to award the *siviløkonom* degree. Some have increased their staff and developed four-year courses, in order to qualify as "authorized" business schools which can award the *siviløkonom* degree. In 1991 the regional college in Kristiansand/Agder also succeeded in becoming accepted as an insider.

4.5 Conclusion

In 1936 the first academic business school was established in Norway. It was a typical business school of the German type, where various aspects of accounting and finance comprised the core subjects on the business administration side, and the ties between business administration and economics were strong.

After World War II the school turned to the United States for its model. As a consequences of the increasing American influence the German influence declined, although some elements remain even today. The most important programme in business administration in Norway still follow the German *Diplomkaufmann* model rather than the American Bachelor/MBA pattern, although MBA degrees were established at NSM and the private Oslo Business School in the later 1980s.

The German influence is also evident in the basic vocabulary established by Coward and others in the 1940s. There also seems to be a growing interest in Norwegian business schools today in developing closer contact with the European research community. However, at this level contact has so far been maintained primarily at conferences held mainly in English, since knowledge of German and French has gradually been declining among Norwegian scholars.

As regards institutional developments we have seen that NSEBA occupied a privileged position with the exclusive right to award the degree and title of *siviløkonom* up to 1985, when this right was extended to NSM and the Bodø Graduate Business School. The NSM's strategy to transform itself from a practically oriented to an academic business school was successful; the process was also assisted by several external circumstances. The growing number of Norwegian students studying abroad helped to encourage the expansion of the domestic capacity, as well as promoting more liberal views on the way academic business education should be organized. The tendency at NSEBA and at other institutions of higher education to adopt certain elements in their financing and organization which are typical of private institutions, may also have helped to generate a more dynamic view of the relation between the private and the public sector in business education.

The mergers in 1992 between NSM and two other schools, the Norwegian School of Marketing and the Oslo Business School, have created a new situation in the Norwegian system of business education. The dichotomy between the public and private sectors in business education still exists, but there is now only one dominant private business school. Even though the public regional colleges in Bodø and Kristiansand have been authorized to award the *siviløkonom* degree, NSEBA in Bergen is still undeniably the dominant public business school.

This concentration will not necessarily lead to an intensification of the competition between the dominant private and the dominant public business school. The result could be greater cooperation, since the process of concentration has created a more orderly situation. This new situation may make it easier for the government to take political steps to develop a more homogeneous system of business education in Norway.

References

Amdam, R. P., 1993, *For egen regning. BI og den økonomisk-administrative utdanningen 1943–1993* (The history of the Norwegian School of Management 1943–1993), Oslo: Universitetsforlaget.
— 1994, "Foreign Influence on the Education of Norwegian Managers before World War II", to be published in *Business History*.
Amdam, R. P. & Mordt, G., 1992, "Utdanningskonjunkturer" (Educational Cycles), *Norwegian School of Management, Research Report*.
Bakke, E. W., 1959, *A Norwegian Contribution to Executive Development*, Bergen: Norwegian School of Economics and Business Administration.
Bedriftsøkonomen, 1952, 14, No. 9b.
Bedriftsøkonomisk Institutt 1946, *Studieplan for 1946/47*, Oslo: Bedriftsøkonomisk Institutt.
Borch, K. H., 1961, "Elements of a Theory of Insurance", *Journal of Insurance*, 28, September, pp. 35–43.
— 1962, "Equilibrium in a Reinsurance Market", *Econometrica*, 30, No. 3, pp. 424–444.

— 1968, *The Economics of Uncertainty*, Princeton NJ: Princeton University Press.
Brandt, E., 1986, "Minervas sønner og døtre" (Minerva's Sons and Daughters), *NAVF's utredningsinstitutt Notat 5/86*, Oslo: NAVFs utredningsinstitutt.
Coward, D., 1944, *Kostnadsregning i industribedrifter* (Cost Accounting in Industrial Firms), Oslo: Aschehoug & Co.
— 1953, *Økonomisk risiko og usikkerhet* (Economic Risk and Uncertainty), Bergen: Skrifter fra Norges Handelshøyskole.
— 1980, *Studier i bedriftsøkonomi. Utvalgte artikler av professor dr. philos. Dag Coward* (Studies in Business Administration. Selected Papers by Professor Doctor Dag Coward), Bergen: Norges Handelshøyskole.
Engwall, L., 1992, *Mercury Meets Minerva*, Oxford: Pergamon.
Hagen, K. P., 1990, "Nobelprisen i økonomi for 1990" (The Nobel Prizes for Economics in 1990), *Sosialøkonomen*, 44, No. 11, pp. 10–12.
Handelshøjskolen i Århus 50 år (The History of Århus School of Economics), Århus: Handelshøjskolen i Århus.
Jensen, O. H. 1980, "Bedriftsøkonomen Dag Coward" (The Business Administration Scholar Dag Coward), In: Coward, D., 1980, *Studier i bedriftsøkonomi. Utvalgte artikler av professor dr. philos. Dag Coward* (Studies in Business Administration. Selected Papers by Professor Doctor Dag Coward), Bergen: Norges Handelshøyskole.
Jensen, O. H. & Strømme Svendsen, A., 1986, *Norges Handelshøyskole femti år* (The Norwegian School of Economics Fifty Years), Bergen: Norges Handelshøyskole.
Kristensson, R., 1936, *Omkostninger i bedriftsøkonomisk teori og kalkulasjon* (Costs in Business Administration Theory and Calculation), Bergen: Eides.
Locke, R., 1989, *Management and Higher Education since 1940. The Influence of America and Japan on West Germany, Great Britain, and France*, Cambridge: Cambridge University Press.
Mossin, J., 1966, "Equilibrium in a Capital Asset Market", *Econometrica*, 34, No. 4, pp. 768–783.
Norges Handelshøyskole 1936/37–1953/54, *Beretninger for året* ..... (Annual Reports), Bergen: Norges Handelshøyskole.
Paulson. E. W., 1940, *Norsk regnskapslovgivning. En bedriftsøkonomisk studie* (Norwegian Accounting Laws. A Study in Business Administration), Oslo: Aschehoug.
Vibaek, J. & Kobbernagel, J., 1980, *Foreningen til Unge Handelsmaends Uddannnelse 1880–1980* (The Association for the Education of Young Merchants 1880–1980), København: Nyt Nordisk Forlag Arnold Busck.
Wallerstedt, E., 1988, *Oscar Sillén, Professor och praktiker. Några drag i företagsekonomiämnets tidiga utveckling vid Handelshögskolan i Stockholm* (Oscar Sillén. Professor and Practician. Some Features of the Early Development of Business Administration at the Stockholm School of Economics), Uppsala: Acta Universitatis Upsaliensis, Studia Oeconomiae Negotiorum 30, Stockholm: Almqvist & Wiksell.

Chapter 5
Academic Management Education in the Netherlands

Huibert de Man and Luchien Karsten
Open University of the Netherlands and State University Groningen

5.1 Introduction

Academic management education in the Netherlands is a recent phenomenon. Faculties of business studies (*bedrijfskunde*) were founded in the 1960s and 1970s. Since the 1980s they have attracted increasing numbers of students, and in quantitative terms the field of business studies can now certainly be called a success. Nonetheless the integration of business studies into the university is still a problem, due to the tension between the scientific values of the academic world and the pragmatism of business studies. This is reflected for instance in the question of giving form and content to scientific research in the field of management. In the labour market the business graduate is still a relatively new figure, whose position and status are still uncertain. The future of business studies, although it looks bright, is not clear.

To understand the present situation and the potential for the future we need to look first at the history of the discipline. Only by examining its roots can we gain some insight into the cultural context in which academic management education is embedded. We follow Robert Locke in thus searching for cultural configurations that are deeply embedded in national history. By looking at our own past we try to reveal the ideas, values and institutional structures (Locke, 1989, p. 2) which continue to condition the way we deal with academic management education in the Netherlands.

In the Netherlands as in other countries the development of academic management education represents an interaction between an original national heritage and new, predominantly North American, ideas on management. The new ideas, for which Locke has coined the term "the new paradigm", spread across the world after the Second World War, and went hand in hand with the development of a new type of business school which teaches an interdisciplinary science of management. According to this new paradigm management is regarded as a profession which requires the combined application of methods from a variety of sciences. In contrast to the older business schools, which taught knowledge and techniques that were considered useful to the manager, attention now came to focus on management itself. Management was redefined as decision-making. In this sense "management" was an invention of the business schools. Knowledge derived from the social, economic and technical sciences had to be combined in managerial decision-making. This means that the manager needs to have received an interdisciplinary education, involving mathematics and natural sciences as well as engineering and behavioural science. Management itself is a "science of sciences", requiring methods for combining eclectical knowledge with practical problem-solving. Formal models borrowed from mathematics and systems theory were seen as important instruments for achieving integration.

This was roughly the new idea of a scientific approach to management (as described by Locke), which originated in the United States of America and became visible there in the new business school curricula of the 1950s. These curricula then became the models for countries in Europe which wanted to bring their management up to American standards. This was also what happened in the Netherlands.

The new ideas were received in a country which had strong traditions in management and industrial engineering, and educational institutions dealing with subjects and courses relevant to the managerial situations. The reception of the new North American ideas thus occurred in a context characterized by ideas and institutions whose roots went back to the beginning of the century.

The first signs of a scientific approach to management in the Netherlands appeared somewhere around 1900. We can begin our present survey roughly a decade earlier when the industrialization of the Netherlands had reached a decisive stage, and can then follow the development of management thinking and management education to the present day.

The sections of this chapter correspond to historical periods. Section 5.2 deals with the period between 1890 and 1940, when accountants and mechanical engineers laid the foundations of a Dutch tradition of management thought and practice. Section 5.3 looks at the introduction of North American management ideas in connection with the economic and social recovery of the Netherlands after five years of German occupation. It deals with the period from 1945 to 1960. Section 5.4 treats the foundation of faculties of business studies (business schools) in the period 1960 to 1977. Section 5.5 analyse the further development of the business schools after 1977, while a few concluding remarks on the Dutch development of academic management education conclude the chapter in Section 5.6.

5.2 The Rise of the Management Professions (1890–1940)

5.2.1 Up to the First World War (1890–1918)

5.2.1.1 Background

The industrialization of the Netherlands came late. There were some beginnings from 1870 onwards, but the process of industrialization entered upon a decisive phase only after 1890. Employment in agriculture declined sharply in the first decades of the present century, while industry was attracting increasing numbers of workers. Particularly significant was the growth of employment in the machine industry around 1900 (De Jonge, 1976). The average size of enterprises was growing, but had not yet led to the professionalization of management or the manager's role. Most entrepreneurs at that time had either a commercial or a technical background (Lambers, 1959, p. 106).

Up to the First World War the word "entrepreneur" had strong commercial overtones. Young industrialists were often looked upon with some contempt in commercial circles, because industry was often financed by borrowed money. The hegemony of the commercial community and the related feelings of class superiority still dominated their view (Klein, 1966). This image of the entrepreneur changed radically, however, with the rapid rise in the number of joint stock companies.

5.2.1.2 Accountants

As enterprises grew in both size and number, management and organizational questions began to attract increasing attention. Accountants and bookkeepers were among the first to show such an interest. Following the British example, accountants founded the Dutch Institute of Accountants in 1895 to provide professional training, and thus to limit dilettantism in the auditing and consulting services now required by the limited liability companies (De Vries, 1985, p. 39). J. G. Ch. Volmer, one of the founders of the Institute, wanted to see accounting practice brought up to the British standard, it would thus be necessary for the institute to establish its own examinations.

In 1906 disagreement arose between the senior and junior members of the Institute regarding the relative importance of theory and practice. The ambitions of the junior members were personified by Th. Limperg Jr. who led an open attack on the alleged conservatism and prejudices of the old guard. He left the Institute, and together with several others, including Volmer, founded the Dutch Accountants Association in 1907. This initiative was successful. Limperg contributed greatly to making accounting a respected profession (De Vries, 1985, p. 55).

The accounting profession made an impact mainly on the field of financial control (auditing), and on consulting connected with the problems of attracting outside capital. Internal management problems were generally solved on the basis of experience. With the increase in size and complexity of companies and the growth of staff departments, the need arose for a new type of management expertise. The question of internal organization first arose among the technically oriented entrepreneurs and managing directors of companies. Here the expertise of engineers had proved useful abroad. In the Netherlands there was a growing need for education with this orientation.

5.2.1.3 Engineers

Since the early nineteenth century there had been plans to establish institutes for trade and industry as part of the university system. Louis Napoleon had considered the idea of founding an institute on the lines of the French *École Polytechnique*. King William I had declared in a Royal Decree in 1825 that the universities should be involved in applied education. Some professors took this seriously, but the various attempts to provide higher technical education at the universities all failed. This situation finally changed following another Royal Decree in 1842, which provided for the foundation of a Royal Academy for the education of civil engineers. This new 'civil' education (i.e. not military, like that provided by the existing institution in Breda) was to be located in Delft. After some conflict concerning school discipline, the Academy became a Polytechnic as part of the restructuring of the national educational system in 1864. This was a disappointment to the civil engineers, who had hoped that the school would be reorganized as an institution of scientific education, i.e. with full academic status.

The educational reform of 1864 institutionalized a dichotomy between theory and practice that was to remain typical of the Dutch situation for a long time to come, even at the level of secondary education. The practical 'civil school' (HBS) was founded as a complement to the existing classical high school, the polytechnic became part of the vocationally oriented, lower-status stream of higher education.

In the second half of the nineteen century the new civil engineers found employment not only in hydraulic engineering and in the construction and exploitation of the railways, but also in industry. The engineer J. C. van Marken, one of the first Delft civil engineers, called attention to the organization of companies. In 1893 this managing director of the Yeast and Methylated Spirit Works in Delft, who had a strong social conscience, expressed a wish to see a curriculum for social engineering included in the existing education in technical engineering. Such a curriculum should deal not only with economics but also with social questions: labour legislation, trade unions, measures taken by employers in the interest of their employees, pay agreements, participation, co-operation, arbitration, housing, savings agreements, pension schemes, medical insurance, normal working hours etc. He also emphasized the relevance of health and hygiene, referring to the increasing complaints of fatigue at work. Character as well as knowledge is an important asset of the future engineer.

In 1904 some members of the Delft polytechnic staff visited the U.S.

World Exhibition in St. Louis, to acquaint themselves with industrial developments and with ways in which curricula could be designed to match them. The influential Society for Commerce and Industry and the Ministry of Foreign Affairs financed their trip. The journal of the Society published an extensive report on the flood of industrial innovations, and a report on visits to several American universities. The applied nature of the science studied at these institutions was spoken of with admiration (Bierens de Haan, 1952, p. 142). This report and Van Marken's comments certainly both played a part in the discussions on improving the engineering curriculum at Delft.

In 1904 the Polytechnic was upgraded from a *Hogere school* to a *Hoogeschool*, due to legal changes. As a 'Politechnique' it was now able to offer education on an academic level. In 1907 the board of the Polytechnic asked the government to institute a chair of Management and Accounting. The subject was considered important, as engineers tended increasingly to find jobs not in the public sector but in private enterprise; in business an engineer without a knowledge of bookkeeping would find it difficult to obtain any of the higher positions. The government agreed to the proposal, and in 1908 the first chair in Management and Accounting was held by J. G. C. Volmer.

Volmer was the first advocate of Taylorism in the Netherlands. A Dutch translation of Taylor's *Shop Management* (1903) appeared in 1909. Engineers were developing an increasing interest in scientific management and the rationalization of production processes. Volmer was convinced that Taylor's approach would entail advantages for both labour and capital.

Van Marken had already seen very clearly that attention should also be paid to the living and working conditions of the workers. An engineering curriculum that does not take such realities into account is bound to alienate itself from practice. Although the Dutch business world was not receptive to such criticism, some experiments were made in Taylorist management to assess its effects.

5.2.2 First World War

In spite of the scepticism that prevailed during the First World War, Volmer advocated the Taylor system at a general meeting of the Society for Commerce and Industry in 1915. Although he was convinced that the growth of prosperity would be served by co-operation between employer and employees, he did not wish to present Taylor's system as the new management gospel. Further scientific exploration of time and motion systems was needed to assess their accuracy (Bloemen, 1988, p. 99). Volmer used every means to convince the employers of the usefulness of the Taylor system. He managed to persuade the general board of the Society for Commerce and Industry to prepare a proposal for a number of Delft professors to make a study trip to the United States, but the lack of financial support from the business world indicated a lack of any real enthusiasm. The conditions of the war then prevented the plan from being realized, and it was postponed indefinitely.

Some enterprises experimented with scientific management. In 1911 Philips had hired some engineers to introduce new machinery and together with some features of Taylorism. The same sort of development could be noted in the artillery workshops of Hembrug, where the mechanical engineer J. F. Quanjer—who had published a pamphlet on the advantages of Taylorism in 1913—was employed. Impressed by the American time and motion studies, the engineer P. Persant Snoep filmed the work of a glassblower of Leerdam in 1917, to analyse his daily activities (Bloemen, 1988).

But the role of the engineers began to acquire more importance especially from 1916 on, as it became increasingly difficult to procure machines and raw materials grew more scarce; all this stimulated a search for efficiency measures. Industrialization, (iron smelting, shipbuilding, machine construction), gained momentum from the pressure of the wartime conditions, but acquired a somewhat improvised character. This led to an excessive variety of materials and of finished and semifinished products on the market.

The Foundation for Normalization in the Netherlands was founded to promote uniformity in standards and norms.

Engineers played an active part in the development of norms and standards for machines, tools and products. Their success led to plans for a permanent institute. In 1918 the Central Normalization Bureau was founded on the initiative of the Royal Institute of Engineers and the Society for Commerce and Industry. E. Hijmans was its first director.

5.2.3 The Interwar Years (1918–1940)

5.2.3.1 Management Consultants

The experiences of the First World War reinforced recognition of the usefulness of management consulting. Not only engineers but also accountants stressed the distinctive contribution of consultants to the field of management. The accountants had better training in economics now, which made them useful as consultants to business enterprises. In the exercise of consultancy assignments accountants would frequently meet engineers, advising on technical aspects of management. In 1917 the Order of Consulting Engineers had been founded to give the advisory work carried out by engineers a formal basis (De Vries, 1985, p. 187).

The Society for Commerce and Industry kept worrying about the consequences of possible bottlenecks in production. Hijmans responded to these signals. Together with his former fellow-student V. Van Gogh he founded the Advisory Bureau for Organization and Metalworking. This bureau gave advice in the field of labour-saving methods, the division of tasks, the purchase of tools, improvements in factory buildings and lay-out, and improvements on the shop-floor and in the office.

Up to 1925 this bureau remained the only one of its kind in the Netherlands. But that year the engineer J. M. Louwerse, who had worked with Hijmans and Van Gogh, founded his own advisory bureau (Bloemen, 1990).

Meanwhile, accountants had also become active in the consultancy field. In the 1920s, problems connected with cost-price, the division of tasks and planning had become an important issue not only in business but also in government. To improve the efficiency of government organizations at local and national levels, a clear financial picture was needed of the functioning of government organizations; such a picture could be provided by accountants.

In 1923, a Retrenchment and Efficiency Congress was organized to underline the importance of efficiency and rationalization. Here, in his opening speech, Volmer presented the case for scientific management. The organizing committee consisting of engineers, accountants, industrial consultants and retrenchment inspectors, did not stop there. Some of them went on to found the Dutch Institute for Efficiency (NIVE). It was their intention to bring together accountants and engineers, as well as administrative and technical managers. The Institute's objective was to communicate the latest insights in the field of scientific management to those directly concerned: the managers. Fundamental research was seen as a condition for the fulfilment of this task. Co-operation with the universities seemed the obvious answer.

5.2.3.2 The Academization of Accounting: Business Economics

Initially it had looked as though the differences between the training of engineers and accountants would be small. In Delft, engineers were taught by the accountant Volmer, who also lectured together with Th. Limperg Jr. in Rotterdam, where in 1913 a Superior School of Commerce had been founded (Stuyvenberg, 1963, p. 44).

The two subjects diverged, however, as accountants became concerned about the scientific status of their discipline and emphasized its relation to general economics. The subject known as the "general doctrine of bookkeeping" was increasingly criticized. Limperg played a central role in the process whereby accounting drifted away from the prevailing practical tradition of management.

When Limperg was appointed to the new faculty of Economics at Amsterdam university in 1922, he explained the nature of the problem in his inaugural lecture. He criticized management (*bedrijfsleer*) as being an artificial doctrine (*kunstleer*). Management can only become scientific in the form of business economics, as a specialized field within (general) economics (*staathuishoudkunde*) based on the concept of an "economic motive". Business economics was a new academic specialization. Limperg expected much of it. Business economists would play a major part in research in business (Limperg, 1950, p. 20).

Limperg emphasized the difference between the business economist (the accountant) and the engineer. The accountant should not be involved in the social tasks which engineers often considered to be part of their advisory work. And engineers should not deal with accounting.

Limperg was rather negative about much consulting work in management: it lacked a scientific, i.e. an economic, basis. This problem had been aggravated, in his view, by an approach deriving from Germany, where Eugen Schmalenbach had developed a doctrine of management (*Betriebswirtschaftslehre*) for practical men which smacked of the "artificial doctrine" (*Kunstlehre*). The German bookkeepers were trained on the job and were little inclined towards scientific analysis. This, according to Limperg, had led to an antithesis between the "doctrine" and business economics (*Betriebswirtschaftslehre*) a dichotomy which had its origins in a lack of understanding on the part of Schmalenbach and his group of the essence of their own profession and of economics (Limperg, 1950, p. 33). Neither bookkeepers nor engineers nor technicians were spared this criticism. None of these groups did Limperg consider to have the necessary economic competence; he was thus emphasizing the distinctive competence of his own new profession, while also creating barriers between accountants and other professionals in the field of management.

N. J. Polak, who had been appointed professor of management (*bedrijfsleer*) at Rotterdam, agreed with Limperg's criticism. But agreement on this basic point could not prevent the differences between Rotterdam and Amsterdam from growing. At the Superior School of Commerce in Rotterdam problems, as defined in practice, remained the main focus. In contrast, all efforts in Amsterdam were directed at reducing practical questions to economic problems. Different and incompatible epistemological positions were at stake. Rotterdam seemed to cling to the inductive, experience-based approach as originally developed at the German *Handelshochschulen*. Amsterdam took an a-priorist, analytical, deductive position (Van Rossum, 1979, p. 216). And in the Netherlands as in Germany, the tension in this debate, became noticeable, between the existing academic tradition and the practice-oriented "superior school" (*hogeschool*).

In Rotterdam the engineer and practical man, J. Goudriaan, was not at all happy with the view of his Amsterdam colleagues. In his opinion business economics was too ready to reduce business problems to purely economic dimensions. He suggested an alternative curriculum to comprise five functional areas of management: technical, commercial, socio-economic, administrative, and financial. Students should be trained to develop a broad view of business and an open attitude towards co-operation with others. The business economists should also be trained in the qualities of the entrepreneur (Goudriaan, 1932). In 1935 Goudriaan was appointed professor of management at Delft. It was to take thirty years before his ideas would be realized.

In the interwar years organization and management were not the concern of engineers and accountants alone. In NIVE, "organization" was seen as more than just an economic or technical issue (Bertels, 1982, p. 97). The human side of enterprise should not be forgotten.

5.2.3.3 Psychotechnics

The journal *Administratieve Arbeid* (Administrative Labour) regularly devoted space to rational work methods which could lead to reforms in the technico-economic and social fields. The editors wanted to draw attention to the human side of organization and to avoid the pitfalls of scientific management in America, where the psychological effects on employees had been neglected.

The German H. Münsterberg was well known in this field. While teaching at Harvard he criticized the American approach. Taylor had pointed out the relevance of personnel selection, but in Münsterberg's view this aspect had not been sufficiently developed. Experiments under psychologists were needed to evolve a scientific approach to the human factor in business. Münsterberg himself was in favour of a "human factors psychology" or "psychotechnics"; the use of psychological tests could improve labour productivity and job satisfaction. These subjects had already been addressed in his study *Psychologie und Wirtschaftsleben* (Psychology and Economic Life) in 1913.

In the Netherlands the idea of a science of labour was launched by a Dutch language teacher, Jac. van Ginneken, the psychologist, F. Roels, who would later become professor of psychology at Utrecht university. Out of the wide range of subjects in the science of labour, they concentrated on personnel selection and career choice. They opened a bureau in this field, the Central Psychological Professional Office. The Protestants created their own organization in 1921, the Christian Psychological Centre, under the supervision of Professor J. Waterink of the Protestant Free University of Amsterdam.

The psychotechnicians claimed to pay more attention to the human being in the organization than the engineers, whom they criticized for being interested in people only as part of a labour force; the subjective experience of the worker was totally neglected. Personnel departments and training activities could serve to counteract the tendency to disregard the human aspect. However, the institutes in the field of psychotechnics did not attract much attention.

5.2.4 Interpretation: the Dutch Heritage

The process of industrialization from 1890 onwards created the conditions for the rise of various professional groups within the field of management. In the course of this process, three groups developed their own identity: engineers, accountants and psychologists.

The difference in developments on the engineering and accountancy sides is interesting. Both had firm roots in practice before becoming accepted as academic disciplines. The engineers remained outside the old universities but succeeded in raising the status of the polytechnic to an academic level, without however fully adopting the culture of the (Humboldt) university. Practice continued to enjoy high status there.

Accountants, on the other hand, made their way into the existing academic culture, by giving up part of their practical orientation. This change in professional culture was symbolized by a new name for the discipline: business economics, regarded as part of the science of economics. This process of academization found its fullest expression at the old and respected university of Amsterdam. At the Superior School of Economics in Rotterdam (not a university), the practical orientation was not so easily given up.

The dichotomy between theory and practice was a fundamental feature of the development in the Netherlands, since it lay at the heart of the whole prevailing educational system. The elitist education at the classical high school and the university was strictly separated from the practice-oriented forms of education for the middle classes. Since management was by nature a practical subject, its acceptance in the existing academic system posed a problem. In principle there were two solutions. One was to preserve the practical, experience-based and inductive character and to create educational institutions outside the existing universities, but to demand academic status for them. This is what happened in the case of engineering in Delft and business economics in Rotterdam. The other solution was to assimilate academic values, which was the essence of Limperg's work.

Apart from the dichotomy between theory and practice, different attitudes toward social problems are an interesting feature in the development of the professions associated with management. Between 1890 and 1940 the roles of the accountant and the engineer became clarified. The engineer was in close touch with the social reality of work; in the Netherlands concern regarding social matters can be seen at quite an early stage in the development of industrial engineering. The accountants worked at a greater distance from the production process and were less involved in social issues; this distance was reinforced by the evolving culture of business economics as an academic discipline.

Industrial psychology first developed in counterpoint to the economic and technical approaches to management. Its moral inspiration was related to religious views of the industrialization process in the denominationally divided Netherlands. Before the Second World War industrial psychology had not yet developed to become a profession of practical relevance.

Thus, before the Second World War the position of the professional approaches to management can be summarized as follows. The practical engineering approach with its base in management consulting, was in a strong position. Engineers were also interested in social aspects of work and organization. On the business economics or accounting side there was a tendency toward academization, which meant a move away from practical management issues. In Rotterdam a more practical approach to business economics was being developed. In counterpoint to the technical and economic approaches to management, there were the beginnings of a psychological approach to work and organization.

This was the heritage of Dutch management thinking and practice which would form the backdrop against which the introduction of North American management ideas would take place after the Second World War. The idea of the business school and of a new paradigm of management would confront the culturally conditioned antithesis between theory and practice, the special role of the engineers and the recently acquired academic status of business economics.

5.3 New Management Ideas and the Reconstruction of the Economy (1945–1960)

5.3.1 Economic Recovery and North American Influences

The period of war and occupation damaged the Netherlands even more than other countries. The Germans had carried off much of the heavy machinery, and the labour force had been forced to work in German industry. Before the war, Germany had been the country's most important trading partner. Allied policy reduced economic relations between the Netherlands and Germany to a minimum after the war, which made the country highly dependent on the other Benelux countries and Great Britain. This in turn strengthened the Atlantic orientation of the Netherlands, even in cultural and scientific contexts. The intellectual influence of Germany, once so important, had almost ceased to exist.

The loss of what is now Indonesia in 1949 and the end of a long colonial era, also affected the economic situation. The combined effects of the war, the occupation and the loss of the former colonies forced the Netherlands to renew its industries and expand its industrial production. Employers, trade unions and the government created the conditions for this process of modernization and industrialization through a centrally controlled system of industrial relations. Wages were kept low to improve the competitive position of Dutch export industry (Windmuller, 1969). The Atlantic orientation of the Netherlands also applied to management. It was felt that the new truths would come from North America. Britain played an important intermediary role.

Management consultants cited the progress in the United States in the field of management and organization. B. W. Berenschot, the founder of one of the most important consulting firms in the Netherlands, stressed the superiority of North American management techniques in the public lecture he held on his appointment as professor of management at Delft in 1950 (Berenschot, 1950). He referred to the disregard for questions of organization and coordination in Dutch firms on the part of managers, both those with technical and those with commercial backgrounds. He also mentioned the underdevelopment of leadership skills in Dutch managers, who continued to believe that leaders are born, not made. One last weakness which he mentioned was the poor exchange of ideas between industry, research institutes and schools. If the Netherlands was to attain the same level of labour productivity as the United states, managers and workers would have to radically change their mentalities.

The problem was thus defined as a lack of labour productivity. In the United States this had been recognized as a core problem of post-war Europe. The belief was widely held that the lack of labour productivity would create tensions and conflicts: fertile soil for communist movements. The European Recovery Program, announced in 1947, rested on the assumption that the political problems of Europe could be transformed into technical ones, which could be solved "when old European ways of conducting business and old habits of class conflict gave way to American methods of scientific management and corporative collaboration" (Hogan, 1987, p. 19). The technical assistance programme organized by the Economic Cooperation Administration at the end of 1948 was directly relevant to the development of management practice and education in Europe. The programme's goal was to "stimulate greater efficiency in industrial production through the introduction of American production techniques, styles of business organization, and labour-management partnerships" (Hogan, 1987, p. 142). "Productivity teams" were organized which cooperated with industry, labour unions and government in the European countries.

In the Netherlands a productivity team of this kind was to be the origin of COP, a national committee which would play a major role in the propagation of North American management ideas, especially by organizing visits to leading business schools (Koenen & Plantenga, 1987).[1]

---

[1] Its original name was *Contactcommissie Opvoering Productiviteit* (Contact Committee for the Improvement of Productivity). As *Commissie Opvoering Productiviteit* it became a standing committee of the new Public Business Organization (PBO), the structure of tripartite consultation of Employers, Labour unions and Government on national and industry levels.

5.3.2 Industrial Engineering and Human Relations

In the era of reconstruction the subject of industrial engineering came into its own. The introduction of scientific management techniques remained in the hands of the consulting firms and the specialist departments of large companies. The consulting firms specializing in industrial engineering evolved in a continuous line of descent, whereby new consulting firms grew out of existing ones. Through Louwerse, who had worked with Hijmans and Van Gogh, all consultancy bureaus are related historically to Hijmans (Gosselink, 1988). The engineer Berenschot, who had worked with Louwerse since 1925, was the central figure in the post-war consulting firms in the management field. From his business many others sprang which still dominate the field. Hijmans remained the *eminence grise* in this field almost until his death in 1987.

The consulting firms grew in both size and number. By 1950 the estimated number of business consultants employed by such firms was 250, the estimated number of enterprises served by them was 500, most of them relatively large organizations (Berenschot, 1950, p. 7).

The scope of industrial engineering was being extended. More attention was being paid to the social aspect of organization and to problems of organizational structure. On the national level industrial engineers contributed to a general system of job classification known as the "normalized method".

Consultants were not only helping to improve labour productivity in industry. They were also active in governmental organizations and state-owned enterprises, where particular attention was paid to problems of structure (lines of authority, staff-line relations, etc.).

The development of ideas on organization and management took place in these consultancy firms. Academic institutions did not contribute much to the practice of management or organization. Novel ideas on operational management, such as Operations Research, were not yet part of the intellectual baggage of the consulting engineers.

As we have seen, the Dutch engineers who worked as consultants in the field of management had been interested in the social aspects of management from the very beginning. They believed in a technical approach to social problems and addressed such things as the division of tasks, hygiene, remuneration systems etc. The role of psychologists and sociologists and their approaches to social problems was quite modest at this stage.

This situation changed after the Second World War, when the Human Relations movement invaded European business. The new socio-psychological ideas of this school found especially fertile soil in the Netherlands. The ideas fitted the existing management culture, which already had a strong social side, and were consonant with the postwar climate of co-operation between labour, government and employers.

An important factor was the rapid process of industrialization after the war. The Netherlands, traditionally dominated by commerce, transport and agriculture had no well-developed industrial culture. New industries were often established in agricultural regions where the populations were not yet used to life in the factory.

The British Tavistock Institute of Human Relations was an important intermediary for the introduction of Human Relations to the Netherlands. The Institute brought together psychologists and psychiatrists who wanted to apply experiences gained during the Second World War to business organizations. The term "sociatry" was invented for this approach (Van Elteren, 1987).

A special role in the introduction of Human Relations ideas was played by the Foundation of True Service. This foundation was established in 1945 under the inspiration of the Moral Rearmament Movement; its aim was to formulate and propagate a new Christian ethic for business and society, and it had its beginnings during the occupation among a number of employers who were also involved in the creation of the Labour Foundation, an important ingredient of the post-war reconstruction of Dutch industrial relations. L. Neher, general director of PTT, was the chairman of the new organization.[2] Its central mission was to create an ethic which would enable people to resist the temptations of totalitarian movements such as Fascism or communism. An important task, derived from this idealistic mission, concerned the propagation of ideas that would promote healthy human relations in industry. To realize this, managers would have to be trained to recognize their responsibility for the functioning of their workforce as human beings. Labour productivity would also profit (Gosselink, 1988, p. 40).

In 1947 the Foundation of True Service and the Dutch Institute for Preventive Medicine (NIPG) founded the Dutch Institute for Personnel Management where the new ideals would be put into effect. The new institute organized a large training programme for lower and middle managers, following the North American and British example of "Training Within Industry" (TWI), to be known in the Netherlands as BKT (*Bedrijfskadertraining*). Similar methods of training had already attracted attention during the war, particularly in Philips, where the ideas of A. Carrard had attracted the attention of management (Boone, 1954, pp. 29–35). When the Dutch Institute of Personnel Management was founded, it was granted a national monopoly on BKT by the Dutch government. Thousands of managers were trained in the early 1950s in BKT, attending courses on work instruction, work methods and human relations at work.

The Dutch Institute of Preventive Medicine (NIPG) related human rela-

---

[2] L. Neher, an autodidact who rose from the ranks of the Dutch Post and Telephone Company, PTT, was managing director from November 1945 to October 1954, with a break between March 1947 and February 1949.

tions to the more general question of mental health. Contact with the Tavistock Institute of Human Relations was lively. NIPG played a pioneering role in industrial psychology, and represented a breeding-ground for talent in this young discipline. Many researchers of NIPG were to play an important part in management education and research in the 1960s and 1970s. It was here that Hutte, the moving spirit behind much intellectual work at NIPG, developed his "sociatric approach" to organization, before becoming professor of social psychology at Groningen University. Others, such as M. Mulder, H. J. van Beinum and M. R. Van Gils, later to become professors in the field of management, all spent some years at NIPG, where the foundations were laid for a strong movement in social management and personnel policy in the Netherlands.

5.3.3 Business Economics

All the development in management thinking in the 1950s which we have been looking at, took place to begin with outside the academic world, in networks of business organizations, government, industrial relations institutions and consulting firms. Business economists were not greatly involved in this development. While engineers and the advocates of Human Relations worked primarily in the world of practice, business economists were working hard to make their subject a science.

In the Dutch situation, where business economics and general economics (macro and micro) were taught in the *same* faculty, the unity of economic science was emphasized.

In the relevant curricula the importance of subsidiary or ("minor") subjects was reduced in favour of the main or "major" economic subjects, and increasing attention was paid to abstract economic theories. A serious limitation of this approach was the lack of mathematical training for students, and further mathematical training thus became part of the curriculum.

There were outside pressures to integrate sociology into the economic curriculum. The problems of public policy and business management would require a broad intellectual overview. Such pressures were successfully resisted, however. At Groningen University, for example, the historical and sociological approach to economics had to give way to the mainstream of neoclassical economics, although socio-economic history remained part of the curriculum (Kastelein, Bijsterveld & Van der Meulen, 1988). Although sociology was taught at the Rotterdam School of Economics (the former Superior School of Commerce), this did not lead to integration. Only at the Tilburg Schools of Economics, was there some integration of the social and economic sciences.

The situation in the economic faculties in the 1950s was not favourable to the introduction of management as an integrated subject. On the one hand, the concentrated focus on the purely economic aspects led to other important subjects, such as personnel and organization, being neglected. On the other hand, the lack of mathematical training among business economists was probably still an impediment to the introduction of the new mathematical techniques of operations research. Business economics departments did not provide the ideal conditions for introducing the "new paradigm of management", the idea embodied in the American business school.

Business economics thus remained tuned to the German cost-accounting traditions, but despite the obstacles mentioned above North American influences did make themselves felt. Operations Research, which had been developed in the United States and British armies, was introduced. The behavioural theories of the firm, as developed by Herbert Simon and his colleagues, reached the business economics departments in the late 1950s, although they never became part of the mainstream of Dutch economic thought. The distinction between finance and accounting, traditionally one integrated subject in Dutch business economics, may also have been introduced as a consequence of North American influences. However, the German background of Dutch business economics, reflected in an emphasis on cost accounting, remains evident even to day. As for the subject of internal organization, the business economics departments tended to concentrate on classical issues of formal structure.

5.3.4 Pressures on the Dutch Academic System

The Dutch university of the 1950s was still an elite institution with long periods of study and a culture emphasizing the value of knowledge *per se* and tending to decline responsibility for vocational training except for the traditional professions of medicine and the law. The special position of technical education (Delft) has already been mentioned. This model of academic education did not seem to fit well with the growing pressure on the university to contribute to the process of modernization and industrialization after the Second World War. Government and business spokesmen proclaimed the need for a change in the model of academic education (cf. e.g. *Rapport van de Contactcommissie Bedrijfsleven-Hoger Onderwijs*, 1957). American examples were also cited in this discussion. Suggestions put forward by business and government included shorter periods of study (the bachelor's degree was often mentioned as a possibility here), a greater practical orientation, and the explicit responsibility of the university for the development of social awareness and personal skills in the students.

The minor role of the universities in the development of managerial talent can be compared with the importance of internal training institutes, especially in large government bureaucracies and state-owned enterprises. The education of officers in the Dutch army and navy as well as the educational system of the Catholic church were early examples of a type of education which was also found in PTT and the Dutch Railways. The residental school was a key concept at PTT, which had its own training institute, Voorlinden; it was also an ingredient in the vocational education scheme for international commercial managers, with a special school, Nijenrode, being founded in 1946 (cf. below). Common to all these schools was the idea of forming a "corps" with its own culture (Van Doorn, 1966, pp. 194–195). The schools provided a route whereby ambitious young men with a secondary school background and mostly from middle class families could enter the managerial hierarchies. In the technologically advanced industrial corporations like Philips, the Dutch State Mines, Hoogovens (blast furnaces) and Royal Dutch-Shell (oil) the various departments of the Delft Polytechnic had the same homogenizing function as these schools. For a managerial career in a bank, young men with a secondary school background would be trained on the job, as management trainees.

The industrialization process in the Netherlands resulted in a shortage of engineers. The monopolistic position of the Delft Polytechnic came to an end in 1951, when it was decided to found a polytechnic in Eindhoven with the help of a gift of money from Philips. A polytechnic in the east of the Netherlands, in Twente, was also considered. Attempts to change the philosophy and structure of academic education were made in these new institutions: experiments were made in connection with the bachelor's degree, with a tutorial system and with the "campus" idea (Groenman, Van Hasselt & Van Heek, 1959). There were also attempts to integrate behavioural science into the engineering curriculum. This would eventually lead to the foundation of business schools in Eindhoven and Twente.

It took some time before the ideas for a new type of academic education which were launched in the 1950s were implemented, and they had no visible effect on management education in the 1950s and early 1960s. The engineering and psychological approaches to management and organization remained largely outside academia.

5.3.5 Moves towards the Business School

However, the whole question of management education was taken up by academics and spokesmen for industry (large companies and multi-nationals), in discussions inspired by the North American example and the availability of Marshall funds. In 1952 a group of leading managers and the director of NIPG visited the United States to study Management Development. In their report, entitled "Who Will Succeed Us?" (*Wie volgt ons op*, 1952), the creation of a management development institute was advocated in cooperation with existing consulting firms and universities. Further discussion of academic management education was also encouraged by the foundation of the International University Contact for Management Education, initiated by Berenschot in 1952. In 1956 A. Wattel, later to become the intellectual father of the Groningen School of Management but at the time still a student of Business Economics, spent some time in the United States. He paid visits to Wharton, MIT and Harvard, on a basis of which he wrote his dissertation on Management Development (Wattel, 1962). In a report on his experiences in American business schools (Wattel, 1956), he put forward some ideas for a business school curriculum. He emphasized the desirability of a broad intellectual background and specialization in at least one functional field of business. He showed himself to be more in favour of (the renewed) Wharton, Cornell and MIT than of Harvard, and was convinced of the necessity of a good grounding in mathematics. At that time he did not deem it necessary to have business schools in the Netherlands, because the necessary courses could easily be added to existing syllabuses.

Meanwhile, management development activities were being organized outside the academic world by various private institutes related to the consulting community, albeit with the frequent participation of university professors. The Dutch Institute for Efficiency (NIVE) provided courses in all fields of management, with an emphasis on production and financial control. In 1953 NCD (the Dutch Centre for Directors) was founded, organizing a wide variety of conferences and study meetings. The Study Centre for Business Policy was founded in Arnhem the same year by Akzo, Unilever, Philips, DSM, Hoogovens and the large Dutch banks, to provide educational courses for the higher levels of management in big business.[3] The foundation of the Interacademic Foundation for Organization Studies (SIOO) in 1958 showed the growing interest of the academic world in management development.

Although not (yet) part of the academic world, the foundation in 1946 of Nijenrode, the school for international commercial managers, should be mentioned in this context. It was founded with a view to providing specialized courses of short duration (a two-year programme) for management positions in foreign trade and commerce. Its official name was the Dutch Training Institute for Foreign Countries. Over the years Nijenrode evolved to become a fully-fledged business school.

5.4 The Founding of Business Schools (1960–1977)

5.4.1 Business Economics and the Social Sciences

In the faculties of economics the emphasis on scientific rigour and general economic theory still persisted, and a good deal of attention was paid to mathematical models and techniques. The advance of electronic data-pro-

---

[3] *Stichting Studiecentrum Bedrijfsbeleid* was founded in 1953 on the initiative of the *Nederlandse Maatschappij voor Nijverheid en Handel* (Dutch Society for Industry and Commerce). In its early years the institute was called *Berg en Dal*, after the hotel where its meetings were held. In 1983 the institute changed its name to *Semafor, Senior Management Forum*.

cessing introduced new ideas into the departments of business economics. As indicated above, operations research and management science were introduced alongside the more traditional cost-accounting techniques. Linear programming and related techniques were applied to operational planning problems, and the first business games were introduced. The new behavioural theories of the firm, as developed by Simon, Cyert and March were an innovative element in the departments of business economics, which until then had been dominated by a belief in perfect rationality. Marketing and corporate planning, not well developed in the Dutch business economics tradition, were also imported from the Anglo-Saxon world. Systems theory and systems analysis became part of a new evolving language of organization theory which was to supplement the existing Dutch tradition of business economics.[4]

The social science faculties—sociology, psychology and education—were growing fast in the 1960s and early 1970s. Ideas on the social aspects of management were developed by departments of industrial psychology, social psychology and organizational sociology. These departments, which were often involved in practical projects connected with human relations, work design and consultation at work, imported the ideas on work and organization from America and Britian, and developed them further.

At Leyden university the sociologist Lammers propagated the North American sociology of organizations and linked it to ideas about participation and consultation in work organizations. At the protestant Free University of Amsterdam, the sociologist H. J. van Zuthem developed his views on the integration of the enterprise and conducted a number of field experiments focusing on the responsibility of the employee. Social scientists with a background in the Dutch Institute of Preventive Medicine (NIPG) played a vital role in the introduction of new ideas on organization and personnel policy. The sociotechnical line of research, originating in the Brittish Tavistock Institute of Human Relations, was applied in field experiments by H. J. van Beinum and others (Van Beinum, 1963; Van Beinum, Van Gils & Verhagen, 1968). Sociotechnical ideas were also used in field experiments on the re-structuring of work at Philips (Den Hertog, 1977). In the 1970s there was a growing interest in power and conflict in organizations, often in the context of industrial relations and personnel policy.

Although the new developments in sociology and psychology were concerned with managerial problems, the university departments of industrial psychology and sociology did not directly train managers. But by way of action research and organizational change projects, managers were indirectly affected by the new ideas. Further, and more directly, these ideas reached managers through the growing personnel departments of large organiza-

---

[4] Especially active in this field was the *Systeemgroep Nederland*, a multi-disciplinary group of academics interested in systems theory, founded in 1970 by Professor A. Hanken.

tions, where academically trained sociologists and psychologists were being employed in increasing numbers. As we shall now see, the social scientists ultimately played a major role in the creation of business schools in the Netherlands.

5.4.2 The Birth of Business Schools

In the 1960s and early 1970s academic education still played a minor role in the careers of Dutch managers. In 1960 only 12 per cent of the CEOs of Dutch limited liability companies held academic degrees (Becker, 1968). The corresponding figure in the United States at the time was 60 per cent.[5] Not only had Dutch executives a relatively low level of education, they were also fairly elderly, and would soon have to be replaced. Internal recruitment led to a suboptimal allocation of managerial manpower in Dutch companies.

However, a growing number of academically trained employees were now entering Dutch business organizations, in particular lawyers, business economists and engineers. Official reports still predicted a shortage of academically trained managers in the future. In 1961 a delegation of representatives of Dutch universities (business economics departments) and industry paid a visit to the United States, resulting in a report on the future of academic education in management and organization (*Onderwijs en Onderzoek inzake Leiding van Bedrijven en Instellingen*, 1964).

The productivity community, COP, was involved in this American trip, while the initiative actually came from the International University Contact for Management Education. Following the report, a study committee was formed. It consisted of representatives of business and university professors, among them Berenschot. The 1964 report reckoned that there were 120,000 positions in the Netherlands for which an education in management and organization would be appropriate. The report presented the basic outlines for a Dutch (academic) business school: post-bachelor courses of study on an interdisciplinary basis. It was suggested that the teachers for such courses would have to be trained abroad. Preparatory activities on the part of committees in 1969 from these two universities was to lead to the foundation of the *Interfaculteit Bedrijfskunde Delft*, now in Rotterdam (Brevoord & Kamp, 1971).

When it came to the development of business studies in the polytechnics, an important part was played by *Neher Report*. In 1960, as a successor to the earlier Contact Committee for Industry and Higher Education, the minister of education, J. M. L. Th. Cals, set up the Committee on Technical Education and Social Sciences. Its chairman was Neher, the former director gen-

---

[5] This comparison did not allow for the differences in educational systems between the two countries. The result was probably an underestimation of the Dutch manager.

eral of PTT who had been active in the field before (see p. 97). The 1962 report (*Rapport van de Commissie Technische Studie en Maatschappijwetenschappen*, 1962) emphasized the importance of the social sciences in the education of engineers. The social sciences would prepare the young engineer for the complexities of modern industrial society. Explicit reference was made to the rapid process of industrialization which was taking place in the Netherlands and which demanded a new attitude on the part of the engineers. They should possess some knowledge of the internal workings of the modern organization and of the structure of the national and international environment. Philosophy, psychology, economics (including organization theory) and law should be integrated into the curriculum of the *Technische Hogescholen*, with a view to extending the intellectual and moral horizons of the engineers. These subjects should account for at least 5 per cent of the curriculum. Apart from this general recommendation directed at all specializations, the committee commented upon the proposal of the *Technische Hogeschool Eindhoven* to establish a new curriculum for business studies, based on recognition that technological development and new forms of international economic cooperation would call for a new type of engineer who knew something of economic, social and psychological processes.

The curriculum then being designed at Eindhoven was to have a technical basis. In later years management subjects would account for 70 per cent of the syllabus, though this proportion was reduced to 30 per cent in subsequent proposals. The committee took a positive view of experimenting in business studies at Eindhoven, but did not advise the minister to incorporate this new discipline into the Academic Statute.

In the department of mechanical engineering at Eindhoven a special option which included management was introduced in 1962. Some management subjects had been introduced into the syllabus as early as 1958. As we have seen, a fully-fledged business studies curriculum was being planned, due to start in 1965. Meanwhile syllabuses with a strong element of management studies were to be offered in other departments as well. In 1966 fifty students embarked on business studies. In 1969 the post-propaedetical curriculum, i.e. studies after the first year, was replaced by a full five-year curriculum. In 1972 the discipline of business studies was officially incorporated into the Academic Statute.

The growing interest in management education in the 1960s was also reflected in the above-mentioned dissertation on management development (Wattel, 1962). Some years later a gift from the Rotterdamsche Bank N.V. enabled the sociologist H.A. Becker to write a dissertation entitled *Management as a Profession* (Becker, 1968). The shortage of trained managers and the lack of professionalization among Dutch managers were central themes in this dissertation.

The lack of professional training among the managers of middle-sized business organizations was being increasingly recognized as a cause of the problems of family-owned firms. For example the question was discussed at a conference on family firms organized by the Dutch Centre for managers (NCD) in 1966. The trend towards rationalization and concentration was making its impact on management: the paternalistic style of the owner-manager was becoming outdated (Horringa, 1966, Chapter III). It was time for professional managers to take the helm.

In 1966 and 1967 a practice-oriented management journal, *Doelmatig Bedrijfsbeheer,* devoted a series of articles to the business school of the future (*Naar een business school in Nederland*, 1966/67). Representatives of business and private institutes of management education as well as university professors (business economists) all gave their views on the subject. Among the academics the business economists of the Rotterdam school were particularly enthusiastic. Meanwhile, a beginning had already been made in Rotterdam where a gift from Royal Dutch-Shell, followed by gifts from other large companies and banks, enabled the start of the Foundation for Management and Organization. In April 1969 six faculties in Rotterdam and Delft decided to found the School of Management. These were the faculties of economics, law and social sciences at the Rotterdam School of Economics, and the departments of mechanical engineering, civil engineering and general science at the *Technische Hoogeschool Delft*. The official foundation date was 23 June 1969.

In the east of the Netherlands a new polytechnic was opened in 1964. It was inspired by American models: the students were to live on the campus and the bachelor's degree was introduced. Business studies for a higher degree started in 1968.

In 1967 talks began at Groningen University between the department of business economics and some departments in the Faculty of Social Sciences. These talks resulted in plans to create a business studies (management) curriculum. Not until 1976, however, were these plans realized. The first students arrived in September 1977.

During the 1970s the existing school for international commerce, Nijenrode, took several steps towards becoming an academic business school. In 1972 it introduced the three-year Bachelor of Business Administration (BBA) course, which continued to be its main course of study. It would take another ten years for Nijenrode to acquire full academic status in 1982.

5.5 The Growth of Academic Business Schools (1977–1992)

5.5.1 Evolution of the Schools

The business schools were founded in a period when the universities were expanding in an unprecedented fashion. From the small elite institution of the 1950s, the university developed to become a system of mass education in the 1960s and 1970s. In 1968, for example, 5,139 academic graduates entered the labour market; in 1974 this number had risen to 8,430; in 1979 the number of graduates was 10,617 (*Vijfentachtig jaren statistiek in tijdreeksen*, 1984).

In the 1960s and early 1970s the faculties of social science were growing even faster than the average rate. The cultural climate of this period favoured the young social sciences. The democracy movement had strong roots in the social faculties.

Business economics showed a different evolution. The percentage of students studying business economics, for example, even decreased slightly between 1965 and 1975, from 10 to 9 per cent of the total number of students. The total number of students in the new business schools remained fairly modest until the early 1980s, when less than 700 students commenced their business studies each year.

From 1980 onwards, however, we can see a combination of general retrenchment and stagnation in the Dutch academic world and the spectacular growth of the new business schools. In 1989 there were already over 6,000 business students; in 1985 there had been less than 4,000. This growth coincided with a generally deteriorating situation for young academics on the labour market, which encouraged a labour-market-related choice of courses. Another factor which stimulated the growth of the business schools was the change in attitudes towards business and entrepreneurship in Dutch society. An industrial career was becoming increasingly preferred to work in government or public sector organizations. This preference for a business career did not only favour the young field of business studies, however; business economics also profited. Apart from the growing interest of students in economics, these departments also profited from the limits imposed on admission (*numerus fixus*) to business studies by the government. For many students, economics was their second choice.

In Table 5.1 we show the numbers of students beginning and successfully finishing business studies between 1966 and 1987. A comparison, in terms of numbers of graduates, with the combined universities (and polytechnics) as a whole and with business economics is shown in Table 5.2

The growth of the business (management) faculties was interesting to the universities because it could compensate for the expected decrease in students in other faculties. This gave the new business faculties a strong position in the academic world, which in turn tended to promote further growth. For the business schools themselves this growth created problems. It became increasingly difficult to find enough qualified professors and other staff, and to allot sufficient time and energy to research.

Table 5.1 *Numbers of First-year Students (Entrants) and Numbers of Graduates in Dutch Business Studies 1966/67–1986/87*

Year	Entrants	Graduate
1966/67	50	0
1967/68	50	0
1968/69	125	1
1969/70	125	1
1970/71	200	7
1971/72	229	28
1972/73	178	79
1973/74	181	120
1974/75	224	120
1975/76	280	179
1976/77	284	148
1977/78	374	178
1978/79	448	183
1979/80	560	198
1980/81	634	202
1981/82	679	229
1982/83	1,068	274
1983/84	1,141	347
1984/85	1,397	390
1985/86	984	414
1986/87	1,205	561

Note: The numbers in the table are slightly different from those obtained from the Centraal Bureau voor de Statistiek. The numbers in this table are based on data collected by ourselves with the help of the faculties.

5.5.2 Government Policy: the Two-phase Structure and the Financing of Research

The development of business studies was strongly influenced by government policy on higher education. The first business courses started as second-degree courses. The introduction of the "two phase structure" (*twee-fasen structuur*) has forced all business faculties to re-design their programmes as four-year courses.[6] Since 1982 the business faculties have recruited their first-year students among school leavers from the secondary schools which qualify their pupils for university entrance. This change in course structure encouraged the growth of the business faculties. The Delft School of Management moved to Rotterdam and became part of Erasmus Univer-

---

[6] The original idea was to divide each programme into two phases. In fact, only the first phase has been realized in most cases, so that the in practice two-phase policy only led to a considerable shortening of curricula.

Table 5.2 *Number of Graduates at Dutch Universities: General, Business Economics and Business Studies*

	1974/75	1979/80	1985/86	1986/87	1987/88
Economics	812	807	1,232	1,513	2,033
Business Studies:					
Technical	85	93	135	262	289
General	46	100	291	387	330
Total	131	193	426	649	619
All Faculties	9,928	10,127	13,504	15,164	20,667

Source: *Zakboek onderwijsstatistieken*, 1989.

sity, at the same time as the two-phase structure was being introduced. A second-phase course of study, leading to a (US) MBA degree, was created alongside the new first-phase course. The commercial school at Nijenrode—until then regarded as an institution of higher vocational education—acquired academic status with the introduction of the two-phase structure. At Nijmegen Catholic University the creation of a new faculty of policy science was followed by moves towards a full first-phase course-business studies. This recent school, which opened in 1990, brings the number of faculties offering a first-phase course in business studies to six, namely Eindhoven, Rotterdam, Twente, Groningen, Nijenrode and Nijmegen.

A course in business studies with full academic status has recently been established in the Open university of the Netherlands, which was founded in 1984 under inspiration from the British Open university. In contrast to the faculties mentioned above, this seventh academic business school, which employs distance tuition, mainly attracts students with previous managerial experience. The business courses are now attracting some 7,000 students, but only a small proportion (10–20 per cent) of them are expected to obtain an academic degree in business studies.[7] Most of them choose a few of the constituent courses only.

Another aspect of government policy involved a change in the financing of academic research. According to what is known as the "conditional financing of research" it became mandatory on the faculties to formulate research programmes and to report their results. Negative results would eventually lead to a loss of financial resources.

---

[7] The proportion of students who express the *intention* to work for a full academic degree is higher: 26 per cent for students who have already completed at least one course (*Visitatiecommissie Open universiteit*, 1990).

These two aspects of government policy, the two-phase structure and the system of conditionally financed research, forced the new business schools out of their previous standing somewhat apart from the academic world and into existing academic patterns. Research and basic scientific education had never been the strongest suit in the business schools, but had to become so now.

5.5.3 The Labour Market for Graduates

Up to now it has been fairly possible for the labour market and in particular large companies to absorb the growing numbers of graduates. The distance between small businesses and the business school is still difficult to bridge. Apart from the cultural gap, small businesses lack the resources and practical possibilities for turning the generalist trained at a business school into a useful employee. In 1984 the consulting firm McKinsey was still predicting an almost insatiable demand for business school graduates in the Netherlands, or more exactly a yearly demand of 7,000 (*Symposium Bedrijfskunde*, 1984). When this prediction was made, large companies in the Netherlands were competing for the best students in order to counteract the shortage that demographic developments were expected to produce. At the same time they were also compensating for their own caution in the years around 1980, when uncertain economic prospects were inhibiting recruitment. There were thus special reasons for the "boom" in the market for management trainees in the mid-1980s and it could not be expected to last.

From interviews held with recruitment departments and top managers in large industrial companies in 1986 and 1987, we gained a strong impression that the business school graduates were not being sought for their specific knowledge; rather, they were generally regarded as interchangeable with graduates of business economics or even law, or with the graduates of the higher vocational schools of commerce and technology. The business graduate was taken on as a management trainee in internal systems of management development in much the same way as the secondary school leavers had been taken on some twenty years before. Because of their general background business school graduates are suitable for jobs in marketing, personnel and other jobs of a not too technically sophisticated nature. Flexibility, the result of multidisciplinary training, is the most important motive for employing business school graduates. A recent survey by D. Veldhorst of the employers' association VNO (*Strategie BBW 1992–2000*, 1991) has shown that for more specialized functions such as production, finance and accounting, and research and development, employers prefer graduates of (business) economics, natural science or engineering. To a question about their academic education, graduates of Eindhoven, Rotterdam and Twente replied that they felt deficient not so much in knowledge as in certain practical skills such as negotiation, oral presentation, report writing, systems design and software use, an answer which reflects the nature of jobs where business school graduates are to be found (Van Dam, Keizer & Kempen, 1990): most start in staff positions and move on into management a few years later.

Although the faculties of business studies are still optimistic about the labour market for graduates, there are also signs that the prospects for business school graduates may become less favourable in the near future. The effects of the growth in business schools and many related forms of education around 1985, are now showing on the labour market. At the same time companies taking on young academics are beginning to recognize the limitations of the general business education for young people without prior specialization. Finally, economic development in the Netherlands during 1990 and 1991 has led to caution on the part of both private and public employers when it comes to taking on new managerial personnel. The result may well be a surplus of business school graduates on the labour market in the near future. Students seem to be expecting this: in 1991, for the first time in the history of the business schools, there was a drop in the number of first-year students. However, fluctuations of this kind on the labour market do not give any clear indication of the long-term trend in accepting business school as a preparation for managerial positions.

5.5.4 Business Studies as a Science and as a Profession

At the start, the idea of an integrated science played an important part in the new academic business schools. The first staff members in the new faculties of business studies, who came from economics, behavioural science, applied mathematics and engineering, faced the problem of defining the scientific identity of the new discipline in terms that were acceptable to the academic community. Systems theory in various forms was often seen as a means whereby the various disciplinary and functional approaches to management and organization could be integrated.

At the same time, however, the new faculties also maintained their existing practice-oriented approach to management, in which scientific research played virtually no part at all. The spectacular growth in student numbers in the 1980s reinforced this tendency: the development of the curriculum and teaching took precedence over research.

We thus have a typical tension between the idea of a unified science of management which still echoes the American belief in a New Paradigm of Management in the 1950s, and the pragmatic view of management which has its roots in the past and has been reinforced by the increase in student numbers. As a result of this tension it is understandable that professors in the field of business studies are still worrying about the scientific status of their discipline.

5.6 Conclusion

The short history of management education in the Netherlands presented in this chapter shows how the North American idea of the business school, and the underlying paradigm of business studies, were absorbed into an existing national context. We have emphasized the contribution made by engineers and business economists to Dutch management thinking and practice before the influence of the new paradigm of business studies appeared.

The two currents in Dutch management thinking reflect two kinds of development, with different views of management and different positions in the academic world. The engineering approach, closely linked to practice and often possessing an awareness of the problems on the shopfloor, was part of the practical and vocationally oriented world of the polytechnics. Business economics, which was closely connected with the accounting profession had a predominantly financial orientation and was not concerned with the problems of the shopfloor; it succeeded in becoming academically accepted by firmly inserting itself into the economics faculties. But we have also seen how the tension between managerial practice and economic theory continued to play a part in business economics.

When the idea of a unified science of management—business studies—was introduced after the Second World War, it came up against high barriers. First of all, it met with the general contempt of the academic world—especially outside the polytechnics—for practice-oriented subjects and vocational training. Secondly, the introduction of business studies had to take the existence of business economics into account.

The development of business studies followed two paths. At the polytechnics of Eindhoven and Twente it was relatively easy for "technical business studies" to develop out of mechanical and industrial engineering. General business studies, which evolved at Delft (Rotterdam) and Groningen, followed another pattern. The accepted position of business economics and its strong links with the accounting profession can be seen as an important reason for the negative attitude of the faculties of economics to the idea of the business school and the related paradigm of management. As a result, new faculties were founded. These faculties felt the need to legitimate their existence in the academic world by demonstrating their scientific credibility. This explains the strong emphasis in the late 1970s and early 1980s on the unique paradigm of management which distinguished business studies from the other sciences. The need to achieve the formal recognition of business studies in the Academic Statute reinforced this search for a unifying idea based on an interdisciplinary methodology.

With the acceptance if not the recognition of business studies in the academic world and the spectacular rise in student numbers, the role of a unifying idea of an interdisciplinary science of management seems to have been pushed into the background. Specialization in the curriculum and research programme is becoming more important. Meanwhile, the departments of business economics are developing an ever broader view of management and offering interdisciplinary courses of study, so that the difference between business economics and business studies is becoming blurred. A glance at the subjects and curricula of the various schools reveals that the difference between courses with an "engineering" or a "general" background is becoming less and less pronounced.

Thus, much of the debate surrounding the introduction of business studies into the academic world seems to be coming to an end. New issues concerning the role of the academic institutions in the education of managers are appearing in the Netherlands as elsewhere. By reflecting on our own past with its rich variety of approaches to management and education, we may find it easier to confront these issues with a fresh eye.

References

Becker, H. A., 1968, *Management als beroep: Kenmerken van de Managersgroepering in Sociologisch Perspectief*, Den Haag: Martinus Nijhoff.

Beinum, H. J. van, 1963, *Een Organisatie in Beweging: Een sociaal-psychologisch veldexperiment bij de postcheque—en girodienst*, Leiden: H.E. Stenfert-Kroese N.V.

Beinum, H. J. J. van, Gils, M. R. van & Verhagen, E.J., 1968, *Taakontwerp en Werkorganisatie*, Den Haag: COP-SER.

Berenschot, B. W., 1950, *Welke betekenis kan de studie van de wetenschappelijke bedrijfsorganisatie hebben voor de verhoging van de arbeidsproduktiviteit*, Rede uitgesproken bij de aanvaarding van het ambt van buitengewoon hoogleraar aan de Technische hogeschool te Delft, Delft, 11 October.

Bertels, K., 1982, "Hoe arbeid en sociologie elkaar niet kregen; Nederland 1820–1920", *Grafiet*, 2, pp. 72–103.

Bierens de Haan, J., 1952, *Van Oeconomische Tak tot Nederlandsche Maatschappij voor Nijverheid en Handel 1777–1952*, Haarlem: Tjeenk Willink.

Bloemen, E. S. A., 1988, *Scientific Management in Nederland 1900–1930*, Amsterdam: NEHA.

— 1990, "Bedrijfsadviseurs in het interbellum; het Adviesbureau voor Bedrijfsorganisatie van ir. J.M. Louwerse, 1925–1938", *Jaarboek voor de Geschiedenis van Bedrijf en Techniek*, deel 7, Utrecht: Stichting JBGTB, pp. 191–219.

Boone, P. C., 1954, *Mens en Medemens in het Bedrijf*, Bussum: Voorhoeve.

Brands, J., 1963, *Een halve eeuw bedrijfseconomie 1913–1963*, Leiden: Stenfert Kroese.

Brevoord, C. & Kamp, J. J., 1971, *Bedrijfskundig Journaal, in opdracht van de Commissie opvoering Produktiviteit van de Sociaal-Economische Raad*, Leiden: Stenfert Kroese.

Dael, J. van, 1938, *De geschiedenis der psychotechniek van het bedrijfsleven*, Public Lecture, Nijmegen/Utrecht.

— 1991, "Vijftig jaar bedrijfskunde, 1965–2015", *Bedrijfskunde*, No. 63, pp. 4–12.

Dam, C. van, Keizer, J. A. & Kempen, P. M., 1990, "Living Apart Together?: Over de spanning tussen theorie en praktijk in de bedrijfkunde", *Bedrijfskunde*, No. 62, pp. 173–187.

Dam, C. van (ed.),1989, *Bedrijfskunde op Weg naar 1990*, Deventer: Kluwer Bedrijfswetenschapen.
Doorn, J. A. A. van, 1966, *Organisatie en maatschappij: sociologische opstellen*, Leiden: Stenfert Kroese.
Elteren, M. C. M. van, 1987, "Tussen opvoering van arbeidsproduktiviteit en ethiek; de receptie van de "human relations"-benadering in Nederland (1945–1960)", *Psychologie en Maatschappij*, 41, pp. 339–353.
— 1989, "Arbeidssociatrie en bedrijfsleven in Nederland", *Sociale Wetenschappen*, 30, pp. 239–277.
Feyter, C. de, 1986, "Amerika en de Nederlandse economische wetenschap", *Grafiet*, 6, pp. 150–167.
Fortuyn, W. S. P., 1983, *Kerncijfers 1945–1983 van de Sociaal-Economische Ontwikkeling in Nederland: Expansie en Stagnatie*, Kluwer: Deventer.
Gils, M. R. van, 1991, "Van Dam en de zin en onzin van de algemene bedrijfskunde", *Bedrijfskunde*, 63, pp. 17–20.
Gosselink, F. J., 1986, *Organisatiekunde in historisch perspectief*, Onderzoeksrapport 8617/0, Rotterdam: Erasmus Universiteit.
— 1988, *Ontwikkelingen in de Organisatiekunde: Organisatiekunde en Maatschappelijke Kontekst*, Rotterdam: Proefschrift.
Goudriaan, J., 1932, "De ontwikkeling van de Bedrijfsleer als Toegepaste Wetenschap", in: de Jongh, J. G. *et al.*, *Bedrijfseconomische Studiën: een verzameling herdrukken van redevoeringen, referaten en artikelen*, Haarlem: De Erven F. Bohn, pp. 534–554.
Groenman, S., Hasselt, R. van & van Heek, F., 1959, *De Vestiging van Hoger Onderwijs in Oost-Nederland: een nadere uitwerking*, Enschede.
Hertog, J. F. den, 1977, *Werkstructurering: Ervaringen met Alternatieve Werkorganisaties binnen het Philips Bedrijf*, Alphen aan den Rijn: Samsom.
Hijmans, E., 1948, *Hoofdlijnen der Toegepaste Organisatie*. Deventer/Batavia: Kluwer.
— 1950, *De Toekomst van onze Arbeid*. Leiden: Stenfert Kroese.
Hogan, M. J., 1987, *The Marshall Plan: America, Britain, and the Reconstruction of Western Europe*, Cambridge/New York: Cambridge University Press.
Horringa, D., 1966, *Ondernemingsbestuur in de Moderne Samenleving*, Utrecht/Antwerpen: Het Spectrum.
Jonge, J. A. de, 1976, *De industrialisatie in Nederland*. Nijmegen: SUN.
Karsten, L., 1990, *De achturendag*, Amsterdam: IISG.
Kastelein, T., Bijsterveld, K. & Meulen, H. van der, 1988, *Een eigenzinnige koers,: 40 jaar Faculteit der Economische Wetenschappen in Groningen*, Groningen: Rijksuniversiteit Groningen.
Klein, P. W., 1966, *Traditionele ondernemers en economische groei in Nederland 1850–1914*, Public lecture, Rotterdam.
Koenen, S. & Plantenga, J. (eds.), 1986, *Amerika en de sociale wetenschappen in Nederland*, Utrecht: Grafiet.
Lambers, H. W., 1959, "De industriële ondernemer in een bewegende economische orde", in: M. Rooy, *Ondernemend Nederland*, Leiden, pp. 96–121.
Lammers, C. J., 1963, *Het Koninklijke Instituut voor de Marine. Een sociologische Analyse van de inlijving van groepen adspirant-officieren in de zeemacht*, Assen: Van Gorcum.
— (ed.), 1965, *Medezeggenschap en Overleg in het Bedrijf*, Utrecht/Antwerpen: Het Spectrum.

Lijftogt, S. G., 1966, *De genormaliseerde methode voor werkclassificatie, waardering en kritiek*, Proefschrift, Utrecht.
Limperg, T., 1950, "Het object der bedrijfshuishoudkunde voor de accountant", in: *Vijfentwintig jaar Maandblad voor Accountancy en Bedrijfshuishoudkunde*, Purmerend: Muusses, pp. 24–52.
Lintsen, H., 1980, *Ingenieurs in Nederland in de Negentiende Eeuw*, Den Haag: Martinus Nijhoff.
Locke, R. R., 1984, *The End of the Practical Man: Entrepreneurship and Higher Education in Germany, France, and Great Britain, 1880–1940*, Greenwich Conn.: JAI Press.
Locke, R. R., 1989, *Management and Higher Education since 1940. The Influence of America and Japan on West Germany, Great Britain and France*, Cambridge: Cambridge University Press.
Maas, A., 1988, *Ongedefinieerde Ruimten: Sociaal-symbolische configuraties*, Delft: Eburon.
Maastrigt, A. J. van & Metzemaekers, L. A. V. M., 1983, *Een eeuw in balans: De wordingsgeschiedenis van Moret en Limperg, 1883–1983*, Nijmegen: Thieme.
Man, H. de, 1988, *Organizational Change in its Context: A Theoretical and Empirical Study of the Linkages between Organizational Change Projects and their Administrative, Strategic and Institutional Environment*, Delft: Eburon.
Meulen, R. ter & Hoorn, W. van, 1982, "Psychotechniek en menselijke verhoudingen. Bedrijfspsychologie in Nederland tijdens en kort na het Interbellum", *Grafiet*, No. 1.
"Naar een business school in Nederland", 1966/67, *Doelmatig Bedrijfsbeheer*, 18/19.
Onderwijs en Onderzoek inzake Leiding van Bedrijven en Instellingen, 1964, Den Haag: Commissie Opvoering Productiviteit/sociaal-Economische Raad.
Polak, N. J., 1953, "Het huidige stadium en de naaste taak van de bedrijfsleer", in: H.T. Go en J.P. Kikkert (eds.), *Verspreide Geschriften van prof. dr. N.J. Polak*, Purmerend: Muusses, pp. 1–15.
Rapport van de Commissie Technische Studie en Maatschappijwetenschappen, 1962, november.
Rapport van de Contactcommissie Bedrijfsleven-Hoger Onderwijs, 1957, 17 mei, Den Haag.
Rossum, W. van, 1979, *Wetenschappelijke ontwikkeling als een sociologisch probleem met speciale aandacht voor ontwikkelingen in de Nederlandse bedrijfseconomie*, dissertatie, Amsterdam.
Strategie BBW 1992–2000, 1991, Heerlen: Open universiteit.
Stuyvenberg, J. H. van, 1963, *De Nederlandsche Economische Hoogeschool 1913–1963*, Rotterdam: Nijgh van Ditmar.
Symposium Bedrijfskunde, 1984, 29–30 november, Noordwijk, 's-Gravenhage: Ministerie van Onderwijs en Wetenschapppen.
Taylor, F. W., 1903, *Shop Management*, Presentation at the Saratoga meeting June 1903 (New York: Harper, 1911).
Teulings A. W. M. (ed.), 1978, *Herstructurering van de Industrie: Praktijk, beleid en perspectief*, Alphen aan den Rijn: Samsom.
Vijfentachtig jaren statistiek in tijdreeksen, 1984. Den Haag: Centraal Bureau voor de Statistiek.
Visitatiecommissie Open universiteit, 1990, *De Open universiteit: een tussenbalans*, Den Haag.
Vries, J. de, 1985, *Geschiedenis der Accountancy in Nederland*, Assen: Van Gorcum.

Wattel, A., 1956, *The Teaching of Organization and Management of an Enterprise at Universities and in Industry in the United States: Report of Personal Experiences*, Philadelphia: Wharton School of Finance and Commerce, University of Pennsylvania.
— 1962, *Vorming voor Leidinggevende Arbeid in de Onderneming: het economisch-organisatorische vraagstuk van management-development*, Leiden: Stenfert Kroese.
Wie Volgt Ons Op?: Rapport betreffende de Management Development in het Amerikaanse Bedrijfsleven uitgebracht door de Studiegroep Industrie, 1952, Den Haag: Contactgroep Opvoering Productiviteit.
Windmuller, J. P., 1969, *Labor Relations in the Netherlands*, Ithaca, NY: Cornell University Press.
Zakboek onderwijsstatistieken, 1989, Den Haag: Centraal Bureau voor de Statistiek.
Zanden J. L. van & Griffith, R. T., 1989, *Economische geschiedenis van Nederland in de 20e eeuw*, Utrecht: Het Spectrum.
Zuthem, H. J. van, 1961 *De Integratie van de Onderneming als Sociologisch Vraagstuk*, Assen: Van Gorcum.

Chapter 6
Division and Unification of German Business Administration and Management Education

Rüdiger Pieper
Paul-Löbe-Institut, Berlin, Germany

6.1 Introduction

Compared to the history of management thought (Wren, 1987), which to a great extent can be seen as an American invention, the history of business administration and management education in Germany has quite a distinctive character. Up to the Second World War German business administration research was a major influence on management education and research in other European countries, in Japan and, through the export of researchers, even in the United States. After the Second World War, however, as a result of the separation of Germany into two states with divergent political and economic systems, the further development of German business administration was split as well. Whereas in West Germany the pre-war tradition of *Betriebswirtschaftslehre* persisted together with an infusion of American management knowledge, the development in East Germany was largely influenced by Marxist-oriented Russian political economy. Only recently, following German reunification, have the two lines of development become synchronous and a number of new problems have arisen.

The present chapter will focus on this process of separation and subsequent unification of German business administration. It will therefore deal particularly with events in the East, against a background of the pre-war period and developments in the West.[1] The chapter starts with a brief review of the period before the 1950s (Section 6.2); the three following decades will then be addressed in consecutive sections (Section 6.3–6.6); some concluding remarks are made in Section 6.7.

6.2 A Brief Review of the Period Before the 1950s

6.2.1 Business Administration in pre-war Germany

The first German-speaking business schools or *Handelshochschulen*, which like those in Aachen, Leipzig, St. Gallen and Vienna were founded at the

---

[1] For the earlier developments and present theoretical approaches, cf. e.g. Albach (1990) and Wöhe (1990).

turn of the century, had an entirely practical orientation. The courses offered during the two-year period of study were intended to increase the general knowledge of businessmen. The subjects were economics, law, accounting, and foreign languages (Schneider, 1987, p. 129). It took more than a decade before business administration evolved from the various themes dealt with by the German business schools to become a discipline in its own right. After these topics had been systematized in textbooks such as Hellauer (1910), Schär (1911) and Nicklisch (1912), the new discipline came to be known first as *Privatwirtschaftslehre* or *Handelswissenschaft* and later as *Betriebswirtschaftslehre*, abbreviated as BWL (Schneider, 1987, p. 136).[2]

The new discipline had to face the problem of not being accepted as a science, since science was traditionally treated at German universities as corresponding to theory ("pure science"), while applied approaches ("techniques") were regarded as unscientific. As attempts were made to gain acceptance in the scientific community, theoretical approaches increased (e.g. Weyermann & Schönitz, 1912). However, this was a question of some controversy since German industry naturally still needed well-educated managers and advice on practical matters. Certain events such as the inflation of the early 1920s even increased the need for practical advice, especially in the field of accounting. Consequently applied research continued to dominate, while the courses at the German business schools also kept their largely practical orientation. Although this controversy regarding the general orientation of the newly established discipline continued during the 1920s (cf. e.g. Rieger, 1928), the concept of BWL as a *Kunstlehre* (i.e. a technique) presented in Schmalenbach (1911) became widely accepted. In particular Schmalenbach's practical approach and his work on accounting problems during the inflation period (Schmalenbach, 1922) helped to win general public recognition for the discipline as a whole.[3] Schmalenbach was also the first representative of the discipline to be publicly recognized, when in 1919 he became a member of the *Reichswirtschaftsrat*, a committee which advised the German government on economic issues. At that time his work was also making a big impact on the development of business administration in other countries, especially in Scandinavia and Japan; several of his students became professors at German and foreign business schools. In Germany, Schmalenbach still has to be regarded as the founder of that approach to BWL which concentrates mainly on problems of accounting and finance. Even today, the Schmalenbach Society and its journal, *Zeitschrift für betriebswirtschaftliche Forschung*, keep this tradition successfully alive.

---

[2] Two academic journals played a major role in establishing the new discipline: *Zeitschrift für Handelswissenschaftliche Forschung* (today: ZfbF, founded in 1906 (editor, Schmalenbach), and *Zeitschrift für Handelswissenschaft und Handelspraxis* (now DBW), founded in 1908 (editor, Nicklisch).

[3] Besides Schmalenbach, Mahlberg (1922) and Schmidt (1921) developed methods for solving problems resulting from inflation.

Although work psychology in Germany has a long tradition going back to Wilhelm Wundt's laboratory for experimental psychology which was founded at Leipzig University in 1879, the psychological aspects of management were not taught at business schools until the 1920s.[4] Scientists at Wundt's laboratory, however, were deeply involved in research on behavioural aspects of work organization, long before similar research was started in the United States as a result of the Human Relations movement. In the 1920s, they even developed a method of personnel selection, which can be regarded as the model for the assessment centre method.

Whereas in most countries changes in the field of production served as the starting-point for modern management (Wren, 1987; Staehle, 1989), in Germany such changes were defined as technical problems to be handled by technical disciplines such as engineering (Staehle, 1991). As a result the technical universities were the first to include work organization, work psychology and personnel management in both their course curriculum and their research agenda.[5] From the start the technical universities proved in general to be strong competitors in management education. They were the first to offer courses in scientific management. In the 1920s they also started a new degree programme in industrial engineering, which combined engineering and business administration. This competition between business schools and technical universities reflects the dualistic German management system (Staehle, 1991, pp. 19–20), i.e. the division of labour between technical managers (*technischer Direktor*) and commercial managers (*kaufmännischer Direktor*). Especially in companies with a strong technological orientation, a degree in engineering still offers an excellent chance of achieving a top management position.[6]

A discourse on the value orientation of the social sciences which took place between 1909 and 1913 (*Werturteilsstreit*) made an important impact on German business administration. While most social scientists (e.g. Max Weber) argued against any value orientation at all, research in business administration took a turn towards ethical-normative approaches. By adopting explicit norms and values, the leading representatives of the discipline sought to combat the criticism that business administration was solely profit-oriented.[7] Nicklisch (1932) in particular developed a purely normative approach to BWL, aimed not at describing and explaining reality but at changing it according to the norms that he himself was proposing. Instead

---

[4] Much of the research of H. Munsterberg is based on research of Wundt's laboratory. Munsterberg himself was a student of Wundt before he left for Harvard University in 1892.
[5] Chairs in *Betriebswissenschaft* were established in Berlin in 1904, in Aachen in 1906, and in Hannover in 1907.
[6] Other degrees which are regarded as suitable qualifications for a top management position are economics and law.
[7] A significant event in this context was the above-mentioned change in the name of the discipline from *Privatwirtschaftslehre*, which in its wording emphasized free enterprise, to the more neutral sounding *Betriebswirtschaftslehre*.

of profit, he focused on the organization's members, and not then as individuals but as members of a community (*Betriebsgemeinschaft*). Nevertheless, the main emphasis of the research and theoretical work in BWL was still on accounting, which must be regarded as the basis of German business administration for the whole period up to the 1950s.

In the 1930s Nicklisch's normative approach was used by the Nazis for restructuring the economy. Many Jewish and left-wing scientists (e.g. about 15 per cent of all the professors in Berlin) were dismissed during this decade, but even so the Nazi period cannot be regarded as any real turning-point in German management thinking. Nonetheless, in certain disciplines that are relevant to management, the final result of the Nazi regime was to put an end to a long tradition. This is especially true of sociology and the behavioural sciences, where most leading scientists either managed to leave the country (e.g. Kurt Lewin, Erich Fromm, and members of the Frankfurt School) or were killed.[8] Interestingly enough, some of these emigrants later became the founders of the behavioural science approach to management in the United States. This applies especially to Kurt Lewin, the father of leadership research and modern social psychology. It thus took more than thirty years to bring knowledge and research in the behavioural sciences back into German management thinking, and much of what was brought back from the United States is in fact based on the research of these German emigrants (especially Lewin).[9]

6.2.2 The Post-war Years (1945–49): Continuity and Restoration

German universities re-opened in the winter of 1945/46. Whereas most of the professors in the Soviet occupation zone who had been party members were dismissed (in Leipzig, for example, 170 of 222; Heitzer, 1984, p. 41), universities in the West were slow in replacing active Nazis. Often, when someone was dismissed in the West, no replacement was apppointed, although plenty of professors from the areas that had been given to Poland by the allies were looking for new jobs. There was considerable sympathy among both professors and students for those who were dismissed. Nor were any structural changes made in the university system (Kleßmann, 1984, pp. 96–98). The only exceptions were the integration of the *Handelshochschule* in Berlin into the Humboldt University in 1946,[10] and attempts in the Soviet zone to support members of working-class families to get a place on a university programme. In 1949 this led to the establishment of the so-called *Arbeiter- und Bauernfakultäten*, which later played an important role in changing the entire university system in the GDR.

---

[8] Most of those who left, emigrated to the United States.
[9] Similar examples can be mentioned from other fields of social science such as economics, where emigrants like Wassily Leontief and Jacob Marschak played a similar part.
[10] The *Handelshochschule* in Leipzig, however, remained independent.

In business administration—as in most other disciplines—neither curriculum nor teaching methods changed very much in the immediate post-war period. Old pre-war textbooks were often still in use, or new editions were printed, even in the Soviet zone (e.g. Mellerowicz, 1947; Schmalenbach, 1947). Since economic laws remained largely unchanged, old techniques in accounting, for instance, could still be used. In the West the traditional business schools (e.g. Cologne and Frankfurt) soon regained their old reputation in their universities. Some other well-known business schools were later expanded to become full universities (e.g. Mannheim and Nürnberg). During the first decade after the war only a very few new schools were established as part of universities. Thus, like 1933, 1945 cannot be regarded as a turning-point as regards the content of German management thought or the organization of management education (Hundt, 1977).

6.3 The 1950s, a Period of Dominating Theories: Gutenberg in the West and Political Economy in the East

6.3.1 West Germany

In 1951, with the publication of the first volume of Gutenberg's *Grundlagen in die Betriebswirtschaftslehre*, West German BWL acquired a new approach which very soon became dominant (Gutenberg, 1951). However, because of its links with earlier ideas propagated by Rieger and Schmalenbach (Wöhe, 1975, pp. 718–719), it can be regarded as the fulfilment of previous attempts to establish BWL as an accepted scientific discipline. While political economy was an attempt to make BWL political, Gutenberg's approach was quite the opposite. It did not aim primarily to give practical advice to managers, nor did it explicitly include evaluations. Rather, on a microeconomic basis it aimed at a theory of the firm with the major focus on production. According to Gutenberg's so-called factor approach, production was regarded as a combination of labour, machines and the various materials needed for the product itself (raw materials) or, for technical reasons, for the production process. The aim of BWL as he saw it is to look for the most cost-efficient combination. As regards the labour factor, Gutenberg distinguished between ordinary labour and what he called *dispositiver Faktor*, or management in modern terms. By paying particular attention to the special tasks and problems of this *dispositiver Faktor*, Gutenberg was one of the first in his field—at least in Germany—to deal explictly with problems of modern management.

Gutenberg's approach represented a clear shift in the problem orientation of BWL, which until the 1950s had concentrated on problems of accounting. Although it soon gained a dominant position in West Germany, which it kept for almost twenty years, the approach was also criticized, as for instance in the dispute between Gutenberg and Mellerowicz, who moved to the Western part of Berlin in 1950. Mellerowicz considered the GDR's political economy too political to be of practical use to managers and Gutenberg's approach as too theoretical—using almost the same methods as microeconomics, it was heavily based on mathematics (Mellerowicz, 1952). He accused Gutenberg of having abandoned the BWL tradition and of trying to force a merger with economics, such as was in fact being proposed by prominent economists at the time (e.g. Eucken, 1947; Schneider, 1947). Other critics argued that Gutenberg's theory treated human beings as just one production factor amongst others, thus refusing them a more prominent role. This last aspect is still being discussed in West German BWL and is criticized particularly by trade unionists and by scientists with close union links (e.g. Projektgruppe, 1974; Koubek, Küller & Scheibe-Lange, 1980). Nevertheless Gutenberg's work exerted a great influence on the ideas and research of a whole generation of scientists.

6.3.2 East Germany

With the establishment of two states in Germany with divergent political and economic systems, German business administration and management education also split into two directions. While West Germany returned to a certain extent both politically and economically to the traditions of the Weimar Republic, the German Democratic Republic (GDR) tried to establish a new kind of society. Business administration was thus confronted with new requirements: East German politicians expected all scientists to support the establishment of socialism. This was seen as the major goal of any science. Since in their eyes and in the eyes of socialist economists BWL had strong links with capitalism and was more ideological than scientific (e.g. Berger, 1949; Behrens, 1950, 1952; Winternitz, 1950), a reorientation was proposed. However, the degree of reorientation was a debatable point. Behrens, a professor from Leipzig who criticized BWL as an unscientific *Vulgärökonomie* (Behrens, 1950, p. 61), nevertheless described the discipline as an accumulation of various techniques which could be used for all kinds of purposes, including of course the establishment of socialism (Behrens, 1949). Although there was some support for this view (e.g. Lemmnitz, 1949), other economists with tougher political views argued that in socialism BWL needed a political orientation (Winternitz, 1950).

Berger (1949) suggested integrating BWL with political economy, in which case it should concentrate on aspects like production. In contrast to this, non-socialist and more traditional professors like Mellerowicz, who taught at East Berlin's Humboldt University until 1950, opposed any merger with political economy. Like economics, this discipline had a scientific approach which could not be combined with that of BWL. Since Mellerowicz (1949 and 1950) defined his discipline as technical and independent of the existing political and economic system, he refused to include considerations referring to society as a whole. What was important in his eyes was not whether BWL had a capitalist or socialist orientation, but whether it led to economic management or to mismanagement (1950, p. 499). Traditionalists like Mellerowicz soon abandoned the GDR, thus leaving the discipline entirely in the hands of those trying to transform it.[11]

But the transformation of BWL was not enough to satisfy the rulers of East Germany. In 1951, when the GDR inaugurated a second major reform in its university system, BWL was abolished altogether. It was regarded as a purely capitalist discipline and thus completely useless in establishing a socialist society (see e.g. Berger, 1949). From then on and for almost twenty years the GDR had no such discipline as business administration. Issues that BWL had addressed were now included in the newly established discipline *Betriebsökonomik*, which concentrated on organization, administration and planning but was split between various institutes. Not until 1956 were any textbooks available (Arnold, Borchert & Schmidt, 1956). Furthermore, universities no longer offered a coherent programme for management education. On the contrary, in 1955 students could specialize in almost twenty different ways, most commonly associated with particular industries (Nultsch, 1955). Political economy and the political education of the students were now seen as the central issues (Kampfert & Krause, 1960; Auras & Bras, 1962). Consequently, the management selection process also changed: managers were regarded primarily as political functionaries, not as professionals. Thus the main criteria for selecting an individual for a top management position was his or her political opinions and activities. Instead of an MBA or some other academic degree, membership of the socialist party and a training in politics at one of the party's schools, became the prerequisite for a professional career (Pieper, 1990*b*; 1992). Business schools only served to educate people for lower management levels. This situation did not change until 1989, when the socialist party lost control.

In both research and teaching the field in which changes were most urgent was accounting. In 1950, with the establishment of a planned economy and the abolition of profit-making as the prime aim of economic activity, the GDR changed its accounting system and adopted what was called *Wirtschaftliche Rechnungsführung*. The old textbooks and earlier research thus became obsolete, and scientific efforts were therefore concentrated to this area (one of the first books to appear was Behrens, 1952; Oelβner, 1952). As in politics, researchers in the GDR often took Russian studies and experiences as their point of departure. The journal *Sowjetwissenschaft* became their major source of information. Thus, while in West Germany BWL showed a certain continuity, a whole new approach was being tried in the GDR. Since, for political reasons, political education was now of the

---

[11] After leaving the GDR Mellerowicz taught at the Technical University in the Western part of Berlin.

foremost importance, business administration was transformed into political economy. One consequence of this was that applied research became a comparatively neglected field.

6.4 The 1960s: Advance of Management Science and Systems Theory

6.4.1 West Germany

With the strong economic growth in both parts of Germany at the end of the 1950s and during the 1960s, there was growing pressure on management theories and education to pay more attention to practice. New problems arose, especially in the West. They were dealt with by new subdisciplines within BWL, which became more and more fragmented. Whereas Gutenberg (1962) defended his approach on grounds that scientifically based management theories were almost an impossibility, since important aspects of management had to be regarded as closer to art than science and thus not altogether teachable or learnable, other prominent researchers such as Mellerowicz (1963) saw management as an important part of BWL (together with theoretical approaches and techniques such as accounting). But it was not until the 1970s that American management theories were introduced into BWL. In the 1960s practical efforts concentrated on operations research and other aspects of management science, which had been developed by the military in Second World War and which were later transferred to companies. At the end of the 1960s research in this area (especially the use of American research) and the adoption of American management ideas led to completely new approaches in West German BWL (Staehle, 1989; 1991).

6.4.2 East Germany

With the building of the Berlin wall in 1961 the GDR government made it clear that there was no alternative to socialism, and the planned economy had in fact already been established. Now politicians and managers (in GDR terminology, *Leiter*) were looking for ways to run this type of economy more effectively. They therefore needed some practical advice which political economy was unable to provide. Furthermore, after the death of Stalin, the Soviet Union tried to revive the management debate which that had been very lively in the 1920s (Gvisiani, 1974). After some delay East German scientists joined in this discourse. Between 1957 and 1959 there was a very vigorous debate in the monthly journal of the socialist party, *Einheit*, about establishing a new discipline to deal with the socialist type of management known as *Leitungswissenschaft* (Pieper, 1989*a-b*). The main purpose of most of the participants in these discussions was to make East German management thinking more practical and to provide managers with applied knowledge which could be used in management education and development and which could help in solving practical problems (see e.g. Berger, 1957; Friedrich, 1957; Thamm, 1958). Although the first books dealing specifically with management problems were published a few years later, the GDR did not establish a *Leitungswissenschaft* for the time being. Like the Soviet Union, they did so only in the early 1970s.

Nevertheless, the debate on practical problems continued. East German scientists soon caught up with the discourse on cybernetics, operations research and general systems theory. They were interested in using such knowledge to solve both management and general economic problems. This last led to serious conflicts when some scientists were inspired by the ideas of general systems theory to propose profound changes in the country's economic system (Behrens, 1956, 1957; Benary, 1957). They suggested that East German politicians should have adopted the economic laws of socialism, instead of trying to plan all economic activities. Companies could then have been given more scope for acting independently. In the course of Ulbricht's fight against these so-called revisionists, whose proposal to establish a socialist market economy was seen as verging on the anarchistic and leaning too far towards capitalism (Redaktionskollegium, 1957; Kampfert, 1957; Lemmnitz, 1958), the discussion was broken off. Politicians and scientists who had supported the idea of systems theory and economic reforms were dismissed (Staritz, 1985). Research in these fields—although it still existed (e.g. at the Academy of Sciences)—was no longer published. For some years at least systems theory ceased to play an important part in the public debate, although criticism of the current state of management thinking in East Germany continued to be heard. Even Ulbricht (1959) claimed that research was failing to address practical problems as it should, and was instead concerned almost exclusively with ideology and general theoretical questions.[12] A profound change in research policy was thought to be necessary (Redaktionskollegium, 1962). Political economy was now seen as less important (Auras & Braß, 1962; Koziolek, 1960; Mußler, 1962; Redaktionskollegium, 1962).

When the so-called Liberman discussion began in the Soviet Union in 1960–61, East German scientists were able to return to operations research and the ideas of systems theory. In 1963 this led to (and was reinforced by) changes in the economic system (known as the New Economic System or NÖS). Plans were now based not only on purely quantitative goals but on qualitative goals as well. The economic system began to employ indirect control mechanisms such as prices and profit, thereby greatly increasing the scope of choice for East German companies. Thus started a period during

---

[12] Walter Ulbricht (1893–1973) was General Secretary of the Socialist Unity Party from 1950 to 1971 and head of state from 1960 to 1971.

which cybernetics dominated East German management thinking as well as the political and philosophical discourse, a process which was also encouraged by the establishment of the Marxist-Leninist Organization Theory (*Marxistisch-Leninistische Organisationslehre*) which was based on cybernetics, as a new discipline to be used in management education. The use of cybernetics, mathematics and computing was now seen as the main way of increasing productivity and improving the functioning of the economic system, and of promoting the practical orientation of management theory (cf. e.g. Wintgen, 1962). And of course it made planning and the handling of billions of balance sheets during the planning process much easier. Largely for ideological reasons, however, in the mid-1960s the new economic system was regarded as a failure. In the planning period 1969–1970 some reforms were reversed. In 1970 the monetarist coordination instruments which had been at the heart the NÖS, diminished in importance. Cybernetics also lost its prominent role. Instead of being seen as the predominant approach, it was now regarded as one technique amongst others. Some politicians even claimed that a technocratic tendency had almost led to the replacement of Marxist theory by systems theory (e.g. Hager, 1971). Economists also criticized the level of abstraction and the formalism of cybernetics (Hörnig, 1972). With the Eighth Party Congress of the SED in 1971, which marked the shift in power from Ulbricht to Honecker, the predominance of cybernetics in East German management thinking came to an end.[13] Marxist-Leninist Organization Theory was abandoned.

The 1960s saw some further attempts to give East German management theory a more practical orientation. Since companies had become more independent during the period of NÖS, they needed more practical advice. For this reason research in accounting was intensified (cf. e.g. Koziolek, 1960; Kupfernagel & Polaschewski, 1966), while a need for a special discipline dealing with management problems was once again articulated. Socialist management (*Sozialistische Wirtschaftsführung*) was thus introduced as a special discipline for management education and development (Graichen & John, 1964). A special central institute for management development (*Institut für Sozialistische Wirtschaftsführung*, Berlin) was also created and placed under the direct control of the socialist party. Universities and newly founded regional management development institutes started to offer management development programmes, albeit these were still dominated by political topics. Sociological research was intensified; sociology was established as an independent discipline in 1963.[14] In addition, the first attempts

---

[13] Erich Honecker was General Secretary of the Socialist Unity Party from 1971 to 1989 and head of state from 1976 to 1989.
[14] The first publications were Hiebisch & Vorwerg (1965, 1968).

were made to use the results of such research to solve management problems and combine *Sozialistische Wirtschaftsführung* with sociology and the newly created discipline of social psychology.[15]

6.5 The 1970s: New Approaches in the West and the East

6.5.1 West Germany

With the introduction of research results from other disciplines such as general systems theory, operations research and the behavioural sciences, economic activities came to be increasingly regarded in terms of decision-making processes. Heinen (Munich) elaborated this aspect, thus formulating a new approach which, unlike Gutenberg's line, is basically practical, defining BWL as an attempt to improve managerial decision-making (Heinen, 1969, p. 209). Like Gutenberg, Heinen accepted the given aims of economic activities (i.e. profit making in market economies) and developed theories to improve the process of decision-making in companies (Heinen, 1966, 1969, 1971). The decision-making approach (*entscheidungsorientierte BWL*) was also increasingly influenced by knowledge from the behavioural sciences (cf. especially Kirsch, 1977).

Another consequence of the predominance of systems theory in the 1960s was Ulrich's formulation of a systems approach to BWL (Ulrich, 1969). Ulrich used general systems theory to describe economic and managerial activities. Unlike Gutenberg's approach this not only provides explanations or tries to improve managerial decision-making; it also attempts to explore further options for managerial activities. Like the decision-making approach it is interdisciplinary, since it also uses other scientific disciplines and tries to integrate them. This, like Heinen's approach, is still a popular ingredient in West German BWL, especially since it has recently been further elaborated by Swiss researchers, who have included new developments in systems theory, e.g. the idea of autopoiesis.[16]

During the 1970s a third new approach evolved in the West, as American management thought and knowledge from the behavioural sciences were infused into BWL. This infusion was stimulated both by the practical needs of German firms and by the practice of American consulting firms and multinational companies with subsidiaries in West Germany which were already applying American management techniques. Research based on this approach

---

[15] A research team at Schiller University in Jena, headed by Hiebisch and Vorwerg, played a major part in this process. For example, these researchers developed the first management seminars based on behavioural science knowledge. Some of these concepts were published by Vorwerg (1971).

[16] Recent publications which are based on Ulrich's approach use biocybernetic approaches of systems theory (e.g. Ulrich, 1984; Malik, 1986) instead of being based on the older mechanistic school.

concentrated on human behaviour in organizations, thus using the knowledge of the behavioural sciences to explain phenomena such as leadership, group behaviour and motivation (Schanz, 1977, 1978; Staehle, 1991). Some authors such as Kirsch attempted to combine this approach with Heinen's work on managerial decision-making (Kirsch, 1971). Further, American management strategies and techniques such as organization development, which are also based on behavioural science knowledge, were imported into West Germany, generally in the translated works of American authors (Pieper, 1991). Although this approach is popular with managers and companies, several German business schools still refuse to include behavioural science in their curriculum. In most other cases, behavioural science is taught only by professors holding chairs in personnel management, organizational theory or marketing.

Thus during the 1970s the predominance of Gutenberg's ideas came to an end in West Germany, and various new approaches with more practical orientations established themselves on an almost equal footing. This led to a pluralization of the entire discipline, which can be said to be typical of the discourse today. This pluralization had a further aspect: BWL became segmentated into various subdisciplines, a process which can be regarded as reflecting growing specialization. Since the 1960s new fields such as personnel management (*Personalwirtschaftslehre*) and marketing had emerged; for each of them, new chairs were established.

The pluralization of BWL was supported by the enormous growth of German business schools. Several new universities were founded in the 1970s, while the old schools were enlarged.[17] Between 1970 and 1980 the number of students of business administration or the newly established combination of business administration and economics (*Wirtschaftswissenschaften*) doubled, reaching over 47,000, while the number of professors almost quadrupled to approximately 500 (Schneider, 1987, p. 151).

6.5.2 East Germany

The GDR experienced a shift in paradigms at the same time as West Germany but unlike the West it did not allow any pluralization. At the beginning of the 1970s the need for a more practical orientation was articulated by politicians, managers and researchers (e.g. Kupfernagel *et al.*, 1970). This led to the re-establishment of business administration as socialist BWL in 1973, and the establishment of *Leitungswissenschaft* as an independent discipline in 1972. Marxism was naturally still regarded as the base, but the formal structure of *Wirtschaftswissenschaften* again became traditional and similar to that prevailing in West Germany. The discipline as a whole then

---

[17] Today there are about seventy universities which offer four-year courses of study in business administration or *Wirtschaftswissenschaften*.

consisted of economics and business administration. In addition there were several methodological disciplines, with *Leitungswissenschaft* as a special discipline dealing with the management of single companies and the socialist economy as a whole (Autorenkollektiv, 1987); BWL can be seen as an attempt to combine the various disciplines dealing with the problems of specific sectors of the economy (*Zweigökonomien*) and to generalize such knowledge (Autorenkollektiv, 1973/1980). It can thus be regarded as a return to traditional German BWL, which like Heinen's and Gutenberg's ideas in West Germany accepts the given (here socialist) goals of economic activity. East German management research came to resemble research in West Germany (e.g. Friedrich & Gerisch, 1966), although no textbooks or complete approaches were published until the mid-1970s (Tichomirov, 1975; Ladensack & Weidemeier, 1977). One significant difference between the two Germanies, however, was that in the East behavioural aspects were neglected. Another was that although East German researchers were using a vocabulary similar to that of the systems approach in the West, and worked on similar attempts to combine the knowledge of various disciplines into the *Leitungswissenschaft*, they did not succeed in establishing a comparable interdisciplinary systems approach to management.

Leitungswissenschaft derived instead from a different tradition going back to Lenin's publications on socialist management principles (Autorenkollektiv, 1970). In the 1920s Lenin had developed several principles for a socialist type of management that were still regarded as valid in the 1980s (Autorenkollektiv, 1986, pp. 21–59), even during the period of perestroika. Moreover, Lenin had tried to use capitalist approaches such as Taylor's for socialist ends (Gvisiani, 1974). Although such considerations disappeared during Stalin's lifetime, the 1970s saw their renaissance. As early as the late 1960s various books on socialist management were published in the Soviet Union and later translated into German (e.g. Afanasjew, 1969; Tichomirov, 1975). The same is true of critical reviews of capitalist management (Gvisiani, 1974; Autorenkollektiv, 1973/80; Hartmann, 1980). Whereas it was difficult to distinguish different schools of *Leitungswissenschaft* in the GDR, such schools certainly existed in the Soviet Union (Vidmer, 1981). Interestingly enough, they seem to have reflected similar ideas in the West as well as the whole modern history of business administration and management in Eastern Europe: political economy, the empirical and behavioural science approach, cybernetics, and planning (Vidmer, 1981, pp. 6–7).

While management thinking in both parts of Germany in the late 1960s and early 1970s showed strong similarities, and even the quality of research on managerial decision-making and leadership and the systems approach were very similar, the GDR returned to traditional and more orthodox approaches when Honecker came to power. In particular, behavioural science approaches were almost totally neglected when it came to establishing *Leitungswissenschaft*, which had a pure political orientation.

Management education did not change very much during the 1970s. The business schools were still offering programmes divided according to industries, with each school having a different industry orientation. The right political orientation remained the prerequisite for a top management position. However, there was one remarkable trend at this time: the vast majority of students of socialist BWL and of industrial engineering were now women. Up to the 1980s this situation made no impact on the gender distribution of management positions: top managers in East Germany were almost all men.

6.6 After the 1970s

6.6.1 The 1980s: Various Schools of Thought and the Growing Importance of the Human Factor

At least in the case of West Germany the parallel nature of various schools of thought can be said to reflect the situation in the 1980s. Similarly characteristic is a segmentation into highly specialized subdisciplines and a growing orientation towards American management thought (Staehle, 1989). It is even being discussed whether BWL as a whole should be redefined as management theory and *Führungslehre*, the better to fulfil the practical needs of managers (Schneider, 1987; Wunderer, 1988). This increasing emphasis on behavioural approaches to BWL is a result of the growing importance of the human factor in companies: human resource management has come to occupy a prominent role in most Western economies (Pieper, 1990*a*).

The same applies to the GDR. With technological development and the introduction of new technologies into most companies, the constant need for rapid innovation and for the education and motivation of people to support this development is also increasing in the socialist countries (Landa, 1990; Meyer, 1990; Purg, 1990). As in Western management literature, an extensive literature on innovation management and human resource management (this last almost exclusively in connection with innovation) was published in the GDR during the 1980s (e.g. Böhring & Ladensack, 1986; Autorenkollektiv, 1987; 1988). Since technology and human performance were regarded as the sole means for increasing productivity, research concentrated on these areas (Pieper, 1988; 1989*c*). The parallel with the Western situation is obvious, since both societies were facing similar problems in the global market. Thus, what was happening in East German management thinking at that time was a growing infusion of knowledge from the behavioural sciences (e.g. Friedrich & Voß, 1988).

6.6.2 The 1990s: Reunification of the two Germanies and of German Business Administration

With the recent political changes in Germany and the unification of the two Germanies, German business administration and management education are undergoing profound changes. With the abolition of the socialist regime, socialist approaches to management like *Leitungswissenschaft* and socialist BWL have also been abolished. The same is true of most of the institutions which were in charge of management education and development in the former GDR (e.g. *Hochschule für Ökonomie* and *Zentralinstitut für sozialistische Wirtschaftsführung* in Berlin). Instead, West German BWL and western management literature and education have been introduced to fill the knowledge gap in management and business administration that had accumulated among East German managers and researchers over the past forty years.

This knowledge gap is one of the main problems in the restructuring of the economies of the former GDR and of the other East European countries. Neither managers nor professors at business schools have any profound knowledge about such things as marketing, finance, human resource management, organizational behaviour, strategic management or management in general, since they received their training in the traditional socialist disciplines and at institutions with a strong political orientation. Further, they had practically no access to Western management literature, nor were they allowed to attend conferences in the West or to communicate regularly with western colleagues. Whereas business school professors often try to acquire such management knowledge by reading books, attending conferences or affiliating themselves with West German universities, former GDR managers who are still in their old positions have no time to educate themselves. They usually attend short courses offered by a variety of institutions and companies, usually only providing an overview of some particular field. The quality and effectiveness of these courses are also very mixed. Since managers in East Germany also served as politicians within their companies, i.e. as representatives of the socialist regime, and since their selection process was based primarily on political criteria (Pieper, 1992), there are political problems as well. Should the old socialist elite remain in their leading positions? Although in 1990 business journals and the *Treuhand* claimed that there was no alternative to keeping the old GDR management in their former positions, and that most managers were capable of managing their companies even in the new market economy, practical experience has proved quite different.[18] Nowadays *Treuhand* representatives tell the press

---

[18] The *Treuhand* is a state-owned holding company which owns all former GDR companies. Its prime task is the privatization of these companies. The political aim is to abolish the *Treuhand* in the late 1990s, once it has privatized all GDR industry.

that 90 per cent of all the old GDR managers have had to be dismissed, either for political reasons or because they are incapable (*Frankfurter Allgemeine Zeitung*, October 31, 1991).[19] Nevertheless, up to now, no advanced retraining programmes at an academic or business school level have been developed for this group. One reason might be that German business schools are not engaged in management development; on the other hand, this only mirrors the current situation in all the former socialist countries.

The restructuring of East German universities is proving equally difficult. There are political reasons for this, but these are compounded by the fact that most of the professors lack the necessary knowledge. Professors in the natural sciences, on the other hand, have very little difficulty in continuing to teach since their level of knowledge is not very different from that of their colleagues in the West. Nonetheless they, and their institutes, have been evaluated by commissions of scientists from West Germany, to see whether their research and their publications match the quality of similar research in the West. If they do, the relevant institutes—particularly those belonging to the Academy of Science—have been retained or integrated with West German scientific institutions such as the *Max-Planck-Institut*; by the same token university professors could keep their jobs. The state also checked the extent to which professors had been involved in the socialist regime. If they had expelled students for political reasons, for example, or had worked for the secret service, their job security became a matter of critical review.

In other disciplines like political science, sociology, history, economics, and business administration, however, the departments at most East German universities have been dissolved altogether. Professors from West Germany were given the task of re-establishing them with new curricula and, most importantly, new staff. While former East German professors have almost no chance of getting their old jobs back or even of finding a chair at another university, several West German professors have already begun to work at East German universities. But there are still too few of them to provide full programmes, in business administration for example. Guest professors, again from the West, have thus been invited to teach specific courses. Furthermore, the labour market at least for professors in business administration is very tight. In the late 1990s most professors who attained their chairs in the early 1970s will retire. At present there do not seem to be enough young scientists in some of the subdisciplines of business administration with the formal qualifications to work as university professors, particularly in view of all the "new" chairs requiring occupants in the East.[20] It

---

[19] This is especially true for managers who worked in the human resource management department since they had the closest links to both the party and the secret service.

[20] In Germany, the formal qualifications to becoming a university professor are, first, a Ph.D. with a top grade. Secondly, there is the *Habilitation*, which can be described as an additional dissertation. The candidate has to write a book to be evaluated by two professors, and to

will certainly take several years before management education in the former GDR will reach the same standard as that prevailing in the West.

6.7 Concluding Remarks

The question of the further development of German business administration and management education remains a relatively open one. There is controversy about whether business administration should stick to its distinctive character, or whether it should be reformulated along general management theoretical lines, thus orienting itself more towards American management thinking. As BWL student numbers rise and German companies need more managers, German management education is also facing a period of major change: the criteria for successful management are changing due to internationalization and a growing need for integrated knowledge and the management of change, for example. At the same time financial resources are very limited and competition from American and European business schools with MBA-programmes is on the increase (Pieper, 1989d). The outcome as regards the shape of the coming changes, their structure and their content, remains largely open.

References

Adler, N. J., 1986, *International Dimensions of Organizational Behavior*, Boston, MA: PWS-Kent.
Afanasjew, V. G., 1969, *Wissenschaftliche Leitung der Gesellschaft*, Berlin (DDR): Staatsverlag der DDR.
Albach, H., 1990, "Business Administration: History in German-Speaking Countries", In: Grochla, E. *et al.*, *Handbook of German Business Management*, Stuttgart: Poeschel, pp. 246–270.
Arnold, H., Borchert, H. & Schmidt, J., 1956, *Ökonomik der sozialistischen Industrie in der Deutschen Demokratischen Republik*, Berlin (DDR): Die Wirtschaft.
Auras, H. H. & Braβ, H., 1962, "Zum Verhältnis zwischen der politischen Ökonomie des Sozialismus und den Fachökonomiken", *Wirtschaftswissenschaft*, 10, No. 10, pp. 1533–1537.
Autorenkollektiv, 1970, *Die Grundlagen der sozialistischen Wirtschaftsführung in den Werken Lenins und ihre aktuelle Bedeutung*, Berlin (DDR): Dietz.
— 1973/80, *Sozialistische Betriebswirtschaftslehre*, Berlin (DDR): Die Wirtschaft.
— 1986, *Pädagogisch-psychologische Grundlagen der sozialistischen Leitungstätigkeit* (9th ed.), Berlin (DDR): Die Wirtschaft.
— 1987, *Intensivierung-Leitung-Neuerungsprozesse*, Berlin (DDR): Die Wirtschaft.

---

give a lecture. The candidate's work also has to be accepted by the whole faculty, not just by two professors. The GDR had the same system (with dissertation I and dissertation II), although people who were highly valued politically could receive the honorary title of professor. The system is the same in Austria and Switzerland.

— 1988, *Das geistige Potential in den Betrieben*, Berlin (DDR): Dietz Verlag.
Behrens, F., 1949, "Einige Grundprobleme des betrieblichen Rechnungswesens in der Wirtschaftsplanung", *Deutsche Finanzwirtschaft*, 3, No. 6, pp. 218–224.
— 1950, "Ist die Betriebswirtschaftslehre eine Wissenschaft?", *Deutsche Finanzwirtschaft*, 4, No. 2, pp. 57–60.
— 1952, *Zur Methode der politischen Ökonomie*, Berlin (DDR): Akad.-Verlag.
— 1956, "Fragen der Ökonomie und Technik", *Wirtschaftswissenschaft*, 4, Sonderheft 1, pp. 1–5.
— 1957, "Zum Problem der Ausnutzung ökonomischer Gesetze in der Übergangsperiode", *Wirtschaftswissenschaft*, 5, Sonderheft 3, pp. 105–140.
Benary, A., 1957, "Zu Grundproblemen der politischen Ökonomie des Sozialismus in der Übergangsperiode", *Wirtschaftswissenschaft*, 5, Sonderheft 3, pp. 62–94.
Berger, W., 1949, "Karl Marx als Kritiker der modernen Betriebswirtschaftslehre", *Deutsche Finanzwirtschaft*, 3, No. 10, pp. 249–253.
— 1957, "Wie soll die Lehre von der Leitung sozialistischer Betriebe aussehen?", *Einheit*, 12, No. 8, pp. 1014–1021.
Böhring, G. & Ladensack, K., 1986, *Wie Leiter den wissenschaftlich-technischen Fortschritt bewältigen*, Berlin (DDR): Dietz Verlag.
Conrad, P. & Pieper, R., 1990, "Human Resource Management in the Federal Republic of Germany", In: Pieper, R. (ed.), *Human Resource Management—An International Comparison*, Berlin & New York: de Gruyter, pp. 109–139.
Eucken, W., 1947, *Grundlagen der Nationalökonomie*, Godesberg: Küpper.
Frankfurter Allgemeine Zeitung, October 31, 1991.
Friedrich, G., 1957, "Probleme der staatlichen Leitung unserer Industrie", *Einheit*, 12, No. 9, pp. 1134–1140.
Friedrich, G., & Gerisch, R., 1966, "Die Information als Führungsaufgabe in der sozialistischen Industrie", *Wirtschaftswissenschaft*, 14, No. 1, pp. 44–63.
Friedrich, G., Richter, H., Stein, H. & Wittich, G., (eds.), 1987, *Leitung der sozialistischen Wirtschaft. Lehrbuch*, Berlin (DDR): Die Wirtschaft.
Friedrich, W. & Voβ, P. (eds.), 1988, *Sozialpsychologie für die Praxis*, Berlin (DDR): Deutscher Verlag der Wissenschaften.
Graichen, D. & John, F., 1964, "Das neue ökonomische System und die Ausbildung ökonomischer Hoch- und Fachschulkader in der DDR", *Wirtschaftswissenschaft*, 12, No. 11, pp. 1761–1775.
Gutenberg, E., 1951, *Grundlagen der Betriebswirtschaftslehre, Band 1: Die Produktion*, Berlin, Göttingen & Heidelberg: Springer.
— 1962, *Unternehmensführung: Organisation und Entscheidungen*, Wiesbaden: Gabler.
Gvisiani, D. M., 1974, *Management. Analyse bürgerlicher Theorien von Organisation und Leitung*, Berlin (DDR:) Die Wirtschaft.
Hager, K., 1971, "Die entwickelte sozialistische Gesellschaft", *Einheit*, 26, No. 11, pp. 1203–1242.
Hartmann, W. D., 1980, *Management. Kapitalistische Führungstechniken im kritischen Vergleich*, Berlin (DDR): Die Wirtschaft.
— 1988, *Handbuch der Managementtechniken*, Berlin (DDR): Akademie-Verlag.
Heinen, E., 1966, *Das Zielsystem der Unternehmung*, Wiesbaden: Gabler.
— 1969, "Zum Wissenschaftsprogramm der entscheidungsorientierten Betriebswirtschaftslehre", *Zeitschrift für Betriebswirtschaft*, 39, No. 4, pp. 207–220.
— 1971, "Der entscheidungsorientierte Ansatz der Betriebswirtschaftslehre", In: Kortzfleisch, G. von (ed.), *Wissenschaftsprogramm und Ausbildungsziel der Betriebswirtschaftslehre*, Berlin: Duncker und Humbolt, pp. 21–37.
Heitzer, H., 1984, *DDR-Geschichtlicher Überblick*, Berlin (DDR): Dietz Verlag.

Hiebisch, H. & Vorwerg, M. (eds.), 1965, *Sozialpsychologie im Sozialismus*, Berlin (DDR): Deutscher Verlag der Wissenschaften.
— (eds.), 1968, *Einführung in die marxistisch-leninistische Sozial-psychologie*, Berlin (DDR): Deutscher Verlag der Wissenschaften.
Hellauer, J., 1910, *System der Welthandelslehre*, Berlin: Puttkammer & Mühlbrecht.
Hofstede, G., 1980, *Culture's Consequences: International Differences in Work-related Values*, Beverly Hills, CA: Sage.
— 1983, "Motivation, Leadership, and Organizations: Do American Theories Apply Abroad?", *Organizational Dynamics*, 9, No. 1, pp. 42–63.
Hörnig, H., 1972, "Die Aufgabe der Wirtschaftswissenschaften in der Gegenwart", *Einheit*, 27, No. 5.
Hundt, S., 1977, *Zur Theoriegeschichte der Betriebswirtschaftslehre*, Köln: Westdeutscher Verlag.
Kampfert, K., 1957, "Gegen das Aufkommen revisionistischer Auffassungen in den Wirtschaftswissenschaften", *Wirtschaftswissenschaft*, 5, Sonderheft 3, pp. 1–19.
Kampfert, K. & Krause, W., 1960, "Für einen schnellen Umschwung in Lehre und Forschung an den wirtschaftswissenschaftlichen Fakultäten und Hochschulen", *Wirtschaftswissenschaft*, 8, No. 4, pp. 481–501.
Kirsch, W., 1971, *Entscheidungsprozesse*, Wiesbaden: Gabler (3 vols.).
— 1977, *Die Betriebswirtschaftslehre als Führungslehre: Erkenntnisperspektiven, Aussagensysteme, wissenschaftlicher Standort*, München: Institut für Organisation, Universität München.
Kleßmann, C., 1984, *Die doppelte Staatsgründung*, Göttingen: Vandenhoeck und Ruprecht.
Koubek, N., Küller, H. D. & Scheibe-Lange, I., 1980, *Betriebswirtschaftliche Probleme der Mitbestimmung*, Köln: Westdeutscher Verlag.
Koziolek, H., 1960, "Zur Lehre der politischen Ökonomie im Sozialismus", *Wirtschaftswissenschaft*, 8, No. 6, pp. 1030–1045.
Kupfernagel, E. & Polaschewski, E., 1966, "Zur Theorie der Kostenrechnung", *Wirtschaftswissenschaft*, 14, No. 6, pp. 1409–1420.
Kupfernagel, E. et al., 1970, "Über die weitere Entwicklung der sozialistischen Betriebswirtschaft bei der Gestaltung und umfassenden Anwendung des ökonomischen System des Sozialismus in der DDR", *Wirtschaftswissenschaft*, 18, No. 10, pp. 1504–1522.
Ladensack, K. & Weidemeier, A., 1977, *Leitungsentscheidungen—soziale Prozesse im Betrieb*, Berlin (DDR): Die Wirtschaft.
Landa, O., 1990, "Human Resource Management in Czechloslovakia—Management Development as the Key Issue", In: Pieper, R. (ed.), *Human Resource Management. An International Comparison*, Berlin-New York: de Gruyter, pp. 155–176.
Lemmnitz, A., 1949, "Das Rentabilitätsprinzip in der demokratischen Wirtschaft", *Deutsche Finanzwirtschaft*, 3, No. 10, pp. 268, 275–278.
— 1958, "Einige Fragen der wissenschaftlichen und politisch-ideologischen Arbeit unserer Wirtschaftswissenschaftler", *Einheit*, 13, No. 2, pp. 257–267.
Mahlberg, W., 1922, *Bilanztechnik und Bewertung bei schwankender Währung*, Leipzig: Gloeckner (2. ed.).
Malik, F., 1986, *Strategie des Managements komplexer Systeme*, Bern & Stuttgart: Haupt (2. ed.).
Mellerowicz, K., 1947, *Allgemeine Betriebswirtschaftslehre*, Berlin: de Gruyter (5. ed.).
— 1949, "Betriebswirtschaftslehre und politische Ökonomie", *Deutsche Finanzwirtschaft*, 3, No. 15, pp. 519–527.

— 1950, "Wirtschaftsordnung und Betriebsordnung—Das Problem theoretisch betrachtet", *Zeitschrift für Betriebswirtschaft*, 20, No. 8, pp. 497–509.
— 1952, "Eine neue Richtung in der Betriebswirtschaftslehre. Eine Betrachtung zu dem Buch von E. Gutenberg", *Zeitschrift für Betriebswirtschaft*, 22, No. 3, pp. 145–161.
— 1963, *Unternehmenspolitik*, Vol. 1, Freiburg: Haute.
Meyer, H., 1990, "Human Resource Management in the German Democratic Republic: Problems of Availability and the Use of Manpower Potential in the High Qualification Spectrum", In: Pieper, R. (ed.), 1990, *Human Resource Management. An International Comparison*, Berlin & New York: de Gruyter, pp. 177–193.
Milner, B. S. & Tschishow, J. A., 1980, *Amerikanische bürgerliche Theorien der Leitung*, Berlin (DDR): Die Wirtschaft.
Mußler, W., 1962, "Die politische Ökonomie des Sozialismus muß ein wirksames Instrument für die Lösung volkswirtschaftlicher Aufgaben werden", *Einheit*, 17, No. 2.
Nicklisch, H., 1912, *Allgemeine kaufmännische Betriebslehre als Privatwirtschaftslehre des Handels (und der Industrie)*, Leipzig: Poeschel.
— 1932, *Die Betriebswirtschaft*, Stuttgart: Poeschel.
Nultsch, G., 1955, "Über einige Fragen des ökonomischen Studiums", *Wirtschaftswissenschaft*, 3, No. 5, pp. 755–761.
Oelßner, F., 1952, *Über die wirtschaftliche Rechnungsführung*, Berlin (DDR): Die Wirtschaft.
Perridon, L., 1967, "Ansätze und Methodik der Vergleichenden Betriebswirtschaftslehre", *Zeitschrift für Betriebswirtschaft*, 27, pp. 677–686.
— 1975, "Betriebswirtschaftslehre, Vergleichende", in: Grochla, E. & Wittmann, N. (eds.), *Handwörterbuch der Betriebswirtschaft*, Stuttgart: Poeschel, pp. 808–816.
Pieper, R., 1988, *The Management of Technological Change in GDR Combines*, Berlin: Freie Universität Berlin.
— 1989*a*, "Rekonstruktion der Geschichte von Betriebswirtschaftslehre und Leitungswissenschaft in der DDR", *Die Betriebswirtschaft*, 49, No. 5, pp. 577–595.
— (ed.), 1989*b*, *Westliches Management—östliche Leitung. Ein Vergleich von Managementlehre und DDR-Leitungswissenschaft*, Berlin & New York: de Gruyter.
— 1989*c*, "The GDR System for Managing Change: The Managerial Instruments", In: Gerber, M. *et al.* (eds.), *Studies in GDR Culture and Society*, 9, Lanham & New York: University Press, pp. 35–56.
— 1989*d*, *Business Schools in den USA. Mythen und Fakten*, Berlin & New York: de Gruyter.
— 1990*a*, "Introduction", In: Pieper, R. (ed.), *Human Resource Management. An International Comparison*, Berlin & New York: de Gruyter.
— 1990*b*, "Personalmanagement und personalwirtschaftliches Wissen in der DDR—Versuch einer Bestandsaufnahme", In: Pieper, R. (ed.), *Personalmanagement. Von der Plan- zur Marktwirtschaft*, Wiesbaden: Gabler, pp. 7–48.
— 1991, "OD in Germany", *Organization Development Journal*, 8, No. 4, pp. 50–58.
— 1992, "Socialist HRM. An Analysis of HRM Theory and Practice in the Former Socialist Countries in Eastern Europe", *The International Executive*, 34, No. 6, pp. 499–516.
Pieper, R. & Richter, K. (eds.), 1990, *Management. Erfahrungen, Bedingungen, Ansichten*, Berlin (DDR) & Wiesbaden: Die Wirtschaft and de Gruyter.

Projektgruppe im WSI, 1974, *Grundelemente einer Arbeitsorientierten Einzelwirtschaftslehre*, Köln: Westdeutscher Verlag.

Purg, D., 1990, "Human Resource Management in Yugoslavia: Problems and Perspectives", In: Pieper, R. (ed.), *Human Resource Management. An International Comparison*, Berlin & New York: de Gruyter, pp. 143–154.

Redaktionskollegium, 1957, "Das 30.Plenum und die Wirtschaftswissenschaften", *Wirtschaftswissenschaft*, 5, No. 2, pp. 161–165.

— 1962, "Zu den Aufgaben der Wirtschaftswissenschaften nach der 14. Tagung des Zentralkomitees der Sozialistischen Einheitspartei Deutschlands", *Wirtschaftswissenschaft*, 10, No. 2, pp. 161–168.

Rieger, W., 1928, *Einführung in die Privatwirtschaftslehre*, Nürnberg: Krische und Co..

Ronen, S., 1986, *Comparative and Multinational Management*, New York: Wiley.

Schär, J. F., 1911, *Allgemeine Handelsbetriebslehre*, Leipzig: Gloeckner.

Schanz, G., 1977, *Grundlagen der verhaltensorientierten Betriebswirtschaftslehre*, Tübingen: Mohr.

— 1978, *Verhalten in Wirtschaftsorganisationen*, München: Vahlen.

Schmalenbach, E., 1911, "Die Privatwirtschaftslehre als Kunstlehre", *Zeitschrift für handelswissenschaftliche Forschung* 1911/1912, 6, pp.304–316.

— 1922, *Goldmarkbilanz*, Berlin: Springer.

— 1947, *Die dynamische Bilanz*, Leipzig: Meiner (9. ed.).

Schmidt, F., 1921, *Die organische Bilanz im Rahmen der Wirtschaft*, Leipzig: Gloeckner.

Schneider, D., 1987, *Allgemeine Betriebswirtschaftslehre*, München: Vahlen (3. ed.).

— 1947, *Einführung in die Wirtschaftstheorie*, Tübingen: Mohr.

Staehle, W. H., 1991, *Management*, München: Vahlen (6. ed., 1. ed. 1983).

— 1989, "Entwicklung der Managementlehre in Deutschland", in: Pieper, R. (ed.) *Westliches Management—Östliche Leitung*, Berlin & New York: de Gruyter, pp. 13–36.

Staritz, D., 1985, *Geschichte der DDR 1949–1985*, Frankfurt am Main: Suhrkamp.

Thamm, J., 1958, "Wie kann die Leitung unserer sozialistischen Betriebe verbessert werden?", *Einheit*, 13, No. 2, pp. 268–271.

Tichomirov, J. A., 1975, *Die Leitungsentscheidung*, Berlin (DDR): Staatsverlag der DDR.

Ulbricht, W., 1959, *Das Gesetz über den Siebenjahrplan und die Aufgaben der Partei bei der Durchführung des Planes in der Industrie*, Berlin (DDR): Dietz.

Ulrich, H., 1969, *Die Unternehmung als produktives soziales System*, Bern & Stuttgart: Haupt.

— 1984, "Skizze eines allgemeinen Bezugsrahmens für die Managementlehre", In: Ulrich, H. et al. (eds.), *Grundlegung einer allgemeinen Theorie der Gestaltung, Lenkung und Entwicklung zweckorientierter sozialer Systeme*, St. Gallen: Hochschule St. Gallen, Institut für Betriebswirtschaft, pp. 1–30.

Vidmer, R. F., 1981, "The Management Theory 'Jungle' in the USSR", *ISMO*, 11, No. 3/4, pp. 3–22.

Vorwerg, G., 1971, *Führungsfunktion in sozialpsychologischer Sicht*, Berlin (DDR): Deutscher Verlag der Wissenschaften.

Walb, E., 1927, *Kameralwissenschaften und vergleichende Betriebswirtschaftslehre*, Köln: Oskar Müller Verlag.

Weyermann, M. & Schönitz, H., 1912, *Grundlegung und Systematik einer wissenschaftlichen Privatwirtschaftslehre und ihre Pflege an Universitäten und Fachhochschulen*, Karlsruhe: Braun.

Winternitz, J., 1950, "Zur Kritik der betriebswirtschaftlichen Metaphysik", *Deutsche Finanzwirtschaft*, 4, No. 2, pp. 52–57.

Wintgen, G., 1962, "Churchman, C. W., Ackoff R. C. & Arnoff, E. L.: Operations Research. (Buchbesprechung)": *Wirtschaftswissenschaft*, 10, No. 12, pp. 1895–1898.

Wöhe, G., 1975, "Betriebswirtschaftslehre, Entwicklungstendenzen der Gegenwart", In: Grochla, E. & Wittmann, W. (eds.), *Handwörterbuch der Betriebswirtschaft*, Stuttgart: Poeschel, pp. 710–747.

— 1990, "Business Administration: Present Theoretical Approaches", In: Grochla, E. et al., *Handbook of German Business Management*, Stuttgart: Poeschel, pp. 270–291.

Wren, D. A., 1987, *The Evolution of Management Thought*, New York: Wiley.

Wunderer, R. (ed.), 1988, *Betriebswirtschaftslehre als Management- und Führungslehre*, Stuttgart: Poeschl (2. ed.).

Chapter 7
The Japanese System of Academic Management Education

Katsuyuki Nagaoka
Tokyo Keizai University

7.1 Introduction

Much less is known in other countries about the state of academic management education in Japan than about the so-called Japanese management system. If I may give my personal opinion at the very beginning I would say that the *average* quality and level of Japanese academic management education must be classified among the worst of the highly industrialized countries. Compared with the Japanese management system, Japanese academic management education could be said to have no internal quality control mechanism.

To make matters worse, this is not limited to the academic education of management. The same applies equally to academic education in other social sciences. It is a structural consequence of the whole Japanese educational system. In addition, and this may seem strange to outsiders, Japanese employers do not encourage students of business management to continue to a second-degree course. Their recruitment practices can even cause disruptions for students who have chosen such a course. This makes it difficult to improve academic management education in Japan in the short term.

I will first describe several features of management education at Japanese universities, and the employment practices and personnel management in Japanese firms, which are related to academic management education. In the last section, where some recent attempts at the universities to improve academic management education are presented, I will discuss some of the problems facing Japanese universities and the academic management education which they provide.

7.2 Main Features of Academic Management Education in Japan

7.2.1 Predominance of Private Universities

More than 40 years have passed since the whole Japanese educational system was drastically transformed from a German type of model to an American, on the initiative of the occupation forces. Generally speaking, the new academic education in natural sciences, technology, agriculture and

Table 7.1 *Number of Applicants for Admission and New Students (in Thousands) in Japan*

Year	Population at the Age 18	High School Graduates	Applicants for University	New Students
1960	2,000	934	242	163
1975	1,590	1,327	628	424
1990	2,010	1,767	867	492

Source: Ministry of Education, *Basic Statistics of Education 1990*, Vol. 1 and 2, Tokyo 1990 (in Japanese)

Table 7.2 *Number of Students in State, Regional (including Municipal) and Private Universities in Japan*

Department of	State	Regional & Municipal	Private	Total
Economics[a]	31,450	9,383	220,111	260,944
Commerce[b]	3,038	4,190	109,598	116,826
Business Management	3,157	235	62,837	66,229
Management Information	0	427	9,748	10,175

Source: Ministry of Education, *Basic Statistics of Education 1991*, Vol. 2, Tokyo 1991 (in Japanese).
Notes: [a] In many universities which have no independent department of commerce or business management, the department of economics has a division of business management.
[b] Almost all departments of commerce give considerable weight to education in business management.

medicine (referred to below, for the sake of simplicity, as the natural sciences) seems to have achieved a high standard that bears comparison with other countries. But the social sciences differ substantially from their American counterparts and are greatly inferior to them. This remarkable contrast within the Japanese academic education system is connected with the policy for higher education that the Ministry of Education has traditionally adopted.

The ratio of high school students who go on to a higher level of education has been growing rapidly since the beginning of the 1960s (see Table 7.1). It is private universities not state universities, that have accepted most of this growing band of applicants for an academic education. Table 7.2. shows the distribution of students between state, regional (including municipal) and

Table 7.3 *Minimum Number of Teachers Required for a Japanese Department in the Field of Social Sciences*

Prescribed Number of New Students per Year up to	100	200	300	400	500
Teachers in General Education	7	12	15	18	21
Specialist Education	11	14	17	20	23

private universities in commerce and business management. From the figures in the table it can be seen that in order to diagnose the state of academic management education in Japan, the situation of the private universities must be thoroughly examined.

The Ministry of Education in cooperation with the Advisory Council on University Education and the Examination Council on University Foundation decides the guidelines (minimum requisite conditions) for university education. Two important requirements concern the teacher-student ratio and the curriculum. Unless the requirements on these and other points are fulfilled, no new departments nor any increase in the number of registered students in existing departments, will be permitted.

7.2.2 Teacher-Student Ratio

One big problem for the social sciences is the low teacher-student ratio they require. The ratio of teachers to students in the main social sciences is only half that in departments of natural science, and it decreases substantially as the number of students rises (see Table 7.3.).

Reasons for the dominance of private universities, in spite of their financial dependence on student fees, are many. One is that research and education in the social sciences are not as expensive as in the natural sciences. Another is the great and still growing demand for university places. Yet another reason is that the Ministry of Education has only slightly increased the capacity of state universities in the social sciences, in spite of a massive number of applicants. As a result many private universities and departments of social science have been founded recently, and existing departments have been greatly extended.

As the private universities expanded, and academic management education became increasingly widespread in Japan, many universities emerged which were accepting students far beyond the permitted numbers. In 1976 this finally led the Japanese government to decide to subsidize private universities in order to improve the education provided there.[1]

The Ministry of Education distributes the total subsidy budget among the

Table 7.4 *Number of University Teachers and Undergraduate Students in Japan (April 1990–March 1991)*

	State	Regional & Municipal	Private	Total
Teachers				
Full-time	53,765	6,592	63,481	123,838
Part-time	10,323	2,392	28,169	40,884
Students	518,609	64,140	1,550,613	2,133,362

Source: Ministry of Education (1991, Vol.1).

private universities according to the number of teachers and whether or not the teacher-student ratio laid down in the guidelines is being met. In spite of this condition the ratios at the private universities are not much higher than prescribed by the guidelines. The reason for this is that even though the subsidies are attractive to the universities, they only cover at most one quarter of the total cost per teacher. Consequently private universities continue to rely on part-time lecturers (see Table 7.4).

7.2.3 Curriculum

Unlike most European students, Japanese undergraduates have to take one-and-a-half or two-year course of general studies before embarking on their major field. There has been much discussion about whether these courses, which are compulsory according to the guidelines, are really appropriate. Indeed, most students regard them as a mere extension of their high-school education and as an uninteresting obligation. Many universities have begun to give students specialized courses in their major field alongside the general studies, so that the first two years at university do not feel like a period of waiting to get properly started. The Advisory Council on University Education has been trying for several years to change the guidelines regarding the general courses in a more liberal direction. At last, in June 1991, the Ministry of Education decided to liberalize the regulation. Since the sum-

---

[1] The government decided at the same time to raise student fees in the state universities gradually each year. In 1991 the average fees in the social sciences at private universities amounted to 523,313 yen. In the state universities the fees were 375,600 yen per year irrespective of the field of study. In addition new students also had to pay admission fees. In 1991 the average private university admission fee was 255,777 yen in the social sciences. In the state universities it was 226,000 yen.

mer term of 1992, each university can decide the content of its own general courses. But it should be noted here that Japanese students (except in medicine) have hitherto studied their major subject for two or two-and-a-half years only.

According to the guidelines all students are required to take at least 76 units in their major field. This means roughly that students in the social sciences have to complete 18 lecture courses and 2 seminars, each consisting in principle of 60 hours but in reality of about 50 hours only. The social science departments at almost all universities require a little more than this, but never so much more as the departments of natural science.

The guidelines also regulate the minimum course requirements which each department has to fulfil irrespective of department size (see Table 7.5).

Almost all the departments of business administration offer more courses than the minimum required. Larger departments offer their students a much more varied range of courses. One problem that must be solved concerns the division between compulsory and optional courses. During the student movement at the end of the 1960s, Japanese universities reduced the proportion of compulsory relative to optional courses. In addition, optional courses in the departments of business administration have been expanding ever since the 1970s, particularly in the fields of organization theory, management theory, international management, and computer & information. An unintended effect of this expansion can now be observed: many students choose "easy" courses in preference to the more valuable ones. One way of solving this problem could be to establish a compulsory core of courses. In business education, however, we have neither a unified system of business management theory nor a curriculum of which a majority of business administration scholars would immediately approve. Instead there is competition between different approaches and different theories. Furthermore, the level of achievement that different teachers require of their students often varies widely among teachers even within the same department.

7.2.4 Teaching Methods and Level of Achievement Required of Students

Any foreigner who has observed the teaching in Japanese schools notices that Japanese teaching methods are predominantly one-way—from the teachers to the pupils. There is a connection between this method and the number of pupils in a classroom, although pupil numbers are not always the only reason for the adoption of a particular method.

The same one-way teaching method is applied in Japanese undergraduate courses. With some exceptions, the predominant vehicle for teaching in the social sciences is the lecture. There is seldom any discussion. The role of the students is a passive one. As a rule no complementary classes are provided; students are simply expected to study further on their own.

Table 7.5 *Standard Model for the Course Programme for the Establishment of a Business Management Department in Japan (since 1986)*[a]

Principles of Business Management (Minimum requirement: At least one obligatory Course)
Introduction to Business Management [Obligatory]
Principles of Business Management [Obligatory]
Business Economics [Desirable]
History of Management Thought

History of Business and Enterprise (Minimum requirement: At least 1 obligatory Course)
Business History [Obligatory]
Japanese Business History [Obligatory]
History of Industrial Development

Enterprise (Minimum requirement: At least 1 obligatory course, can be replaced by one that is desirable)
Business Enterprise (Forms of Enterprise or Growth of Enterprise) [Obligatory]
Medium and Small Enterprise (Including Venture Business) [Obligatory]
Japanese Enterprises (or Japanese Management System) [Desirable]
Multinational Enterprise [Desirable]
Public Enterprise (Public Utilities)

Business Management (Minimum requirement: At least 3 Obligatory Courses, can be replaced by one that is desirable)
Management Theory [Obligatory]
Strategic Business Management [Desirable]
Organisation Theory [Obligatory]
Labour Management (Including Personel Management) [Obligatory]
Industrial Relations
Business Finance [Obligatory]
Production Control (Including Quality Control) [Obligatory]
Marketing [Obligatory]
Sales Management [Desirable]
International Business
Business Environment [Desirable]
Research and Development

Management Science (Minimum requirement: At least one obligatory course)
Management Science [Obligatory]
Statistics for Business and Management [Desirable]
Mathematics for Business Management
Management Information System [Obligatory]
Programming and Data Processing [Desirable]

Accounting (Minimum requirement: All the obligatory courses and at least one desirable course; one obligatory course can be replaced by one that is desirable)
Bookkeeping [Desirable]
Accounting Theory (Including Financial Statements) [Obligatory]
Cost Accounting [Desirable]
Managerial Accounting [Obligatory]
Business Analysis (Enterprise Assessment)
Auditing [Desirable]
Accounting by Means of Computer

Related Fields
Economics; Commerce; Law; Sociology; Psychology

Source: Ministry of Education (ed., 1988)
Notes: [a] This model is reviewed every seven years by the Examination Council on University Establishment.

Some slight compensation is provided by the seminars, in which numbers are limited to about 20. Students choose a seminar in their major field and attend once a week. The standard case is that students write their graduation thesis as an extension of their seminar study.

It is an open secret that the real level of achievement of B.A. graduates differs very much between universities. The level of achievement differs remarkably even among high-schools graduates, and every department at every university (including the state) holds its own entrance examination. A common first-round entrance examination was introduced in 1979 by the Ministry of Education, but it has merely helped to expose more harshly the existing differences between the universities at entrance level. All high-school students are familiar with a ranking table of universities and university departments, that form a hierarchy according to their entrance levels. No one knows for certain, however, whether the rankings in this table reflect the achievement levels of the subsequent graduates. Some departments may improve their students more, and others less, than might be expected from their entrance rankings.

But one thing is absolutely certain. All questionnaire surveys show that as a daily average the number of hours that students in the social sciences spend on study is considerably lower than it was in their high-school days: Japanese universities are difficult to get into but easy to graduate from. There are no official statistics, but it is commonly held that more than 85–95 per cent of the students graduate in four years.

7.2.5 Graduate Courses and Business Schools

Unlike postgraduate courses in the natural sciences, postgraduate courses in the social sciences are unpopular with students. This is because an M.A. or Ph.D. degree in the social sciences brings no substantial advantages in the Japanese business world—a question that will be addressed in the next section. Current postgraduate courses are attended by a few Japanese students only who wish to pursue a career in the academic world, and by some foreign students whose numbers are now beginning to grow.

For the same reason there are virtually no business schools in Japan as yet.

7.3 Employment and Personnel Management in Japanese Firms and Academic Management Education

7.3.1 Recruitment and its Timing

Every year private Japanese firms and other employers draw up an employment plan for the coming year, which includes a recruitment plan for new graduates. The employment of new graduates is a normal and necessary undertaking for Japanese employers. Although there are more and more examples of people being recruited into the higher levels of a firm's internal hierarchy from outside, the normal recruitment model in large Japanese firms is still lifetime employment with a pay scale based on seniority. Under this system a firm cannot increase the proportion of outsiders at higher levels very much, without the risk of conflicting with the expectations of its existing employees.

The recruitment of undergraduate students is regulated by a kind of gentlemen's agreement about when recruitment activities can begin and the employment examinations can be held. The time is settled by representatives of the employers and the universities under the mediation of the Ministry of Education. According to the agreement the starting date for recruitment activities has hitherto been the 1st of August, and for the official employment examinations which precede the official employment decision, the 1st of October. However, the agreement is being violated with increasing frequency by the employers, who make direct contact with undergraduate students before the official starting date for recruitment activities. Neither employers nor students can afford to wait, when they hear that several other firms have already started their recruitment campaign.

This violation of the agreement can be illustrated by what happened in 1991. This was the last year of a boom, and as early as May (i.e. the second month of the last year of a Japanese student's course) students began to visit the recruitment sections of firms. By the middle of July, i.e. before the summer vacation, most firms had announced their decisions to their preferred applicants. These decisions were called "unofficial", in order to avoid open violation of the regulations. The decisions were not officially binding on the applicants. At the beginning of October employers then held their official employment examinations, and told the applicants their employment decisions. In fact, in most cases the formal examination on the 1st of October was held purely to comply with the agreed formalities.

In all their contacts with one another both students and employers assume that employment will be for life. This means that the employment decision is crucially important for both sides. All employers try to make their first approaches to students at least no later than other employers, in spite of the official agreement. As a result, they interrupt students in their studies during their last summer term. This disorganized competition among employers for better employees, and the corresponding competition among students for better positions, thus disrupts the smooth course of the final stages of a person's university education.

7.3.2 Employment not for Specific Jobs

Whilst employers expect a university graduate to have a good academic education, their recruitment behaviour as described above shows that they nevertheless select employees regardless of their final level of academic achievement. Moreover, another aspect of the employers' recruitment behaviour suggests that they are not greatly interested in what the students have studied.

In the ordinary case of recruiting students from the social sciences, employers fail to distinguish between students of business administration and students of economics or even of law. Employers wanting to recruit staff from among the new graduates do so not on a basis of "that individual for that job", but on such non-specific lines as "x new graduates of the social sciences" or "about x new graduates for our sales department and accounting division".

It is no exaggeration to say that the students who succeed in an employment examination acquire not a specific job, but membership of a specific company. Employers (except small ones) assign them to a job (and not infrequently to the city of their working office too) after they have gone through the training for new employees, allowing to some extent for their individual wishes and aptitudes.

7.3.3 Education and Training in a Lifetime Employment System

All employees who reach retirement age in Japan cease to work on the 31st of March. All new graduates begin to work on the 1st of April, the day after they leave school or university. Japanese firms start by giving their new graduate employees a general introductory course lasting about one month. In large firms and banks this is followed by systematic training lasting anything from three to 12 months, during which the new employees are given individual experience of various places of work. They are then assigned to a regular position, which at this stage is definitely not an administrative post. Thus, they all start their working life in a system of lifetime employment from the same low hierarchical level and at the same rate of pay. In their regular positions they are then given some on-the-job training. After three to five years of work experience, they are regarded as fully-fledged members of staff.

While it is the non-practical nature of academic education that makes long training in firms necessary, it is the lifetime employment system that makes it valuable (Saito, 1988). Japanese organizations which employ new graduates on the assumption of lifetime employment, have a very strong interest in manpower development within the company (Koike, 1981). There are two ways in particular in which this development is handled. First, it is the general and important duty of all superiors, irrespective of the hierarchic level, to "bring up" their subordinates. Secondly, every large firm or big bank or insurance company has its own training institute for various off-the-job training courses. Small banks have a joint training centre for their employees and every government ministry also has its own training centre.

7.3.4 Personnel Management in a Lifetime Employment System

Unlike European firms, Japanese firms do not in principle recruit managers from outside. Internal promotion is the rule. In the case of transfers from a parent company to a management position in a subsidiary the person transferred will normally have had a management position in the parent company. Only in exceptional circumstances, as when a firm lacks know-how and is unable to acquire it quickly—perhaps because of rapid diversification and entry into an unfamiliar market, or the introduction of an unfamiliar system—will a firm try to recruit managers from outside.[2]

In large Japanese firms which take on new university graduates for lifetime employment, the pay scale depends on both seniority and hierarchical level.[3] The employees have a common feeling of shared interests, of a long-term perspective and an expectation that their firm will grow in the long run. On the other hand they compete hard for advancement within the firm. As we have seen they all start equally as new graduates, so their working lives begin from the same baseline. They are all well aware of the competition for advancement, which makes the rivalry more keen. But this hard competition also contributes to the growth of their firm.[4]

As Japanese firms rely essentially on their internal labour market, they often have to undertake job reassignments. Indeed, this is so common that there is a special word for it, "Teiki Idou", which means a regular change in personnel or job. Business firms and other organizations make small or large-scale personnel changes every year, irrespective of whether or not they are introducing a reorganization. Japanese firms also have larger personnel departments at head office than European firms. The personnel department plans and carries out centralized employment and job assignments. Employees accept these changes, so as not to miss an opportunity

---

[2] These cases have been increasing since the 1980s, for the Japanese economy is undergoing radical changes and restructuring and diversification is a common strategy of Japanese firms. But there is still no column advertising managerial posts either in business newspapers or business journals; in contrast several special journals are published for recruiting part-timers and regular employees.

[3] This means that it is quite possible for an old worker to be paid more than a young manager. The income before tax of a CEO in the largest Japanese firms, on the other hand, is estimated to be 13–15 times that of a new university graduate (the income of a new university graduate for the first five years or so is only very little higher than that of a high-school graduate of the same age).

[4] After the Japan National Railroad Corporation had been partitioned and transformed into six stock companies, some of these companies abolished the special employment examination for new university graduates which had formerly been held, and which were similar to a high-level civil service examination. Successful candidates in this examination were promised a special career course with rapid advancement. They were known as the "express trains" and were distinguished from the other staff ("local trains") in the Corporation. It is now said that the abolition of this different category of staff and the introduction of an equal chance of promotion has not only helped to dissolve the sense of "they/us", but has also led to a remarkable increase in applicants for jobs.

for promotion in the future. They even accept job changes calling for difficult adjustments or involving a transfer to another office in another city that may not be welcomed by their families. This readiness to accept unwanted changes is grounded in their recognition that they do not have a specific job based on their vocational qualifications; what they have is membership of this particular company. Moreover, it is normal in Japan that all the members of a person's trade union will be from their own company. This is an important reason why Japanese firms are able to implement an innovation or a restructuring more easily and quickly than European firms.

An employee who changes job naturally receives some off-the-job training, if this is necessary. Large firms also provide off-the-job training for those who are promoted to management positions either before or soon after their promotion. A well-known example of special off-the-job training is the four-month course provided by the various ministries for their higher officers (who have passed a high-level civil service examination). University teachers are called in as lecturers. This example illustrates the tendency of Japanese organizations to provide further education for their members under their own auspices. This is both a cause and an effect of the underdevelopment of postgraduate courses in the social sciences and of the almost total lack of business schools in Japan.

7.3.5 Employment of Students from Postgraduate Courses

Up to the middle of the 1960s only a few second-degree courses in business administration were provided. Their main educational goal was to train university teachers. Partly as a result of the small number of graduate students and partly because of the rather unpractical nature of the education, Japanese firms showed little interest in the holders of higher university degrees. Those with a master's degree who were lucky enough to find jobs in large firms were treated according to the seniority system, as members of staff who had been working for two years after taking their first degree. However, the number of postgraduate courses in business administration and the number of employers who want to employ the graduates of such courses, for example business consulting companies and research institutes, have both been gradually increasing since the 1970s. But there has still been no essential change in attitude on the part of large firms and banks as regards higher degrees in business or management, whereas in the natural sciences and technology most students go on to take a postgraduate course, and firms are all eager to employ people with an M.A. or Ph.D.[5]

It is true that large Japanese firms and banks have recently begun to send their younger staff more often to business schools or postgraduate courses abroad. What they need, however, is not specifically people with an M.A. or an M.B.A., but people who have been educated abroad and who have mastered a foreign language. The direct investments and business operations of Japanese firms in foreign countries, as well as their international money trading, have been increasing rapidly over the last ten years. Few of them, except the big trading companies which have long been involved in trade in an international environment, have enough staff to cope with activities. This is also why they now employ foreigners who have graduated from Japanese second-degree courses.

7.4 Problems connected with the Reform of Academic Management Education

The Japanese education system has some serious problems which can only be solved by fundamental changes. Every year at the time of the entrance examinations for high-schools and universities there are calls for some sort of radical reform in our education system. High-school students study very hard to get into a university with a high standing in the reputation hierarchy. The number of high-school students failing their university entrance examination has increased every year. In 1990 as many as 292,000 students failed to get into a university. Many of these enrolled in private schools, simply to prepare themselves and to improve their chances in next year's entrance examinations. Junior high-school pupils also study hard in order to be accepted by a high-school with a good reputation for getting their students into high-status universities. Many pupils also attend private evening schools or vacation courses to prepare themselves for the entrance examination. But once they have entered a university, they no longer have to work so hard.

In spite of the widespread criticism there has been no fundamental change in the last thirty years. This is the most important problem facing the Japanese education system. To discuss the system as a whole is not our present purpose, however. Our discussion focuses on a more limited problem, namely the improvement of academic management education, given the existing hierarchical ranking of our universities.

The important issue is how, and in what direction, the abilities of students of business administration could be further developed. In this context the fact that student ability at each individual university is fairly uniform due to the hierarchical differences in the entrance levels, might be regarded as something of an advantage: the homogeneous level of achievement of the students on entry should reduce possible teaching problems. Another fa-

---

[5] The number of Japanese students who go on to doctoral programmes in the natural sciences and technology has recently fallen. There are three main reasons for this. First, while the government budget for education and research in universities has stagnated over the last ten years, the research budget and the facilities for experiments in firms have improved enormously and now surpass those at the universities often to quite a remarkable extent. Secondly, scholarships for postgraduate courses are very low. Thirdly, the difference in salary for a Master of Arts or a Ph.D. is negligible.

vourable circumstance is that the departments now have a certain autonomy in deciding the content of their courses, once they have received their charter from the Ministry of Education.

But why have departments of business administration and other social science departments hitherto failed to introduce any significant reforms, although most faculty members consider such reform to be desirable? One reason is certainly the recognition that every fundamental improvement in the present state of affairs will force them to take on additional tasks. They are already responsible not only for teaching but also for various kinds of administrative tasks which American and European university teachers would not accept. Japanese university teachers in the social sciences, including full professors, enjoy no secretary services and have no teaching assistants, except in some of the state universities. Another obstacle to improvement in the educational system is that Japanese universities have no system for evaluating the performance of their teachers. A third problem militating against reform is that there is no satisfactory measure of reform that would be unanimously approved. Opinions differ, and it is always possible to discover drawbacks in a proposed reform in order to protect one's interests or to avoid additional work.

It is a well-known fact that the more non-authoritarian and "closed" an organizational structure is, the more likely it is that new proposals will be rejected and that radical change will be rare. All departments in the Japanese universities have also known failure more than once when reform has been attempted, and have had to be satisfied with small improvements instead. But over the next five years, circumstances will be changing. Although the number of college-minded high school students has been increasing much faster up to now than every prediction or plan of the Ministry of Education expected, the 18-year-old population will begin to decrease from 1992, and the number of applicants for university places is expected to fall rapidly from 1995.[6] Lower-status universities have already set out to grapple seriously with reform. This movement is spreading to other universities, and the decision by the Ministry of Education in 1991 to liberalize the regulation about general courses is giving additional impetus.

Even without these new circumstances the departments of business administration have been making greater efforts to improve their courses compared with other social science faculties, the reason being that as a younger field they have not been bound by an established system of education, and new research fields and approaches have been continually emerging.

In 1976 the deans of business administration in Japanese universities organized the first conference to discuss improvements in management educa-

---

[6] It is anticipated that in the year 2000 the number 18-year-olds will be 1,510,000 and the number of applicants for university will be 649,000 (Sankei-Shinbun-Shakaibu (ed.), 1992, p. 230).

tion. Since then they have been exchanging and discussing their experiences every year, as well as any new attempts. A difficulty which they all face in their attempts to change things is persuading and motivating a majority of their faculty members to adopt reform, and involving other colleagues engaged in the general education courses.

Up to now only a few departments of business administration have reached a stage at which reform has been put in train, and then only in the main subjects. Other departments and programmes are still at the discussion stage. A general assumption from which discussion in this reform movement starts, is that at a time when higher education is becoming almost a popular movement, students have not the same awareness or interests or future prospects as they had before (Saito, 1992).

When Japanese academic management studies and education started as a new field of imported science in the 1920s it had to fight to acquire an academic status equal to that of the older economics discipline (Kataoka, 1990). Economics at that time was imbued with critical ideas reflecting current social conditions. In this context "academic" meant distancing economics from the perception of employers, not to mention business firms, as the bearers of economic development. Further, an important skill required of all university graduates in those days was the ability to read foreign management literature and to glean new knowledge from it. For these reasons academic management studies and education in pre-war Japan were predominantly literature- and theory-oriented (Nagaoka, 1987).

It was often said at that time that an education which is immediately practical and useful, soon becomes unpractical and unusable. This statement still contains a relevant grain of truth, but it was even more applicable when only a limited number of students could and did study at university. But as social and technological changes accumulate and the ratio of students continuing into a higher level of education rises, the more necessary it becomes to reconsider what a truly practical and useful education should consist of. No-one today could advocate an exclusively traditional literature- and theory-oriented education. The traditional one-way teaching method based chiefly on lectures no longer succeeds in sufficiently motivating students to study. Many universities therefore try to offer more classes for introductory and basic courses, and to limit the number of participants per class. At the same time they look for other educational approaches which could activate students.

But the questions on which opinions differ are: what is a "better" education in business administration and what are its most important ingredients? Answering these questions is further complicated by the fact that students do not have any work experience from the business world. Also, they only study business administration for two-and-a-half years. Another complication is that there are scarcely any positions in the business world in Japan, where such vocational qualifications lead to a correspondingly specific job.

Added to which the traditional view still prevails that vocational abilities and skills are best developed through on-the-job training.

Even the teachers at the universities with the highest entrance levels do not believe that they can provide a management education which would enable their graduates to work as competent managers soon after their graduation. The same opinion prevails among Japanese business managers. And Japanese employees would not accept a new graduate as their manager, even if he or she had an M.B.A. To have studied and to possess more theoretical knowledge is a necessary condition for a manager, but it is not yet a sufficient qualification for becoming a top manager. Candidates for such positions must first of all be good members of a work community. They must then gradually prove themselves capable in their work, finally earning recognition as candidates for managerial positions. Only those who have stood such a test step by step and again and again in the course of long service, can become top managers.[7] Thus what is expected of Japanese academic management education, and what it can succeed in giving its students, is not an education for managers but an overall knowledge of business and management and a general ability to learn by themselves in their future lives.

Although opinions differ among faculty members about what a "better" management education would look like, there is a broad consensus about the defects in the present situation. As was mentioned in Section 7.2.3. above, Japanese universities reduced the proportion of compulsory courses during the student movement at the end of the 1960s, and the number of courses offered has been increasing continuously since the 1970s. To begin with these two changes encouraged students to study actively according to their individual intellectual interests (and encouraging efforts by a small number of students can still be seen). But it has also become obvious that on the whole the two changes has been that a great many students choose in an unsystematic and "easy" way instead.

As a result almost all departments of business administration are going to increase the proportion of compulsory courses, often introductory courses such as The Institution of Business Enterprise, Introduction to Economics, Introduction to Business Administration, Data Processing and Management Information Systems, Accounting System and Bookkeeping, and Commerce and the Distribution System. The universities which have introduced more compulsory basic courses have given the students the opportunity to choose one of several (three, four or five) sets for more intensive

---

[7] An exception occurs in the recently growing number of cases of high government officials who generally retire at the age of around fifty-five, when one of their colleagues is appointed the same year to the top position in their Ministry. Many of them are then accepted for a high position in a business organization. The employees in these organizations regard them with ambivalent feelings.

study. The sets which are already being offered or planned in various universities are: functional management, management science, management information systems, finance and accounting, commerce and distribution, money and banking, the management of non-profit organizations, and international business management.

These changes make it more or less inevitable that the courses which have previously been offered to students will have to be rearranged and integrated. It seems to me that those departments of business administration which have succeeded in thoroughly rearranging and reorganizing their courses, have improved the education provided more than those which have only made minor changes. A major reorganization naturally requires a broader consensus among faculty members. In other words, a successful reform of the education provided by Japanese universities depends upon whether or not faculty members can reach such broad consensus.

Universities with lower entrance levels are going to offer students more technical and training courses. But even these universities continue to offer such courses as History of Management Ideas since Frederick W. Taylor and Johann F. Schär and Business History including European and American Business. Foreign enterprise and foreign management theories are also often referred to in other courses, continuing the tradition whereby business management studies in Japan started as an imported science. Thus, I may add here, a characteristic feature of academic management eduction in Japan is that it gives greater weight to the historical and international aspects of business administration than other countries do.

7.5 Conclusions

In the eyes of university teachers in other countries, the efforts to improve academic management education in Japan would certainly appear insufficient. At any rate, what I have described here is the real state of management education in Japanese universities. As we have seen above, its main framework and basic conditions are determined by the Japanese educational system as a whole and by the employment practices and personnel management system in Japanese firms. Students, who generally have no work experience, study business management as their major field for two or two-and-a-half years only. What is thus expected of Japanese academic management education, and what it can give the vast number of students, is not an education for managers but, at most, an overall knowledge of business and management. Each employer then gives new graduates additional on-the-job and off-the job training. Larger employers have their own education and training centres. While it is the unsatisfactory nature of management education at universities that makes training programmes in firms necessary, it is the lifetime employment system that makes it advantageous.

University teachers were not previously unaware of the inadequacy of their management courses, but only recently has a movement to improve management education begun to spread to many universities. Its main aims hitherto are:

1. The integration of more extensive courses and the rearrangement of the courses provided.
2. More compulsory introduction courses, and the intensive study of one field of business studies.
3. The activation of student interest and promotion of a positive attitude to study.

The Ministry of Education's decision in 1991 to deregulate the general education courses on the advice of the Council on University Education, has stimulated this reform movement. The Council on University Education also recommended the Ministry of Education to further extend graduate courses in the social sciences and to give working businessmen more opportunities to study. It will first be necessary to increase the number of faculty staff members, however, and/or to reduce their administrative burden, if such courses are to be started.

References

Kataoka, S., 1990, *Nihon Keiegakusi Jyosetsu* (Introduction to the History of Japanese Business Management Studies), Tokyo: Bunshindo.
Koike, K., 1981, *Nihon no Jyukuren. Sugureta Jinzai-Keisei Sisutemu* (Labour Skills in Japan. An Outstanding System for Manpower Development), Tokyo: Yuhikaku.
Ministry of Education (ed.), 1988, *Daigaku-Shinsa Youran* (Handbook of University Foundation and Examination), Tokyo: Bukyou-kyoukai.
— 1990, *Gakkou Kihon-Chousa Houkokusho* (Basic Statistics of Education. 2 Volumes), Tokyo: Ookurasho-Insatsukyoku.
Nagaoka, K., 1987, "Business Management Study in Japan. Its Development under the Influence of Germany and the USA", *Paper presented at the Symposium on the Relationship between Academic Business Education and Industrial Performance in Europe and Japan*, Brussels, 21–22 May 1987.
Saito, T., 1988, *Gendai no Keiei Kyoiku* (Contemporary Management Education), Tokyo: Chuo-Keizaisha.
— 1992, "Education of Management in Japan—Present and Future", In: *Proceedings of the First International Federation of Scholarly Management (IFSAM) Conference*, Tokyo, 7–9 September 1992, pp. 222–225.
Sankei-Shinbun-Shakaibu, (ed.), *Daigaku o tou. Kouhaisuru Genba karano Houkoko* (Report on University Problems), Tokyo: Sinchousha.

Chapter 8
Management and Higher Education since 1940

Robert R. Locke
University of Hawaii, Manoa, USA

8.1 Introduction

During the twentieth century a veritable explosion has taken place in business studies at American colleges and universities. The United States Office of Education reported that bachelor degrees in business increased from 3.2 per cent of all undergraduates in 1919 to 10 per cent in 1939. By 1949, business baccalaureates numbered 72,187, almost 17 per cent of all first degrees conferred. Even more impressive was the growth in graduate business studies. Harvard was actually founded as a graduate school, but up to World War II it remained an exception. After the war some undergraduate institutions (e.g. U.C.L.A.) transformed themselves into schools exclusively for graduate studies. Others, while retaining undergraduate degrees, added graduate programs. During the ten-year period 1953–63, the number of master's degrees awarded doubled; between 1964 and 1968 they more than quadrupled (6,375 to 29,335), while bachelor degrees in business during the same five-year period almost doubled (from 56,088 to 93,561).

In Europe, even though developments took off mainly after World War II, they have been only slightly less impressive. A few figures can be given to illustrate this progress. Although the business studies movement did not really get underway until the 1960s, twenty years later the number of students majoring in economics or management in European institutions of higher education, relative to total student numbers, ranged from 10.5 per cent in the Federal Republic of Germany to 13.98 per cent in the United Kingdom, which was a deviation of two points from an average of about 12 per cent (Schieb, 1990). These figures are lower than their American equivalents, but they nonetheless show that a great European effort to promote management education has produced splendid results (Luostarinen & Pulkkinen, 1991). Not only were the sacred precincts of undergraduate education massively invaded by the new discipline, but academic post-experience business education also flourished.

Despite this achievement we can still often read negative statements about this education, such as Ivan Fallon's comments in an issue of *The Sunday Times* (21 April 1991). "John Major's thoughts on the value of a university education", he wrote:

> find echoes around the business world—or rather the entrepreneurial world. Jimmy Goldsmith, with never an O-level to his name, feels so strongly about bus-

iness schools that he would probably disinherit one of his children if they went there. If you run your eye down *The Sunday Times* list of the rich, all the top self-made men left school early: Goldsmith was 16, Robert Maxwell is entirely self-educated, Richard Branson has three O-levels, Gerald Ronson was 16, Tiny Roland was 17.... Even John Major probably has more O-levels than the lot of them put together. Goldsmith argues that higher education is destructive of entrepreneurial drive, and this weekend Professor Hugh Murray, director of the City University Business School, says much the same thing. Murray, who has been teaching business for 25 years, reckons business schools do a pretty awful job of training managers. 'The only place where meaningful exercise can be done is in the work place'. Goldsmith would agree. (The Sunday Times, 1991, pp. 4–2)

I suppose that one could rise up in righteous indignation about such Philistinism, and let there be no doubt about it being Philistinism. But Fallon's comment contains facts that are true. Leading men and women, without formal university education, do succeed entrepreneurially. On the other hand, people with excellent educational credentials show no particular entrepreneurial flair. So the question "Does higher education enhance management performance?" is clearly a legitimate one. Answering it seems especially urgent in view of the great amount of resources now being pumped into management education.

The answer could be framed in many ways. I propose to approach it as an historian, since I am one. I mean that I am concerned only to clarify how business ecucation came into existence, not to establish the general principles of management education. In doing so I shall use the Fallon quotation as a reference.

8.2 American Business Education

Even though there are two strong traditions in business education, going back to around 1900, namely the German and the American I intend to focus only on the latter (Locke, 1984). I do so because management education, as opposed to business education, became the focus of attention principally after World War II, and this development was primarily the work of the Americans. Since their influence has been paramount, their achievement needs to be addressed when evaluating the efficacy of academic management education.

In my book *Management and Higher Education Since 1940* (1989), I note that a new paradigm in American management studies emerged after World War II. This paradigm, which consists of the application of science to management problems, took shape rather slowly in the decades preceding the Second World War. Then, under the pressure of unprecedented wartime managerial events, it proceeded apace. The new paradigm in turn prompted a new constellation in higher education, for the application of science to management required a formal education for future managers on a scale hitherto unknown.

This new management education paradigm had two roots. One was economic demand. The Second Industrial Revolution which emerged after 1870 took place in capital-intensive factories. These were characterized by tremendous throughput capacities requiring a continual, regular flow of supplies and secure market outlets. The consequences of this production system were many: the forward and backward integration of the firm, direct marketing, the integration of finance with industry, and the creation of the managerial hierarchies necessary to run the resultant multi-divisional, multi-national corporations. The work of Alfred D. Chandler, Jr., in particular *The Visible Hand: The Managerial Revolution in American Business* (1977) and *Scale and Scope: The Dynamics of Industrial Capitalism* (1990) are germane here. Without these large corporations and the managerial hierarchies that went with them the new paradigm in academic management education would never have been called into existence.

The second source of the new paradigm was the American tradition in higher education as a whole. Americans like to think of their country as a quintessential democracy but it is in fact a meritocracy based on individual talent. Its elite is broad-based, including the leaders of government, the military, business and industry in its ranks. As an elite it is thus quite different from that of Victorian England, which bifurcated into those who ran business and industry and those who were politically and socially dominant (Locke, 1984, 1989, 1993). The American elite by contrast shared and shares common values that are deeply rooted in the nation. Among them is an instrumental view of education, an idea that knowledge can be applied to problem solving in a variety of situations. This has led, in turn, to a great appreciation of intelligence and knowledge among members of the elite, and much knowledge crossover between occupations and professions in their problem solving. Nothing illustrates this better than the interaction between business and the military. American business historians are familiar with this phenomenon. Professor Chandler notes that "the United States Military Academy provided the best training in civil engineering in this country until the 1860s" which led, not surprisingly, to the employment of its graduates in the building of America's railroads (Chandler, 1977, p. 95). This influence, moreover, was managerial as well as technical.

West Pointers working for industry used systems learned at the Point to improve workshop discipline and cost accountability. They were directly involved in working out the "power-knowledge configurations" that brought about the re-organization of factory management and the development of corporate managerialism in this century (Hoskin & Macve, 1988, p. 37).

This education-management connection was not very important in the nineteenth century; most managers were educated exclusively on the shopfloor rather than at college. One major reason for this was the contemporary situation as regards mathematics and science. Not until the twentieth century, indeed, not really until after World War II, was the scientific method (linear programming, mathematical model building, statistics, decision science, etc.) introduced into management studies. The military led the way, as the operations research teams spawned by the war dramatically demonstrated the efficacy of science in management (Waddington, 1940). During the Cold War the application of science to managerial problems grew in the defense establishment, the most impressive example being the employment of linear programming, developed by George Danzig of the RAND Corporation on contract to the U.S. Air Force, to optimize aircraft operations during the Berlin airlift and bombing patterns during the Korean War.

Mathematical modelling and statistical analysis spread in the 1950s from military to civilian governmental agencies, e.g. the Census Bureau, and then to the large corporations. At first the techniques were applied to transportation and production problems, e.g. queue theory; later they were applied to traditional management fields such as finance and marketing. As a result of the impressive results achieved, management education systems became impregnated with mathematics and science; the systems began to expand, initially in the departments of industrial administration in the engineering schools (Case Western, Carnegie Tech, MIT, etc.), where the required knowledge of mathematics and statistics was more readily available, and then in the late 1950s and 1960s in the business schools proper. The systems radically upgraded their admission requirements as regards mathematics, and introduced mathematical models and statistics into their behavioral science courses, as well as their traditional functional management (marketing, finance, etc.), general management, and decision science courses.

Thus the rapid increase in student numbers described at the beginning of this chapter coincided with the shift in the content of business education towards the new science paradigm. The calibre of the students improved despite their greater numbers, as business studies began to enjoy the intellectual respectability in American academia that had previously eluded them. It was this American achievement that captured the attention of the Europeans when, under the impulse of the Marshall Plan, they crossed the Atlantic to learn the secrets of American productivity. Many visitors were persuaded that American management success depended on the thriving system of academic business education which they discovered there and which was developing rapidly before their very eyes. So convinced, they launched the business studies movement in Europe whose fruits have already been mentioned.

Two factors, then, were involved in bringing about the wedding between academia and managerial practice in America. One was the new paradigm—the application of scientific and mathematical knowledge to management—the mastery of which necessitated formal learning in institutions of higher education. The second factor, to some extent a result of the first, was sociological. The Americans created management and, with it, the profession of managers. As in all professions, the claim was that managers possessed special skills and knowledge. The creation of business schools and the M.B.A. degree (Master of Business Administration) were meant to provide the educational qualifications for the new management profession. The idea behind this sociological fact was elitist: that a group of men and women, who had learned the science and art of management, was indespensable; without their managerial skills American business and industry would flounder. Hence, the American achievement has a knowledge and a sociological dimension. Let us look at both using Fallon as a foil.

8.3 Management Knowledge

Since Fallon's point, strictly speaking, is that higher education inhibits entrepreneurship, a distinction should be drawn between entrepreneurship and management. We usually think of entrepreneurs and managers, even successful ones, as cut from different cloths. The entrepreneurs are the creative ones, they bring business into existence, they innovate. The good manager, on the other hand, runs a going concern well. The first issue Fallon raises, then, is: does higher education harm entrepreneurial flair? There are good reasons not to think so.

One has to do with the nature of entrepreneurship proper. Professor Kenichi Yasumuro likes to distinguish between technologically innovative and noninnovative entrepreneurs (Yasumuro, 1993). He claims that people who discuss entrepreneurship usually lump the two together. Fallon does. All the entrepreneurs on his list are famous for making money, not for advancing technology. They contributed nothing to the U.K.'s technological prowess, and indeed, if one were to fault British entrepreneurs it would be for the relative absence among them of technologically creative people. Yasumuro's point is that truly creative entrepreneurship must add to the technological and industrial development of a country; otherwise, however many entrepreneurs there may be, in terms of money-making, the country remains in the stone age. When technologically creative entrepreneurship is at stake, an educational background in science and engineering is important.

But is a business education equally important? Here the knowledge component does seem unimpressive. Indeed, it is hard to show that anything learned at business school promotes entrepreneurship. The proper conclusion is probably that no amount of education produces an entrepreneur, but people with (innate) entrepreneurial talent can benefit enormously from the study of natural science and engineering. The usefulness to entrepreneurship of the techniques learned at business school is not, however, unproblematic.

When we turn from entrepreneurship to management, the merit of a business education is more apparent. However, a distinction needs to be drawn, in terms of usefulness, between education *for* and education *in* management. Before World War II few people thought that management could be taught as an academic discipline, which could then be applied in practice. Business education at the time boiled down to the teaching of functional subjects (accounting, marketing, finance, etc.), in other words auxiliary disciplines that provided managers with information valuable to decision making. This constituted business education *for* management, because it did not seek to make management itself an academic subject. It was the Americans who, on inventing the management profession, made education *in* management the focus of attention at business schools.

To some extent judgements about how well they succeeded have depended on the changing reputation of American management. During the postwar years that judgement was positive; hence the effort to emulate the American business school abroad and the great expansion of such schools at home. The decline in the reputation of American management since 1970 and the collapse of the reputation of social science has meant that faith in academic management research and teaching has declined. The world has seen that, despite their mathematical models for decision and control, despite their systems, despite the fame of their business schools, the American manager has been bested by foreign competitors, often from countries that do not even have business schools such as Germany and Japan.

Thus, Fallon's negative view of the usefulness of business schools currently has the best of the argument. This is true particularly as regards education *in* management, although the value of functional business education *for* management seems to be much more defensible.

Yet there is a profound reason why the Fallon article and what it represents must be challenged: Fallon's critique seems to go beyond business education as such to the usefulness of any kind of higher education to an entrepreneurial life. There is much more to higher education than the preparation of people for a specific job or profession.

There are good reasons, indeed, to believe that the ability of a society or a person to cope with economic and technical change has more to do with general literacy and numeracy than with professional or occupational training. Studies carried out by the European Parliament show

> that the time it takes for the content of education to become outmoded and the speed with which it takes place can be positively correlated with its concreteness (closeness to praxis) and negatively correlated with its level of abstraction. It follows, therefore, that during periods of sudden social change the basic education needed to prepare us for life is worse the more it is related to concrete practical needs. (Wächter, 1980, p. 34).

This conclusion is interesting because it signifies that one should not just try to teach what goes on in practice. It is better, when organizing secondary and higher education, to teach what have been called "key qualifications" (*Schlüsselqualifikationen*). Among these key qualifications are basic and lateral ones. Basic qualifications are those needed for learning, lateral are

Table 8.1 *Key Qualifications*

As Education Goals	BASIC QUALIFICATIONS Expressed Concretely	Acquired Educationally by
logical thinking	logical conclusions	formal logic, algebra
analytical procedures	technical analytical processes	linguistics, analytical geometry
critical thinking	capacity to discuss and dispute	dialectics
structural thinking	classification skill	priority ordering of phenomena
management thinking (*dispositives Denken*)		organisational theory, principles of economics
conceptual thinking		planning techniques

As Education Goals	LATERAL QUALIFICATIONS Expressed Concretely	Acquired Educationally by
information acquisition capacity	nature of information	semantics, information science
	information acquisition	library science, statistics, media science
	understanding information	foreign languages, language structures, speech, knowledge of symbols, graphics, mathematical symbols
	assimilation of information	speed reading, acquisition of specialized vocabularies, elimination of redundancies and repetitions

Source: Locke (1989, p. 219), which is an adaptation of a table in Wächter (1980).

those that permit the individual, who is properly equipped with basic qualifications, to tap the information available in society in order to relearn (Table 8.1).

It is obvious from the table that key qualifications are not really qualifications at all, in the sense of qualifying a person for a particular job or occupation in a specific field. During periods of change such qualifications rapidly become outmoded. Indeed, the Institute for Job Market and Occupational Research in Nuremberg, Germany, has concluded that "it is illusory to believe that quick changes can be made in the training structure, the educational curricula, or in continuing education in order to keep them synchronized with the sudden and constantly changing work world" (Wächter, 1980, p. 34). There is no way, especially during periods of greater ferment, "to make educational institutions serve directly specific professional and occupation needs of the economy". The Institute also quotes a Professor Mertens, who reports

> ...that such a response is not really necessary: For most jobs the bosses in a business or firm find that they want people with entirely different qualifications than those imagined when the original position was advertized. Also positions offered can be filled by people of quite diverse training. Mertens concludes that in numerous cases a complete elimination of bottlenecks and surpluses on the labor market occurs, even if calculations about future educational and occupational structures are wrong. The immininent elasticity of the system is important. (*ibid.*, p. 35)

Since the system seems to be self-regulating and no real bottlenecks appear, we have to ask ourselves why the labor market is capable of adjusting. What in an education makes this flexibility possible? The answer is the acquisition of key qualifications.

Germans make a distinction in their education between making a person *berufsfähig* (capable of doing a job) and *berufsfertig* (ready to do a job). Higher educational institutions in Germany do not intend to make students *berufsfertig*; that is left to business and industry after a student's academic education is completed. Rather, academia feels that its essential role lies in making people *berufsfähig*. This it does by giving students a *Denkschulung* (schooling of the mind), largely by providing them with basic and lateral qualifications. This interpretation of the role of education constitutes an implied criticism of American business schools, which do pretend to make people *berufsfertig*. Perhaps this criticism explains why German (and, it might be added, Japanese) academic business education never became heavily involved in post-experience management education, either in the form of long-term M.B.A. or short-term executive programs. In these countries post-experience education was left to practice.

At the same time, the emphasis on *berufsfähig* education amounts to a strong condemnation of Fallon's educational Philistinism. A managerial corps with key qualifications, acquired to a very great extent from higher education, is flexible and creative. Indeed, this adaptability is one significant cause of business prowess. It is not the skill of a few prognosticators or probabilists to predict the future accurately that determines managerial success (that was the mistaken belief of the age of mathematical modelling), but the ability of people to react quickly and well to events—even unexpected ones—when they come. Fallon's praise of uneducated practitioners is therefore misplaced, precisely because such people lack the basic qualifications essential to adaptability.

8.4 Managerial Motivation

A second aspect of good management is motivation. In the West our conceptions of motivation have usually been individual. The impressive manager is the high-flyer, the innovative, imaginative, hard-driving, risk-taking, competitive leader, who is the opposite of the organization man. And the same could be said of the successful student. Indeed, it is precisely this type of highly creative individual that elite business schools seek to recruit into their M.B.A. programs.

But at the start of this chapter I declared my interest in looking at the sociology of motivation. The Japanese have a proverb which says that the nail that sticks up is hammered down, and the philosophy this expresses seems to pervade Japanese organizations. Hiroko Charles, a Japanese businesswoman (married to an Englishman) who has worked extensively with Japanese and British brokerage firms, has underscored the difference between Japanese and Western management: we find more capable and intelligent individuals in British firms, but Japanese firms are more effective businesses. Japanese firms are often dynamic, risk-taking, quick-learning, flexible, highly competitive collectives, but they are composed of unassuming, modest and indeed rather ordinary organizational men and women. They seem to Westerners to have developed a new idea of group as opposed to individual motivation (Kagona, 1981; Aoki, 1990). And in the competition between individual and group management, the synergy of the latter has proven to be almost irresistible.

Japanese success has meant that the traditional conceptions of management and motivation, with which the West explains its achievements, have become subject to revision. The Ashridge survey of Global Human Resource Management offers a recent and convenient example of how this sort of revisionism is being undertaken (*Economist Intelligent Unit*, 1990). Firms reporting from many countries now talk about management in terms of a whole organizational culture rather than the skill levels of individual managers, for the "mind set and outlook of managers is more important than formal structures and reporting lines (the heart of American traditional individualist management) in bringing about a flexible, yet cohesive organization" (*ibid.*, p. 7). Quoting the management expert Rosabeth Moss Kanter, the conclusions presented in the survey emphasize the superiority of "process over structure", since it is not the way responsibilities are divided but the way people pull together that counts. What is needed, the authors claim, is the creation of transnational organizations, with what Christopher A. Bartlett and Sumantra Ghoshal (*Managing Across Borders*) describe as "integrated networks which share-decision making and where components, products, resources, information and people flow freely between the interdependent units, [...] and dynamic integrative ways of taking decisions through using the commitment of every individual employee to the overall corporate agenda" (*Economist Intelligent Unit*, p. 8) are extant. The highly formalized and institutionalized central mechanisms (a clear attack on Americans) of management have, it stresses, to give way to

> 'co-option', to concensus building with each individual understanding, sharing, and 'internalizing', the company's purpose, values, and key strategies constituting the most effective means of co-ordination. (*loc.cit.*)

Now this shift to group management conceptions profoundly affects the sociology of management education. Japanese managers are among the most highly educated in the world; for instance well over 90 per cent of them have college degrees. But they have not received much academic business instruction. Accordingly, Japan's managerial achievements have not been accompanied by similar achievements in academic management education; indeed, from the perspective of the American business school, Japan has a very poor system of business education. But, from the sociological standpoint an elitist American-type management educational system is ill-suited to group forms of management. If we are thinking in terms of vertical organizational loyalties and firm-specific relational skills, then the role of an outside 'alien' educational institution in the preparation of managers must be radically reduced. Collectivist Japanese management requires in-house training, especially where group cohesion and motivation are concerned, since what counts are not sophisticated management techniques but rational skills which are organization-specific and cannot be learned in business schools.

Thus from the viewpoint of collectivist Japanese-type management, American business school education is actually dysfunctional. The American schools are criticized today for teaching "pseudo-skills when [students] might be getting on-the-job experience or acquiring genuine skills" (Samuelson, 1990, p. 45). Their professors are chastized for "building elegant, abstract models", and their graduates condemned as "... critters with lop-sided brains, icy hearts, and shrunken souls" (Haynes, 1991, p. 4). The problem is the way that the American business school projects a community-disruptive, elitist management mode, not only by what it teaches but by the way its graduates are received, for instance with very high salaries, and the way they are treated, perhaps being given fast-track promotion—ways that undermine the group motivation necessary to the operational efficiency of the firm.

Thus, Fallon's Philistinism represents a popular (above all in the U.K.) but misguided interpretation of the relationship between higher education and management. The more numerate and literate the managers, the more capable they are, not so much because of specific knowledge about how to manage acquired at school, as from the acquisition of basic qualifications that give people, and the organization composed of such people, the flexibility that favors the long-term prospects of the firm. But Fallon's critique of business education stops short where it could have been most telling. Since Fallon himself exudes the ethic of individualism, he fails to see that business education as practised by American and American-influenced business schools disrupts the collectivist forms of management that seem right today.

For the American business school to be useful, therefore, it seems necessary that it should try to promote collectivist management. Could such a transformation of business schools be achieved? Could they try to introduce the sort of participative management forms advocated by the former American Secretary of Labor, Ray Marshall (Marshall, 1987), not just as regards what they teach but also the way they interact institutionally with firms? The answer is, not very easy. To do so, the business schools would have to stop simply reflecting a management system that is in need of reform, and become instead places of informed and thoughtful criticism of American-style management and management education.

References

Aoki, M., 1990, "Towards an Economic Model of the Japanese Firm", *Journal of Economic Literature*, 28, March, pp. 1–27.

Brown, J. & Rose, M. (eds.), 1993, *Entrepreneurship and the Growth of the Firm*, Manchester: Manchester University Press.

Chandler, A. D. Jr., 1977, *The Visible Hand*, Cambridge, MA: Harvard University Press.

— 1990, *Scale and Scope*, Cambridge, MA: Harvard University Press.

Haynes, P., 1991, "Management Education", *The Economist*, March 2, p. 2.

Economist Intelligent Unit, 1990, *The Quest for the Inter-national Manager, A Survey of Global Human Resource Strategies*. Ashbridge: Ashbridge Management Research Group.

Hoskin, K. & Macve, R., 1988, "The Genesis of Accountability: The West Point Connection", *Accounting, Organizations and Society*, 13, No. 1, pp. 37–73.

Kagona, T., et al., 1981, "Mechanistic vs. Organic Management Systems: A Comparative Study of Adaptive Patterns of U.S. and Japanese Firms", *Annals of the School of Business Administration*, 25, Kobe University, Kobe, Japan.

Locke, R. R., 1984, *The End of the Practical Man*, Greenwich, CT: JAI Press.

— 1989, *Management and Higher Ecucation Since 1940*, New York: Cambridge University Press.

— 1993, "Business Education and Managerial Performance: A Study Comparing Japan and America to France, Germany and England", In: Brown, J. & Rose, M. (eds.), *Entrepreneurship and the Growth of the Firm*, Manchester: Manchester University Press.

Luostarinen, R. & Pulkkinen, T., 1991, *International Business Education in European Universities in 1990*. Helsinki: Helsingin Kauppakorkealuolun julkaisuja

Marshall, R., 1987, *Unheard Voices: Labor and Economic Policy in a Competitive World*, New York: Basic Books.

Samuelson, R. J., 1990, "What Good Are B-Schools", *Newsweek*, May 14, p. 45.

Schieb, P.-A., 1990, "Des modèles nationaux où un modèle européen?" *La Revue Francaise de Gestion*, Mars-avril-mai, pp. 105–110.

The Sunday Times, 1991, "Schools of Failure", 21 April, pp. 2–4.
Yasumuro, K., 1993, "Organised Entrepreneurship and the Reconstruction of Japan's Export-Oriented Economy", In: Brown, J. & Rose, M. (eds.), *Entrepreneurship and the Growth of the Firm*, Manchester: Manchester University Press.
Waddington, C. H., 1940, *Science in War*, London: Allen & Unwin.
Wächter, H., 1980, *Praxisbezug des Wirtschaftswissenschaftlichen Studiums*, Expertise für die Studienreformkommission: Wirtschaftswissenschaften.

Chapter 9
Formal Knowledge and Management Education

Richard Whitley
Manchester Business School,
University of Manchester, England

9.1 Introduction

Management education in universities and similar institutions of higher education expanded considerably in North America and many European countries in the 1960s. Although tertiary level education and training in commercial skills and related areas of expertise had developed in a few countries before 1900 (Locke, 1985, 1989; Redlich, 1957), the establishment of business education in leading universities as a legitimate subject for research and high level training has been a largely twentieth century phenomenon (cf. Abbott, 1988, p. 206). This development occurred at different rates and in different ways in Europe and North America, but in the 1960s university level management education became much more widespread in many countries and its dependence on formal academic knowledge more generally acknowledged. Indeed, the dominant conception of the relationships between research based knowledge, the development, assessment and credentialling of managerial skills, and managerial structures and practices changed quite sharply in the 1950s and 1960s, particularly in the USA, and underpinned this growth. This change also was associated with the increasing academic acceptability of management science in the more prestigious universities and has been characterized as a qualitative shift to a new "paradigm" in business studies (Locke, 1989, pp. 1–3).

This new paradigm presumed that managerial skills and problem solving procedures could be derived from formal scientific knowledge and that the craft of managerial practice could be transformed into a science based profession in a comparable manner to engineering and medicine. Whereas most previous knowledge taught in business and commercial schools had been largely based on the structures and practices found in leading firms, and so can be summarized as a codification of current "best practice", the new paradigm sought to develop more abstract and theoretical knowledge which would define and structure managerial expertise. Similarly, while earlier instruction had been based on case studies of particular managerial problems and ways of solving them in practice—most notably at Harvard, but also in Germany (Locke, 1989, pp. 129–134), the new courses and degrees, in contrast, were built around highly formalized theories and models, often expressed in mathematical formalisms, of idealized phenomena. Learning these theories and associated techniques for manipulating data would, it was thought, enable the new "scientific" managers to solve a wide range of problems and provide the foundation for "professional" expertise (Locke, 1989, pp. 159–163). Thus, formal knowledge became seen as the foundation of general managerial skills and the necessary basis for high level academic management education.

These skills in turn were held to be widely applicable across firms and industries so that specific problems and issues were susceptible to general, formal techniques and did not require detailed knowledge of particular sectors. While the earlier form of business education developed skills from codified and synthesized practices, the new paradigm constructed them around formal knowledge and assumed that managerial problems would fit this science based expertise. Because this expertise was more general, more formally coherent and more deductively rigorous, it was seen as naturally more effective and useful than its practice-based predecessor.

The rapid diffusion and acceptance of the new paradigm in the post-war period, especially in the newer business schools in the USA (Locke, 1989, pp. 160–161), was part of a more general expansion of science based education and training. The widespread belief that practical skills should be based on applied science, and that this in turn should be derived from pure science, led to many engineering and other professional training programmes becoming reconstructed around more formal types of knowledge, and skill evaluation dominated by similar methods to those used in the sciences (Divall, 1991). The prestige of science, especially physics, as the dominant source of cognitive authority had been enhanced by its apparent success in generating new military technologies during and after the Second World War, so that it seemed natural to assume that other fields of practice could benefit from a closer dependence on formal scientific knowledge and that high level practical skills should be derived from applied science. Engineering skills thus became seen as essentially scientific, to be taught and assessed in a similar manner to pure science degrees, and engineering knowledge ultimately reducible to scientific theories. This "scientification" of high level technical skills and training, and the overall growth of scientific knowledge in post war society, led some commentators to herald the development of the "knowledgeable society" and the rise of science as an independent factor of production (Lane, 1966; cf. Böhme & Stehr, 1986).

More recent analyses of engineering knowledge and skills have emphasized their distinctive nature and the important role of judgement and tacit knowledge in engineering design (e.g. Seely, 1984; Vincenti, 1984). Additionally, the simple model of applied science, whereby technical knowledge and skills were seen as straightforward derivations of formal scientific knowledge, has become recognized as far too simple. Relationships between scientific and technological knowledge are varied, complex and dynamic, with much twentieth century science itself being substantially dependent on technological developments so that in some fields it is more correct to talk of "technological science" than of "scientized technology" (cf. Böhme et al., 1978; Weingart, 1978). Furthermore, technological knowledge itself has developed in a variety of forms and is incorporated into technical expertise in a number of different ways (Whitley, 1988a).

The inadequacy of the simple view of applied science, and of the direct incorporation of formal knowledge into high level technical skills, is reinforced in the case of management education by the uncertain status of the "pure" scientific knowledge that is being "applied" and the limited success of many science based skills. The belief that economics and behaviourist psychology provide solid foundations for applied social scientific knowledge and effective managerial practices appears rather less convincing in the 1990s than it may have done in the heyday of Keynesian macroeconomic policies. The validity of both orthodox neo-classical economics and laboratory based psychology has been questioned on both epistemological and empirical grounds (see, for example, Caldwell, 1982; Eichner, 1983; Harré & Secord, 1982), and their connections to the management of economic activities in imperfect markets appear rather tenuous to many analysts (e.g. Diesing, 1982; Lindblom, 1990). Indeed, the whole idea that general, abstract knowledge of idealized systems could form the basis of practical skills for managing complex organizations in uncertain, open systems is open to severe dispute, at least in its more simple forms (cf. Whitley, 1988b; 1989).

Perhaps more significant for the fate of the "new paradigm" in business and management studies has been the relative decline of the US economy and the corresponding success of economies organized in quite different ways, principally those of Germany and Japan, where high level management education either does not exist in a comparable form or else is based on different cognitive foundations. Together with different connections between particular educational credentials and access to elite labour markets across industrialized societies, these variations in dominant patterns of economic organization suggest that the US system of training and selecting senior managers of large firms is by no means the only way of ensuring economic success and that the knowledge gained in leading US business schools is neither a necessary nor sufficient basis for generating effective managerial skills. Indeed, the relative decline of some US manufacturing industries has led some writers to accuse these schools of being responsible for the loss of US economic leadership in the world economy, a view which surely overstates the contribution of a relatively small number of elite educational institutions to a very large economic system.

The realisation that US management structures and practices are not the only ways of successfully organising an economy, and that different arrangements for training and selecting managerial cadres can be equally or more effective, means that the "new paradigm" can no longer be assumed to be the only, or most "rational" pattern of structuring knowledge and training in management. It also suggests that the variety of relationships between formal knowledge, training and certification in managerial skills, and managerial recruitment, promotion and careers need to be systematically explained. The simple and straightforward extension of the naive model of applied science in medicine and engineering to management is clearly inadequate. Instead we need to understand how and why relations between formal knowledge, management education and labour markets vary between market economies, and what sorts of connections between different types of knowledge and types of managerial problems are likely to develop in which circumstances.

This understanding requires a more systematic analysis of how formal scientific knowledge is incorporated into academic training programmes, and of how these in turn affect skill use and task performance, than has perhaps been apparent in some discussions of "scientification" and the knowledge society. Increasing academic control of skill definition and assessment has not always led to the reconstitution of skills around formal knowledge, nor has it always resulted in the monopolization of complex tasks by academically trained practitioners, let alone the domination of problem solving practices by scientifically derived procedures. The extent to which formal scientific knowledge—however defined—dominates academic curricula and task performance is a contingent matter which varies considerably across fields, countries and historical periods.

Accordingly, in the next section I consider some of the major ways in which research based knowledge is connected to academic training and certification of high level technical skills and how these latter are linked to work jurisdictions and problem solving activities. The particular nature of managerial practices and skills which have inhibited their academization in some societies are then discussed, as well as their implications for their possible scientification. Finally, I briefly consider the connections between academic control of skill certification, the variety of legitimate audiences for research results and the extent of academic control over rewards and scientific reputations in terms of their consequences for the organization of research fields within management studies.

9.2 Relations Between Formal Knowledge, Practical Skills and Work Practices

In considering relations between formal knowledge and practical skills, it is important to bear in mind that the application of academically certified skills to problem solving is by no means a straightforward matter. First of all, the academic domination of skill development and certification need not imply that complex tasks are always carried out by academically qualified practitioners. Employers are often able to choose non-certified staff for such tasks so that academic skills do not monopolize them. Even where states license practitioners, the definition of jobs and positions is frequently sufficiently flexible to allow a variety of skills to be used.

Secondly, the actual skills being used in complex problem solving activities are often not those inculcated in formal training programmes, as studies of engineering graduates have shown (e.g. Whalley, 1986). Thus, the relations between task definition and performance, skill development and certification and formal knowledge production and application are variable and complex. Who controls these processes and how they are organized obviously affect their interconnections, and the idealized model of "scientized" problem solving which seemed attractive to many in the early discussions of management science represents only one possible set of connections between problems, skills and knowledge—and a rather improbable one. Although a systematic exploration of the critical characteristics of practical problems, skills and formal knowledge and their interrelations is beyond the scope of this chapter, a useful start can be made by distinguishing between: a) academic control over skill definition and certification, b) the incorporation of formal, research based knowledge into these skills, and c) the use of that knowledge in solving problems.

By drawing these distinctions I am emphasizing the variety of knowledges that are incorporated into academic training programmes and the limited role of scientific knowledge in these programmes, as well as the variable role of formal knowledge in complex problem solving activities. As the history of business education in US universities shows, the content of academic courses can be derived from practical experience and descriptive accounts as easily as from formal knowledge, and much medical and legal training in universities is craft based rather than derived from abstract knowledge of idealized phenomena (e.g. Atkinson, 1981; Cicourel, 1986). Depending on how scientific knowledge is conceived, much academic training can be based on non-scientific forms of knowledge and on practitioner generated concepts and techniques.

Academic control of practical skills, then, can be associated with varying degrees of reliance on formal, research based knowledge, as the contrast of finance courses in post 1960 business school programmes with earlier ones readily demonstrates (Smith & Gondzwaard, 1970; Solomon, 1966). It is also associated with varying degrees of control over work jurisdictions and problem selection. For example, the development and certification of engineering skills in most industrialized countries are dominated by academic institutions, often in concert with the state, employers and professional institutions. However, the use of those skills to deal with particular kinds of problems is more controlled by employers than by academics, and engineers in general have limited control over the definition and evaluation of engineering problems. Thus, their ability to monopolize distinctive areas of work and control a specific jurisdiction is quite limited.

On the other hand, professional groups able to dominate particular problem solving activities, such as the professions of law, accounting and medicine in many countries, have become more reliant on university training and certification, even if academics have to share control over skill development with professional elites. As Abbott (1988, p. 207) puts it: "the organised professions by no means conceded control of these university schools (in America); they were in the university but not of it [...] the professors remained professionals first and professors second, a distinct reversal of the German situation." In this case, particular practical skills were developed and assessed in the university in conjunction with practitioner groups and monopolized distinctive activities. However, the key control is exercized here by professional organizations rather than by academics. Thus, the extent to which formal knowledge is incorporated into academically certified skills which monopolize high level and prestigious problem solving activities varies considerably, not least according to the existence of strong professional groups controlling jurisdictions over such activities.

In principle, then, formal research based knowledge varies in its incorporation into academic training programmes and evaluation procedures, academic institutions vary in their ability to control the definition and certification of practical skills, and academically certified skills vary in their monopolization of particular problem solving activities and jurisdiction over distinctive tasks. Increasingly, for example, the results of academic research dominate MBA programmes, at the expense of more informal, practitioner generated knowledge, as academic autonomy from managerial elites has grown. However, such programmes do not monopolize access to leading managerial posts, nor are there specific problems reserved for MBA graduates in the way that certain tasks are monopolized by certified accountants or medical doctors in many countries. In this case, then, increasing incorporation of research based knowledge into training programmes is associated with relatively weak links between formal qualifications and labour market boundaries and work jurisdictions.

These variations suggest that a number of combinations of connections between formal knowledge, skill development and working practices are possible. However, not all of these seem theoretically or empirically likely. For example, training programmes dominated by formal knowledge seem improbable where employers and/or professional associations control skill definition and assessment. The large scale incorporation of research based knowledge into curricula and assessment procedures probably requires considerable academic control over skill development, as the history of engineering education in the USA suggests (cf. Calvert, 1967). Equally, if academic control over skill definition and certification is low, then clearly

Table 9.1 *Types of High-Level Practical Skills*

	Professional Craft Skills	Academic Professional Skills	Competing Research Based Skills	Dominant Research Based Skills
Dependence on Formal Research Based Knowledge	Low	Medium	High	High
Degree of Control over Skill Definition and Certification	Low	Shared with Professional Elite	High	High
Extent of Control over Work Jurisdictions by Academically Certified Skills	Low	High	Low	Medium
Examples	English Accounting English Barristers	Clinical Medicine Law	Financial Analysts Embryonic Professions	O.R. Engineering

academic control over problem solving activities and performance criteria cannot be high. At least four major kinds of practical, high level skills can be distinguished in terms of their dependence on formal, research based knowledge, the extent of academic control over their certification and the significance of academically controlled skills for conducting particular problem solving activities. These are listed in order of increasing academic control in Table 9.1 and will now be briefly outlined.

Professional craft skills are those controlled largely by professional institutions in Anglo-Saxon societies where techniques and methods are acquired either on the job through some sort of apprenticeship, by correspondence courses or through private tutoring organizations dominated by the practitioner elite. Academic training is here largely introductory and does not necessarily guarantee preferential treatment in the professional examinations, nor does academic research play much of a role in those examinations. The most obvious example of this kind of skill today is English accountancy (Geddes, 1992), although it was generally more common in the past.

Academic professional skills have become more widespread in recent decades as universities and formal knowledge have gained prestige and the traditional power of professional elites has declined. Here, curricula have become more linked to scientific research of various kinds and university qualifications are often—though not always—sufficient to become a recognized practitioner, albeit in a subordinate position. However, these skills are not entirely dominated by scientific research based knowledge and are often taught as craft-like forms of expertise and apprenticeship methods within academic institutions. Clinical medicine is perhaps the most notable example, although the extent to which academics share control with professional elites can vary greatly between countries, as (Abbott, 1988, pp. 197–208) has pointed out.

Competing research based skills rely more extensively on formal scientific knowledge and are typically developed in academic training programmes, but have to compete with other sorts of expertise in the labour market to gain employer acceptance. Typically a product of the post war expansion of higher education and increased prestige of formal knowledge, these kinds of skills develop from attempts to "credentialize" occupations and increase entry barriers to certain sorts of work by establishing academic training programmes and claiming expertise on the basis of scientific knowledge. While the development of legal "science" in US law schools may represent an early example of this sort of labour market exclusion (Auerbach, 1971)—although control was here shared with practitioner elites and it is not clear that curricula are entirely dominated by research based knowledge—this kind of "scientification" is mostly a late twentieth-century phenomenon arising from collective social mobility projects in embryonic professions. Unless supported by the state, these are unlikely to be successful, since they threaten to raise wage costs and decrease flexibility, as long as employers are able either to train employees on the job or obtain similar levels of expertise more cheaply on the open labour market.

Dominant research based skills on the other hand combine a high level of dependence on the results of scientific research and training programmes, which means that they are often structured around the categories and frameworks of formal knowledge, with some control over problem selection and allocation. The organization and control of tasks undertaken by those equipped with these kinds of skills is shared by employers, professional associations and state agencies, and so practitioners are more able to monopolize particular kinds of problem and determine performance standards. However, even where employers accept the verdicts of the education system in recruiting, say, engineers or systems analysts, they are unlikely to accept rigid definitions of the sorts of problems these recruits can work on, or depend totally on "professional" judgements of work competence. Rather, they combine and organize these skills in different ways to deal with a variety of complex problems which are not isomorphic with the intellectual problems governing training programmes. The full "scientification" of practical problems would imply their redefinition in terms amenable to research techniques and academic conceptual frameworks, which in turn implies very high levels of control over complex problems and the situations in which they occur (cf. Whitley, 1988*a*).

Formal research based knowledge is also capable, of course, of being directly applied to practical problems and changing the three components of professional practice identified by Abbott (1988, pp. 40–52): diagnosis, inference and treatment. Indeed, this is precisely what the founders of management science saw their new field doing (Locke, 1989; Smiddy & Naum, 1954). Scientific methods were to be developed to solve managerial problems and thus a science of managing would emerge which consisted of formal problem solving techniques and skills. It is important to note here that this was an essentially technique focused conception of science, not a theoretical one and operations research (OR) in general is often regarded as a collection of techniques rather than a theoretically defined scientific field (e.g. Bonder, 1979). As a result, it was not restricted to a specific domain or set of activities. Equally, though, OR practitioners have not been able to claim jurisdiction over particular managerial tasks or areas of work—except perhaps those amenable to formal mathematical modelling. Such a "scientification" of managerial practices has, of course, been beset with difficulties, to the extent that the whole enterprise has been called into question (Ackoff, 1979). As Abbott (1988, p. 55) has pointed out however, the academic goals of rationalization and generalization typically result in formal knowledge being organized in more abstract ways that do not fit practical categories of diagnoses and treatments which make it difficult to translate into improved practices directly. Furthermore, much scientific knowledge deals with "closed" systems which manifest invariant regularities (cf. Bhaskar, 1975, pp. 65–79; Sayer, 1984, pp. 111–114) whereas nearly all practical problem solving involves managing in open systems where such regularities do not often obtain. The direct application of research based knowledge to practical problem solving, then, is usually limited to those areas where control over tasks and their context is so high that they resemble the abstract, closed phenomena and situations constructed by researchers.

A further limitation on the direct applicability of formal research based knowledge to everyday problems stems from the nature of the scientific reward system. In very broad terms, this allocates material and other rewards on the basis of intellectual reputations for contributions to collective intellectual goals (Whitley, 1984). As the modern western sciences became more autonomous from immediate practical goals and gained prestige as the primary sources of cognitive authority, they developed a distinctive form of organization which generated intellectual innovations in a largely conservative manner (cf. Kuhn, 1977). This reputational system rewarded researchers according to the impact their work has upon the work of colleagues/competitors and hence structuring research agenda and priorities. The highest reputations were, and are, given to those scientists who reorganize and redirect the intellectual purposes, concepts and frameworks of entire fields and disciplines. Because such reorganization affects the research strategies and priorities of colleagues, it is rarely easily accepted and radical innovations are therefore infrequent in the sciences. Rather, research is expected to fit in with current conventions and norms about what is significant and how competent work is conducted. Contributions to knowledge are usually, then, restricted in their innovatory degree and scope as major challenges to current intellectual frameworks would threaten the existing reputations, and possibly skills, of the established leaders of the field.

Not all scientific fields have, of course, developed the degree of autonomy, prestige and reputational control over rewards as much of late nineteenth and twentieth-century physics, chemistry and biology. In particular, those fields of research closely connected to the training of practical skills and solution of complex practical problems have developed rather less autonomy from lay elite goals and evaluation standards than many natural sciences. However, the point here is that as academics do gain some autonomy from employers, professional institutions and other influential sponsors, they typically espouse scientific goals and seek intellectual respectability by imitating the dominant reputational system for organizing and controlling research. This means that they increasingly write for each other and seek to influence leading researchers by contributing to their intellectual goals and following the approved style of research. Thus, as knowledge producers become more independent of lay demands, the more they develop distinctive goals and standards for judging the worth of contributions for awarding reputations and so rewards. This, in turn, implies that they focus on intellectual problems which are scientifically significant and develop research skills that are relatively remote from current practitioner interests and techniques. Unless lay audiences remain significant sources of legitimate academic reputations—which arguably is the case in some fields of management studies—the generation of formal knowledge which can be directly applied to everyday problems declines as autonomy increases.

This means that scientific fields which have become firmly established as distinctive and cohesive reputational systems of research organization and control are unlikely to produce knowledge that can be directly applied to practical problems but rather will impinge upon problem solving activities through the development and certification of practical skills, as well as through consultancy. New methods of diagnosis, inference and treatment, then, will develop from formal research based knowledge indirectly through training programmes in fields where rewards are largely reputationally controlled. However, as we have seen, the extent of academic control over practical skills and work jurisdictions varies considerably, as does the extent to which scientific knowledge dominates curricula and assessment standards, and it is worth briefly considering the major factors which affect such "academization" and "scientification".

Overall, academic control of training and certification increases as the universities and their knowledge base become more highly regarded and prestigious in a society. Codification of expertise in general is likely to be high when the state plays a significant role in structuring labour markets and certifying competencies but this need not always result in academic domination of the certification process. Probably a necessary condition for high levels of academization is the relatively low prestige and power of employers' and practitioners' associations so that universities have no significant rivals as guarantors of competence and expertise. Where professional associations are relatively strong and have historically controlled skill definition and examination, as in the case of the English accountancy associations, universities will be less likely to dominate curricula and assessment (cf. Geddes, 1992). This is particularly so where the professional bodies overlap considerably with major employers and are jointly able to control the definition of tasks and standards of performance. Overall, then, academic domination of practical skill development, certification and use is more likely in societies and in fields where: a) practitioner and employer control over task definition and competence standards is weak, b) the state plays an important role in setting standards and maintaining competence levels, c) external labour markets are stronger than internal ones, and d) university certified knowledge is widely seen as a critical component of high level expertise.

These conditions are even more critical for the scientification of practical skills and problem solving activities. For high levels of this to develop, formal scientific knowledge has to become seen as the dominant source of cognitive authority, such that all competing forms of understanding are regarded as inferior, partial and limited. Skills and problems are here standardized around scientific knowledge bases so that the nature of expert work is structured more by academic boundaries than by employers' division of labour and purposes. This implies, of course, that the knowledge produced by researchers is so critical to employers' success that it forms the basis for their activities and pattern of work organization. This, in turn, suggests that practical problems are themselves commensurate with scientific ones, i.e. relatively closed, formally specified and stable, such that formal knowledge can be demonstrably and directly useful in dealing with them.

A further major influence on the development of dominant research based skills is the licensing of problem solving activities by the state. Indeed, it seems likely that a high degree of integration of academically developed and certified skills with control over problem definition, allocation and evaluation is only feasible when the state control access to particular kinds of work through licensing and delegates the training and certification process to universities. For example, the state licensing of engineers and restriction of the title to those who have been trained and examined in specific educational institutions in some countries clearly encourages the integration of formal research based knowledge with skill development and certification and with particular problem solving activities. Even here, though, it should be noted that employers are able to organize these "academic" engineers in a variety of ways and do not have structure tasks around scientific frameworks or topics. Furthermore, they are often able to influence state agencies in setting or revising licensing requirements so that academic control over skills is rarely total. The incorporation of formal research based knowledge into high level practical skills, and their subsequent domination of particular problem solving activities, are, then, highly dependent on the relative influence and control of universities, practitioner elites, employers and the state.

9.3 Formal Knowledge, Managerial Skills and Problem Solving Practices

In the case of managerial skill and work, there are clear limitations to their academization and scientification. First of all, employers retain a strong degree of control over the division of managerial labour, the definition and allocation of managerial tasks and the evaluation of managerial performance. There are few, if any, practitioner based occupational groupings which control the definition of managerial skills and hence could standardize them around academically certified credentials such as the MBA. Relatedly, the sheer variety of managerial tasks within and between organizations, sectors and countries means that no single academically controlled skill could claim a monopoly of all managerial problems. In addition, as I have argued elsewhere (Whitley, 1989), the nature of much managerial work makes it difficult to formalize and standardize particular managerial problems which could be dealt with by high level, standardized skills. The more it involves managing uncertain situations in which interdependencies are high and problems are interconnected, the less it can be reduced to a series of relatively stable, well bounded problems which are amenable to resolution by standard techniques and formal models.

There are then two major, interconnected, reasons for the low level of standardization of managerial skills and work practices in market economies, and so their limited control by academics. First, the nature and variety of managerial problems and, second, the dominant role of employing organizations in determining tasks and performance standards. Managerial work can, of course, be understood in many different ways (e.g. Hales, 1986; Willmott, 1987), but it typically is taken to include the organization and control of work and resources for competitive purposes. The economic function of management can be seen as organizing human and material resources in ways which add value to them by combining them and directing their use in particular ways (cf. Penrose, 1980; Whitley, 1987). Which resources are to be organized and controlled in firms are decided by property rights owners and their delegated managers in capitalist societies, and this forms part of the more entrepreneurial function of management.

How they are to be organized is equally decentralized to economic actors and their agents so that firms can, and do, develop distinctive patterns of work organization and control. This means that managerial tasks and problems are often differently structured and organized in different firms and industries, as well as across countries. Furthermore, the need to compete with other firms means that resources and tasks often have to change as competitors alter their activities and so the nature of managerial problems does not remain stable. As a result, many, if not most, managerial problems and tasks are highly variable and idiosyncratic. Even where distinctive industrial recipes (Spender, 1989) have become institutionalized, and organizations follow the dominant ways of doing business in a particular sector, the organization of managerial work within firms can vary considerably and, of course, does so between industrial sectors.

This variability and change in managerial problems and tasks mean that skills developed for dealing with particular kinds of problems with standardized procedures will be less effective for managers than where tasks can be largely separated from their context, are fairly stable and do not vary greatly across situations. Many medical skills of diagnosis, inference and treatment, for instance, assume that illness can be decomposed into separate problems that do not differ much between patients and can be treated by fairly standard remedies irrespective of their contexts. In contrast, much managerial work involves dealing with problems that are quite interdependent with other parts of the organization, are specific to this particular firm, market and industry and not readily reduced to a general, standard syndrome that can be treated by a specific technique (Whitley, 1989). As a result, the more managerial skills become based on formalized, standardized problem solving techniques which presume the decomposable, stable, well bounded and standard nature of managerial problems the less likely they are to be effective.

This lack of applicability of highly standardized certified skills based on formal models of idealized problems in management is reinforced by the high level of employer control over work and performance standards. Partly because of the variety and change of managerial tasks, together with the ready availability of market based performance measures as alternatives to professional standards, employers are able to exert much more control over the definition and assessment of managerial skills than in the traditional professions. Additionally, since managerial work is inherently organizational, and employers decide the shape and mode of operation of administrative structures as a result of delegated powers from property rights holders, neither practitioner elites nor academics can control the definition of managerial problems nor insist on particular standardized skills monopolizing specific areas of work. While some practical skills are quite standardized in some countries, such as Germany, and these can structure the organization and structure of tasks, as Maurice *et al.* (1986) have shown, the freedom of employers to determine the nature and structure of managerial work, together with its organizational and dynamic nature, severely restricts both the standardization of managerial problems and the institutionalization of academically certified skills as necessary credentials for managerial posts.

This is especially so for the more senior roles in complex organizations which involve managing high levels of uncertainty. Problems and tasks are more vaguely defined, rapidly shifting and interdependent than at lower levels of organizational hierarchies, solutions are also more difficult to specify and outcomes not very clearly connected to particular actions or decisions. Thus, the applicability of standard problem solving procedures and models of idealized systems to senior managerial tasks is not high and credentials based on such formal knowledge are unlikely to become widely accepted by employers for such roles.

However, where organizations are more able to control their environment and have developed internal procedures and mechanisms for stabilizing tasks, managerial problems may be more decomposable, separable from their contexts and capable of resolution with fairly standardized techniques and models. These may, of course, be derived from current "best practices" as much as from formal research based knowledge, but the central point here is that academically certified skills based on formal knowledge of idealized, abstract phenomena and situations are only likely to prove effective and gain acceptance from employers for posts dealing with fairly clearly specified, separate and controllable problems.

It follows, of course, that such skills are unlikely to be as effective as their possessors move up the administrative hierarchy and so are unlikely to monopolize access to senior positions. Thus, the more academically controlled and certified skills based on formalized and standardized models succeed in colonizing particular departments and activities in large organizations, the less likely are those units to be central to managerial careers and the organizational dominant coalition.

This lack of a strong connection between standardized, academically certified skills based on formal knowledge and access to senior managerial positions does not, of course, mean that managerial skills have not become more influenced by academic knowledge and institutions, although it is important to remain aware of the difference between managerial expertise as practiced in organizations, and reified in organizational handbooks and procedures, and as developed and certified in academic training programmes. The growth of MBA programmes from leading universities in Anglo-Saxon societies indicates an increase in the incorporation of formal knowledge into the training of formally certified managers but does not imply that the skills used by managers have necessarily become more research based. Instead it suggests a growing academization and credentialization of formal managerial skills in some societies, together with a possible greater distance developing between formal skills and actual managerial practices.

The greater academic control over formal training programmes in business and management since the end of the Second World War, and the corresponding growth of formal knowledge in these programmes, reflect the increasing autonomy of business schools in the leading universities from managerial elites which in turn has been reinforced by the growth in student demand for high level management education in many countries. This demand has enabled academics to insist on their standards for evaluating competence and to develop curricula which followed research interests and results rather than practical knowledge and current "best practice". Increasingly, then, advanced management education has become research based and more remote from current managerial work practices. This increase in student demand, in turn, reflects, of course, the belief that such training and certification improves job and career prospects because employers pay higher wages and provide better opportunities for MBAs and similar qualifications. This belief, and to some extent this practice, do not, though, imply that these academically controlled programmes develop useful skills from the knowledge that is taught, rather they select highly ambitious and qualified candidates for intensive training which enables employers to rely on the verdicts of elite universities (cf. Whitley *et al.*, 1981, pp. 211–216).

Furthermore, it should be noted that the expansion of high level post graduate management education has been greatest in the Anglo-Saxon countries and that others, such as Japan, have very low levels of university training in business and management. These differences reflect significant differences in dominant patterns of business organization, as well as national systems of education and training (Lane, 1989; Maurice *et al.*, 1980; 1986). For example, the greater level of diversification of economic activities controlled by large firms in the USA and UK compared to those in Germany and Japan (Clark, 1979; Kono, 1984, pp. 74–86) has encouraged the development of more general management roles at lower levels of the hierarchy in the former countries, and a greater reliance on financial skills and techniques for assessing performance across divisions and controlling diverse operations.

The rapid growth of the MBA degree as the passport to senior managerial positions in the USA over the past 3 decades, although not in all industries (Collins, 1975), is, then, partly due to the expansion of large US firms across industrial sectors and the considerable mobility of managers between them. Credentialization of managerial skills by academic programmes is clearly easier in this situation than where firms and managers tend to remain in particular sectors and managerial skills are quite firm and industry specific.

In summary, then, the highly contextual, interdependent and dynamic nature of many managerial problems, and high level of employer control over managerial tasks and role definition, severely limit the extent to which academic institutions are able to control the definition and assessment of managerial skills. The varied and changing nature of managerial structures and roles across industries, markets and countries means that employers are most unlikely to rely on the academic definition and certification of managerial competencies, and formal research-based knowledge is rarely directly applicable to practical problems. However, the rapid expansion of university business education, together with the widespread belief in formal scientific knowledge as the basis for high level expertise, have resulted in the considerable growth of management research and in its domination of curricula. The high demand for undergraduate and postgraduate management education in many western countries since the 1960s has increased researchers' autonomy from practitioners' goals and standards and enabled them to increase academic control over skill development and assessment. It has also increased the number of researchers competing for academic reputations, and their dependence on academic colleagues for recognition and promotion, which in turn has encouraged the proliferation of research specialisms in management research and the formation of new sub-fields. The extent to which researchers, and their intellectual objectives, are independent of practitioners' standards does, though, vary between these specialisms, as does their control over curricula and the value of the skills they certify in managerial labour markets. These variations are linked to the structure of the reputational organization governing researchers' work and the nature of the knowledge produced in ways that will now be discussed.

9.4 Knowledge Production and Skills Development in Management Research

In considering connections between the structure of research communities, the organization and control of training programmes and the nature of intellectual goals and standards in different areas of management studies, a central dimension is the extent of reputational control over access to key resources and rewards. This refers to the degree to which researchers depend on collegiate intellectual reputations among specialist colleagues for their contributions to collective goals in order to gain material rewards. High levels of reputational control imply strong, specialist researcher control over intellectual objectives, standards of intellectual significance and of intellectual competence. This means that scientists who seek appointments at leading institutions, tenure and promotion, as well as control over research facilities and related resources, have to convince the leaders of their specialism that their research significantly advances knowledge in terms of the field's particular intellectual goals and so gain high scientific reputations. In this sort of work organization, then, reputations mediate access to rewards (Whitley, 1984).

The most effective way of gaining reputations in sciences where such collegiate control is high is to influence other colleagues' research strategies and perceptions of dominant objectives. By redirecting or reinterpreting the prevailing intellectual focus of the field, scientists obviously have much more impact on the work of colleagues than if they simply fill in small pieces of the prevailing Kuhnian "puzzle". Equally, contributions that are directed to highly deviant goals which appear irrelevant and/or illegitimate to specialist colleagues are unlikely to lead to high reputations and so to material rewards. For example, attempts to publish studies of financial markets that do not follow the established approach based on orthodox, neo-classical economies are unlikely to be successful, at least as far as the leading journals are concerned, and even if they do become published are unlikely to make a serious impact (cf, Friend, 1973; 1977). High levels of reputational control, then, imply a strong concern with contributing to collective intellectual goals and influencing the work of specialist colleagues.

Low levels of reputational control of scientific communities, on the other hand, imply that researchers have only limited influence on the selection of intellectual priorities and competence standards. Here, reputations can be obtained for contributions to a variety of objectives and rewards obtained by reaching a large, non-specialist audience—such as management consultants and managerial elites. Rather than focusing on research topics and approaches that are expected to influence leading specialist colleague/competitors, scientists in these sorts of fields are able to undertake research which could be of interest to a wider range of audiences and seek reputations for contributions to a variety of goals. Dependence on particular fellow specialists for access to resources and rewards is clearly lower here.

Variations in the degree of reputational control over intellectual standards and access to resources have significant consequences for the organization and type of research that is carried out in different scientific fields. In turn, they are substantially affected by differences in a number of contextual factors, of which a key one in management studies and other research fields connected to the development and certification of practical skills is the extent of academic control over the skill definition and assessment, together with the overall value of academically certified skills in the labour market and their privileged access to highly regarded activities and functions. The key relations between these contextual variables, the degree of reputational control and the organization of research are summarized in Figure 9:1 and will now be briefly discussed.

Increasing reputational control over intellectual standards of significance and competence implies increasing dependence on the verdicts and assessments of specialist colleagues. This in turn encourages the standardization of research approaches and techniques as scientists focus on convincing the specific audience of specialists of the merits of their research and have to demonstrate their competence by using the established procedures in the appropriate way. Contributions based on methods from other fields or more general discursive approaches will not be publishable in this situation. Thus, research skills are more uniform and specialized in sciences where reputational control is high, and relatively remote from everyday competencies since communication is limited to particular colleagues. Reputational con-

Figure 9.1 *Connections between contextual factors, reputational control and the organisation of research.*

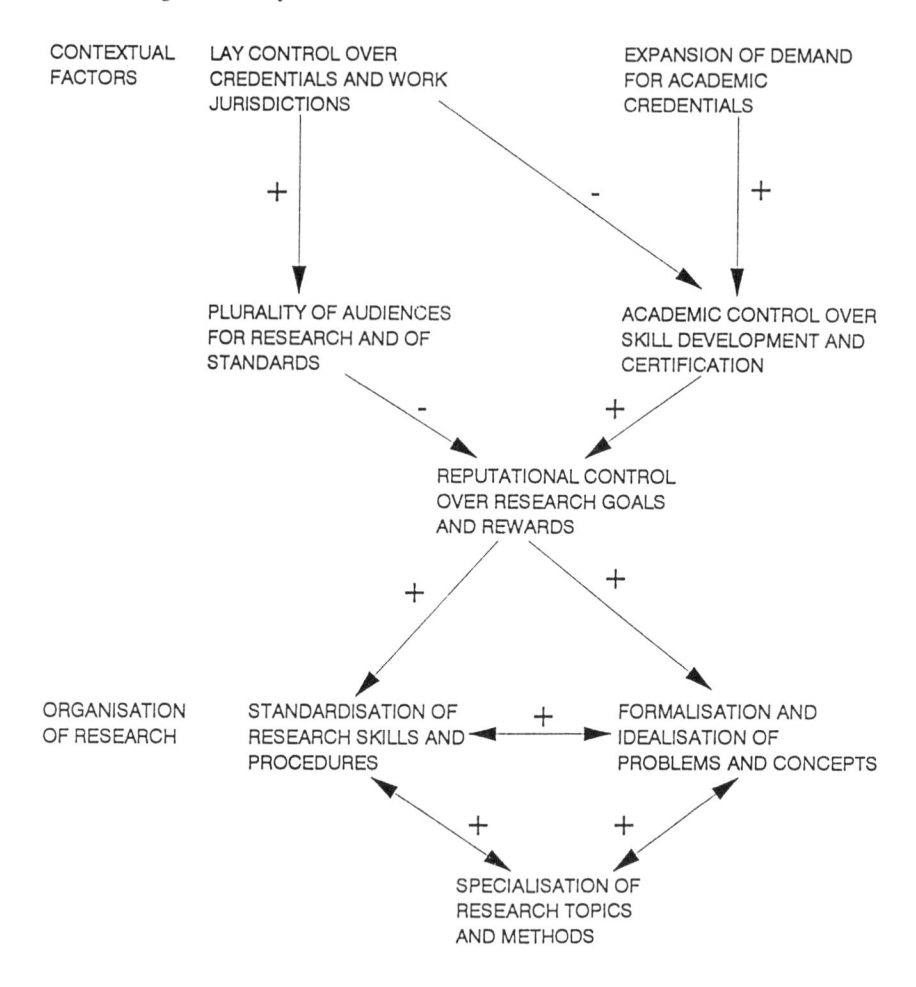

```
CONTEXTUAL    LAY CONTROL OVER                    EXPANSION OF DEMAND
FACTORS       CREDENTIALS AND WORK                FOR ACADEMIC
              JURISDICTIONS                       CREDENTIALS

                  +              -                    +
                  ↓                                    ↓
              PLURALITY OF AUDIENCES            ACADEMIC CONTROL OVER
              FOR RESEARCH AND OF               SKILL DEVELOPMENT AND
              STANDARDS                         CERTIFICATION
                         -              +
                          ↘            ↙
                      REPUTATIONAL CONTROL
                      OVER RESEARCH GOALS
                      AND REWARDS
                         +        +
                        ↙          ↘
ORGANISATION    STANDARDISATION OF    +    FORMALISATION AND
OF RESEARCH     RESEARCH SKILLS AND  ↔     IDEALISATION OF
                PROCEDURES                 PROBLEMS AND CONCEPTS
                         +        +
                          ↘      ↙
                      SPECIALISATION OF
                      RESEARCH TOPICS
                      AND METHODS
```

trol seems to be greater, for example, in financial economies and operations research than in, say, strategic management research, and so research methods are more standardized, esoteric and formally taught in those areas (cf. Churchman, 1970; Klamer and Colander, 1990; Whitley, 1986*a*).

Greater dependence on one's colleagues also leads to a specialization of research topics and issues around currently important concerns. This in turn implies a growing distance between central research problems and broader issues which might be of more general interest as researchers become more internally focused. Since reputations and rewards depend on contributing to specialist intellectual goals, the nature of research problems and approaches become more specialized and remote from everyday concerns as reputational control increases. Again the contrast of research topics in financial economies and OR with those in strategic management illustrates this point (cf. Whitley, 1986a; 1988b).

The standardization of research skills and specialization of problems and issues are often associated with considerable abstraction and formalization of phenomena and their properties in fields with high levels of reputational control. This is because researchers seeking intellectual autonomy and collective control over resources and reputations typically try to establish distinctive specialist identities on the basis of pursuing separate intellectual goals and/or using novel skills and procedures. This involves demarcating problems and methods both from everyday concerns and from related scientific ones which is facilitated by formulating them in abstract and idealized ways. Additionally, reputational control is clearly easier to maintain and reproduce when phenomena and techniques are highly formalized and abstract since research competence can then be readily defined and assessed and the boundaries of the field be clearly specified and policed. Conversely, the closer are descriptions of phenomena and research approaches to everyday language and understandings, the more difficult is it to distinguish between specialist skills and contributions from those of non-specialists and maintain distinctive intellectual identities.

This tendency to abstraction and formalization is reinforced by strong competition over theoretical contributions in fields where key resources are scarce and/or expensive and control over them is concentrated in the hands of the reputational elite. In high energy physics and astronomy, for example, access to key experimental apparatus is rationed because of its cost and applicants for machine time have to demonstrate the intellectual merits of their project in terms of its likely contribution to theoretical goals (Collins, 1975, pp. 506–514; Gaston, 1973). This means that the theoretical implications of research projects are more systematically discussed in such fields and are the focus of more sustained debate than in sciences where mutual dependence and competition is less intense. Generally, the more attention is focused on the theoretical issues and significance of research results, we would expect greater concern with the precision and formalization of theoretical models, albeit not perhaps always to the extent of theoretical physics. This concern with theoretical clarity and formalisms further encourages abstraction and idealization of phenomena and systems as scientists compete for reputations by emphasizing the general, theoretical significance of their work at the expense of its descriptive adequacy.

While no field in management studies approaches the competitive intensity of high energy physics, or even the concern with theoretical issues of orthodox economics, perhaps financial economics comes closest to this type of reputational organization and its central focus on theoretical analyses of idealized systems (Whitley, 1986a; 1986b). In contrast, work in operations research seems less concerned with theoretical debates and contributions rarely spell out in detail their theoretical implications or seek to dominate research agenda, despite the high degree of skill standardization and formalization (cf. Dando & Bennett, 1981). Perhaps this is due to the widespread availability of posts and relative cheapness of research resources.

High levels of reputational control imply considerable academic control over curricula and training programmes because they could not be sustained in situations where practitioner-based knowledge was regarded as a valid foundation for skill development. In this case, researchers would legitimately seek reputations from practitioner elites by synthesizing and disseminating current "best practices" to a general audience rather than concentrating on specialist goals and priorities. Ensuring that skill development programmes are based on formal research dependent knowledge both justifies academic research and devalues lay forms of knowledge and, by extension, those who seek recognition from lay elites. Reputational control thus depends on, and reinforces, academic control over curricula and certification standards.

The major influences on the degree of reputational control over goals and rewards in fields closely connected to the development of practical skills are, of course, the importance of lay control over skill definition and credentialization, and the related plurality of legitimate audiences for research results and variety of intellectual standards, and the converse degree of academic autonomy over curriculum development and skill certification. As already mentioned, the latter has been greatly enhanced by the expansion of student demand for management education so that even where practitioner control over practical skills remains high, academics can still develop distinctive research goals and insist on reputational standards when making appointment and promotion decisions, as in the case of English accounting departments (Geddes, 1992). Where, on the other hand, practitioners and other groups are legitimate audiences for academic researchers to seek reputations from, obviously the extent of collegiate control over research goals and approaches will be less, and researchers could publish in practitioner oriented journals without losing their academic standing.

In general, the extent of reputational control over research goals and standards in these skill related fields reflects the balance of these divergent contextual factors. This balance changes the result of managerial fashions and labour market developments, together with broader developments in education and training systems and major social institutions. Because student demand is ultimately dependent on employer demand for their credentials, curricula and skills can never become completely divorced from the labour market, and the overall evaluation of the training process made by managerial recruiters. Thus, knowledge production and evaluation in these fields is always more open to multiple audiences and criteria of significance than where researchers have been able to gain more control over key resources. Consequently, management research fields will remain relatively pluralistic and, at least rhetorically, maintain a connection with currently topical managerial problems and issues. Individual subfields do, of course, vary in their closeness to managerial audiences, and so in the extent of reputational control over goals and rewards, but business and management studies as a whole will continue to reflect the different pressures of lay elites and fluctuating labour market demand, on the one hand, and student demand and the desire to gain academic autonomy and prestige on the other hand.

9.5 Conclusions

This brief discussion of formal knowledge and management education has emphasized the varied and changing nature of connections between research-based knowledge, the development and certification of technical expertise and control over work jurisdictions and practices. This variety occurs both across fields, and historical periods as well as between countries, and clearly demonstrates the inadequacy of conventional accounts of applied science and of the new "paradigm" of business education and management of science. The role of new formal knowledge produced by universities and research organizations in developing practical expertise is highly interdependent with the ways in which that expertise is controlled and certified, and with the ways that jurisdiction over different problem solving activities is organized. These patterns differ considerably across nation states and between areas of expertise, and there are no good reasons to expect them all to converge on a single model of "scientification". Indeed, there are substantive grounds for doubting that complex problems in uncertain situations are amenable to procedures derived from formal scientific knowledge. This is especially so for senior managerial problems in market economies.

The analysis of how scientific knowledge has affected high level practical skills and work practices in management, then, requires consideration of the variety of types of research based knowledge and their connections to everyday practical understandings, of the institutions governing skill definition, development and certification and of the organization and control of managerial work in different sectors and countries. This last phenomenon, in turn, reflects more general patterns of business organization which vary significantly between institutional contexts, as the recent success of East Asian economies so strikingly demonstrates (Redding, 1990; Whitley, 1992). It therefore implies the integration of studies of knowledge production and the organization of research, of systems of skill development and certification and of the organization of high level expert work. The sociology of scientific knowledge and institutions, the sociology of the professions and technical expertise and the analysis of managerial work and business organization are all important contributing fields for this task. Additionally, it is important to note that such an analysis requires the analytical separation of formal knowledge from education and training, from skill certification and from work jurisdiction and practices. In order to examine the different ways in which knowledge, skills and practices are related, they clearly need to be first distinguished in a theoretically coherent manner. In this chapter I have suggested some of the ways in which these phenomena are interconnected and the factors responsible for them as a preliminary attempt at such an examination.

References

Abbott, A., 1988, *The System of Professions*, Chicago, IL: University of Chicago Press.

Ackoff, R. L., 1979, "The Future of Operational Research is Past", *Journal of the Operational Research Society*, 30, No. 2, pp. 93–104.

Atkinson, P. A., 1981, *The Clinical Experience: the Construction and Reconstruction of Medical Reality*, Farnborough: Gower.

Auerbach, J. S., 1971, "Enmity and Amity: Law Teachers and Practitioners, 1900–22", *Perspectives in American History*, 5, pp. 551–601.

Bhaskar, R., 1975, *A Realist Theory of Science*, Leeds: Leeds Books.

Böhme, G., Daele, W. van den & Krohn, W., 1978, "The 'Scientification' of Technology", In: Krohn, W., Layton, E. T. & Weingart, P. (eds.), *The Dynamics of Science and Technology. Social Values, Technical Norms and Scientific Criteria in the Development of Knowledge* (Sociology of the Sciences Yearbook 2), Dordrecht: Reidel, pp. 291–250.

Böhme, G. & Stehr, N., 1986, "The Growing Impact of Scientific Knowledge on Social Relations", In: Böhme, G. & Stehr, N. (eds.), *The Knowledge Society. The Growing Impact of Scientific Knowledge on Social Relations* (Sociology of the Sciences Yearbook 10), Dordrecht: Reidel, pp. 7–29.

Bonder, S. C., 1979, "Changing the Future of Operations Research", *Operations Research*, 27, No. 2, pp. 209–224.

Caldwell, B., 1982, *Beyond Positivism*, London: Allen and Unwin.

Calvert, M. A., 1967, *The Mechanical Engineer in America, 1830–1900*, Baltimore, MD: John Hopkins University Press.

Churchman, C. W., 1970, "Operations Research as a Profession", *Management Science*, 17, No. 2, pp. B37-B53.

Cicourel, A., 1986, "The Reproduction of Objective Knowledge: Commonsense Reasoning in Medical Decision-making", In: Böhme, G. & Stehr, N. (eds.), *The Knowledge Society. The Growing Impact of Scientific Knowledge on Social Relations* (Sociology of the Sciences Yearbook 10), Dordrecht: Reidel, pp. 87–122.

Clark, R., 1979, *The Japanese Company*, New Haven, CT: Yale University Press.

Collins, R., 1975, *Conflict Sociology*, New York: Academic Press.

Dando, M. R. & Bennett P. G., 1981, "A Kuhnian Crisis in Management Science?", *Journal of the Operational Research Society*, 32, No. 2, pp. 91–103.

Diesing, P., 1982, *Science and Ideology in the Policy Sciences*, New York: Aldine.

Divall, C., 1991, "Fundamental Science versus Design: Employers and Engineering Studies in British Universities, 1935–1976", *Minerva*, 29, No. 2, pp. 167–194.

Eichner, A. S., 1983, "Why Economics is not yet a Science", In: Eichner, A. S. (ed.), *Why Economics is not yet a Science*, London: Macmillan, pp. 205–241.

Friend, I., 1973, "Mythodology in Finance", *Journal of Finance*, 28, No. 2, pp. 257–282.

— 1977, "Recent Developments in Finance", *Journal of Banking and Finance*, 1, October, pp. 103–117.
Gaston, J., 1973, *Originality and Competition in Sciences*, Chicago, IL: Chicago University Press.
Geddes, B., 1992, "Explaining the Gap? A Sociological Analysis of the Relationship between Research and Practice in Accounting", *Paper Presented to an EIASM Workshop on "The Relationship between Accounting Research and Accounting Practice"*, Manchester, June 1992.
Hales, C., 1986, "What Do Managers Do?", *Journal of Management Studies*, 23, January, pp. 88–115.
Harré, R. & Secord, P. F., 1982, *The Explanation of Social Behaviour*, Oxford: Blackwell.
Klamer, A. & Colander, D., 1990, *The Making of an Economist*, Boulder: Westview.
Kono, T., 1984, *Strategy and Structure of Japanese Enterprise*, London: Macmillan.
Kuhn, T. S., 1977, "The Essential Tension: Tradition and Innovation in Scientific Research", In: Kuhn, T. S., *The Essential Tension*, Chicago, IL: University of Chicago Press, pp. 225–239.
Lane, C., 1989, *Management and Labour in Europe*, Aldershot: Edward Elgar.
Lane, R. E., 1966, "The Decline of Politics and Ideology in a Knowledgeable Society", *American Sociological Review*, 31, No. 5, pp. 649–662.
Lindblom, C., 1990, *Inquiry and Change*, New Haven, CT: Yale University Press.
Locke, R. R., 1985, "Business Education in Germany: Past Systems and Current Practice", *Business History Review*, 59, Summer, pp. 232–253.
— 1989, *Management and Higher Education Since 1940*, Cambridge: Cambridge University Press.
Maurice, M., Sorge, A. & Warner, W., 1980, "Societal Differences in Organising Manufacturing Units", *Organization Studies*, 1, pp. 59–86.
Maurice, M., Sellier, F. & Silvestre, J.-J., 1986, *The Social Foundations of Industrial Power*, Boston, MA: MIT Press.
Penrose, E., 1980, *The Theory of the Growth of the Firm*, Oxford: Basil Blackwell (2. ed., 1. ed. 1959).
Redlich, F., 1957, "Academic Education for Business: Its Development and the Contribution of Ignaz Jastrow (1856–1937). In Commemoration of the Hundredth Anniversary of Jastrow's Birth", *Business History Review*, 31, Spring, pp. 35–91.
Redding, G., 1990, *The Spirit of Chinese Capitalism*, Berlin: de Gruyter.
Sayer, A., 1984, *Method in Social Science*, London: Hutchinson.
Seely, B. E., 1984, "The Scientific Mystique in Engineering. Highway Research at the Bureau of Public Roads", *Technology and Culture*, 25, No.4, pp. 798–831.
Smiddy, H. F. & Naum, L., 1954, "Evolution of a 'Science of Managing' in America", *Management Science*, 1, No. 1, pp. 1–31.
Smith, K. V. & Goudzwaard, M. B., 1970, "Survey of Investment Management: Teaching versus Practice", *Journal of Finance*, 25, No. 2, pp. 329–47.
Solomon, E., 1966, "What Should We Teach in a Course in Business Finance?", *Journal of Finance*, 21, No. 2, pp. 411–415.
Spender, J. C., 1989, *Industrial Recipes*, Oxford: Blackwell.
Vincenti, W., 1984, "Technological Knowledge without Science. The Innovation of Flush Riveting in American Airplanes", *Technology and Culture*, 25, No. 3, pp. 540–576.
Weingart, P., 1978, "The Relation between Science and Technology—A Sociological Explanation", In: Krohn, W. *et al.* (eds.), *The Dynamics of Science and Technology*, Dordrecht: Reidel, pp. 251–286.
Whalley, P., 1986, *The Social Production of Technical Work*, London: Macmillan.

Whitley, R., 1984, *The Intellectual and Social Organisation of the Sciences*, Oxford: Oxford University Press.

— 1986a, "The Transformation of Business Finance into Financial Economics: The Roles of Academic Expansion and Changes in U. S. Capital Markets", *Accounting, Organizations and Society*, 11, No. 2, pp. 171–192.

— 1986b, "The Structure and Context of Economics as a Scientific Field", *Research in the History of Economic Thought and Methodology*, 4, Greenwich, CT: JAI Press, pp. 179–209.

— 1987, "Taking Firms Seriously as Economic Actors: Towards a Sociology of Firm Behaviour", *Organization Studies*, 8, No. 2, pp. 125–147.

— 1988a, "The Transformation of Expertise by New Knowledge: Contingencies and Limits to Skill Scientification", *Social Science Information*, 27, No. 3, pp. 391–420.

— 1988b, "The Management Sciences and Managerial Skills", *Organization Studies*, 9, No. 1, pp. 47–68.

— 1989, "On The Nature of Managerial Tasks and Skills. Their Distinguishing Characteristics and Organization", *Journal of Management Studies*, 26, No. 3, pp. 209–224.

Whitley, R., 1992, *Business Systems in East Asia*, London: Sage.

Whitley, R., Thomas, A. & Marceau, J., 1981, *Masters of Business?*, London: Tavistock.

Willmott, H., 1987, "Studying Managerial Work: A Critique and a Proposal", *Journal of Management Studies*, 24, No. 3, pp. 249–270.

Bibliography

Abbott, A., 1988, *The System of Professions*, Chicago, IL: University of Chicago Press.
Ackoff, R. L., 1979, "The Future of Operational Research is Past", *Journal of the Operational Research Society*, 30, No. 2, pp. 93–104.
Adler, N. J., 1986, *International Dimensions of Organizational Behavior*, Boston, MA: PWS-Kent.
Afanasjew, V. G., 1969, *Wissenschaftliche Leitung der Gesellschaft*, Berlin (DDR): Staatsverlag der DDR.
Albach, H., 1990, "Business Administration: History in German-Speaking Countries", In: Grochla, E. et al., *Handbook of German Business Management*, Stuttgart: Poeschel, pp. 246–270.
Amdam, 1993, *For egen regning. BI og den økonomisk-administrative utdanningen 1943–1993* (The history of the Norwegian School of Management 1943–1993), Oslo: Universitetsforlaget.
— 1994, "Foreign Influence on the Education of Norwegian Managers before World War II" to be published in *Business History*.
Amdam, R. P. & Mordt, G., 1992, "Utdanningskonjunkturer" (Educational Cycles), *Norwegian School of Management, Research Report*.
Annerstedt, C., 1912, *Upsala universitets historia, Bihang 3* (History of Uppsala University, Appendix 3), Uppsala: Almqvist & Wiksell.
— 1913, *Upsala universitets historia, Band 3:1* (History of Uppsala University, Volume 3:1), Uppsala: Almqvist & Wiksell.
— 1914, *Upsala universitets historia, Band 3:2* (History of Uppsala University, Volume 3:2), Uppsala: Almqvist & Wiksell.
Aoki, M., 1990, "Towards an Economic Model of the Japanese Firm", *Journal of Economic Literature*, 28, March, pp. 1–27.
Arnold, H., Borchert, H. & Schmidt, J., 1956, *Ökonomik der sozialistischen Industrie in der Deutschen Demokratischen Republik*, Berlin (DDR): Die Wirtschaft.
Atkinson, P. A., 1981, *The Clinical Experience: the Construction and Reconstruction of Medical Reality*, Farnborough: Gower.
Auerbach, J. S., 1971, "Enmity and Amity: Law Teachers and Practitioners, 1900–22", *Perspectives in American History*, 5, pp. 551–601.
Auras, H. H. & Braβ, H., 1962, "Zum Verhältnis zwischen der politischen Ökonomie des Sozialismus und den Fachökonomiken", *Wirtschaftswissenschaft*, 10, No. 10, pp. 1533–1537.
Autorenkollektiv, 1970, *Die Grundlagen der sozialistischen Wirtschaftsführung in den Werken Lenins und ihre aktuelle Bedeutung*, Berlin (DDR): Dietz.
— 1973/80, *Sozialistische Betriebswirtschaftslehre*, Berlin (DDR): Die Wirtschaft.
— 1986, *Pädagogisch-psychologische Grundlagen der sozialistischen Leitungstätigkeit* (9th ed.), Berlin (DDR): Die Wirtschaft.
— 1987, *Intensivierung-Leitung-Neuerungsprozesse*, Berlin (DDR): Die Wirtschaft.
— 1988, *Das geistige Potential in den Betrieben*, Berlin (DDR): Dietz Verlag.
Bakke, E. W., 1959, *A Norwegian Contribution to Executive Development*, Bergen: Norwegian School of Economics and Business Administration.

Becker, H. A., 1968, *Management als beroep: Kenmerken van de Managersgroepering in Sociologisch Perspectief*, Den Haag: Martinus Nijhoff.

Bedriftsøkonomen, 1952, 14, No. 9b.

Bedriftsøkonomisk Institutt 1946, *Studieplan for 1946/47*, Oslo: Bedriftsøkonomisk Institutt

Behrens, F., 1949, "Einige Grundprobleme des betrieblichen Rechnungswesens in der Wirtschaftsplanung", *Deutsche Finanzwirtschaft*, 3, No. 6, pp. 218–224.

— 1950, "Ist die Betriebswirtschaftslehre eine Wissenschaft?", *Deutsche Finanzwirtschaft*, 4, No. 2, pp. 57–60.

— 1952, *Zur Methode der politischen Ökonomie*, Berlin (DDR): Akad.-Verlag.

— 1956, "Fragen der Ökonomie und Technik", *Wirtschaftswissenschaft*, 4, Sonderheft 1, pp. 1–5.

— 1957, "Zum Problem der Ausnutzung ökonomischer Gesetze in der Übergangsperiode", *Wirtschaftswissenschaft*, 5, Sonderheft 3, pp. 105–140.

Behrman, J. N. & Levin, R. I., 1984, "Are Business Schools Doing their Job?", *Harvard Business Review*, 62, January/February, pp. 140–147.

Beinum, H. J. van, 1963, *Een Organisatie in Beweging: Een sociaal-psychologisch veldexperiment bij de postcheque—en girodienst*, Leiden: H.E. Stenfert-Kroese N.V.

Beinum, H. J. J. van, Gils, M. R. van & Verhagen, E.J., 1968, *Taakontwerp en Werkorganisatie*, Den Haag: COP-SER.

Benary, A., 1957, "Zu Grundproblemen der politischen Ökonomie des Sozialismus in der Übergangsperiode", *Wirtschaftswissenschaft*, 5, Sonderheft 3, pp. 62–94.

Berch, A., 1746, *Sätt, at igenom politisk arithmetica utröna länders och rikens hushåldning* (Means to Ascertain the Economy of Countries and States through Political Arithmetics), Uppsala: Ferrner.

— 1747, *Inledning til almänna hushålningen, innefattande grunder til politie, oeconomie och cameral wetenskaperne [...]* (Introduction to General Administration Including the Basis for Political, Economic and Fiscal Sciences), Uppsala: Ferrner.

— 1749, *Tal om den proportion, som de studerande ärfordra til de ledige beställningar i riket, hållet för den academiska ungdomen i Upsala [...] då han afträdde rectoratet D. 17 junii 1749. Öfversatt från det latinska [...] af H. L.* (Speech about the Proportion between the Number Students and Employment Openings in the Country, Made to the Academic Youth in Uppsala when he Resigned from the Vice-Chancellorship on 17 June 1749. Translated from the Latin [...] by H. L.) Uppsala: Akad. Program.

— 1759, "Anmärkningar öfver de svenska plogar" (Remarks on Swedish Ploughs), I: *Vetenskaps-Akademiens Handlingar*, Stockholm: Kungl. Vetenskapsakademien.

— 1761, *Quod ad illustrem*, Uppsala: Akad. Program.

— 1763, *Ut florens bonarum artium*, Uppsala: Akad. Program.

Berch, A. & Westbeck, G., 1747, *Tankeförsök om särskilda näringars idkande* (Intellectual Efforts on the Practising of Certain Industries), Uppsala.

Berenschot, B. W., 1950, *Welke betekenis kan de studie van de wetenschappelijke bedrijfsorganisatie hebben voor de verhoging van de arbeidsproduktiviteit*, Rede uitgesproken bij de aanvaarding van het ambt van buitengewoon hoogleraar aan de Technische hogeschool te Delft, Delft, 11 October.

Berg, G., 1979, "Anders Berch—en forskar- och lärargestalt i 1700-talets Uppsala" (Anders Berch—A Teacher and Researcher in the Eighteenth Century Uppsala), In: *Tal över blandade ämnen*, Collegium Curiosorum Novum årsbok 1977–78, Uppsala: Carmina, pp. 7–25.

Berg, I., 1970, *Education and Jobs: The Great Training Robbery*, New York: Praeger.
Berger, P. L. & Luckmann, T., 1966, *The Social Construction of Reality: A Treatise in the Sociology of Knowledge*, Garden City, NY: Doubleday.
Berger, W., 1949, "Karl Marx als Kritiker der modernen Betriebswirtschaftslehre", *Deutsche Finanzwirtschaft*, 3, No. 10, pp. 249–253.
— 1957, "Wie soll die Lehre von der Leitung sozialistischer Betriebe aussehen?", *Einheit*, 12, No. 8, pp. 1014–1021.
Berglund, H., 1933, *Handelshögskolan i Göteborg. Tioårsöversikt 1923–1933* (Gothenburg School of Economics. An Overview for the Ten Years 1923–1933), Göteborg: Handelshögskolan i Göteborg.
Berglund, H. & Grönfors, K. (eds.), 1977, *Handelshögskolan i Göteborg 1923–1971. En minnesbok* (The Gothenburg School of Economics 1923–1971. A Memorial Publication), Göteborg: Västsvenska Akademibokhandeln.
Bertels, K., 1982, "Hoe arbeid en sociologie elkaar niet kregen; Nederland 1820–1920", *Grafiet*, 2, pp. 72–103.
Bhaskar, R., 1975, *A Realist Theory of Science*, Leeds: Leeds Books.
Bierens de Haan, J., 1952, *Van Oeconomische Tak tot Nederlandsche Maatschappij voor Nijverheid en Handel 1777–1952*, Haarlem: Tjeenk Willink.
Blaug, M., 1976, "The Empirical Status of Human Capital Theory: A Slightly Jaundiced Survey", *Journal of Economic Literature*, 14, No. 3, pp. 827–855.
Bloemen, E. S. A., 1988, *Scientific Management in Nederland 1900–1930*, Amsterdam: NEHA.
— 1990, "Bedrijfsadviseurs in het interbellum; het Adviesbureau voor Bedrijfsorganisatie van ir. J.M. Louwerse, 1925–1938", *Jaarboek voor de Geschiedenis van Bedrijf en Techniek*, deel 7, Utrecht: Stichting JBGTB, pp. 191–219.
Bolin, E. & Dahlberg, L., 1975, *Dagens storföretagsledare* (Top Managers of Today), Stockholm: SNS.
Bonder, S. C., 1979, "Changing the Future of Operations Research", *Operations Research*, 27, No. 2, pp. 209–224.
Boone, P. C., 1954, *Mens en Medemens in het Bedrijf*, Bussum: Voorhoeve.
Borch, K. H., 1961, "Elements of a Theory of Insurance", *Journal of Insurance*, 28, September, pp. 35–43.
— 1962, "Equilibrium in a Reinsurance Market", *Econometrica*, 30, No. 3, pp. 424–444.
— 1968, *The Economics of Uncertainty*, Princeton NJ: Princeton University Press.
Brands, J., 1963, *Een halve eeuw bedrijfseconomie 1913–1963*, Leiden: Stenfert Kroese.
Brandt, E., 1986, "Minervas sønner og døtre" (Minerva's Sons and Daughters), *NAVF's utredningsinstitutt Notat 5/86*, Oslo: NAVFs utredningsinstitutt.
Brevoord, C. & Kamp, J. J., 1971, *Bedrijfskundig Journaal, in opdracht van de Commissie opvoering Produktiviteit van de Sociaal-Economische Raad*, Leiden: Stenfert Kroese.
Brown, J. & Rose, M. (eds.), 1993, *Entrepreneurship and the Growth of the Firm*, Manchester: Manchester University Press.
Byrt, W. (ed.), 1989, *Management Education. An International Survey*, London: Routledge.
Böhme, G., Daele, W. van den & Krohn, W., 1978, "The 'Scientification' of Technology", In: Krohn, W., Layton, E. T. & Weingart, P. (eds.), *The Dynamics of Science and Technology. Social Values, Technical Norms and Scientific Criteria in the Development of Knowledge* (Sociology of the Sciences Yearbook 2), Dordrecht: Reidel, pp. 291–250.

Böhme, G. & Stehr, N., 1986, "The Growing Impact of Scientific Knowledge on Social Relations", In: Böhme, G. & Stehr, N. (eds.), *The Knowledge Society. The Growing Impact of Scientific Knowledge on Social Relations* (Sociology of the Sciences Yearbook 10), Dordrecht: Reidel, pp. 7–29.

Böhring, G. & Ladensack, K., 1986, *Wie Leiter den wissenschaftlich-technischen Fortschritt bewältigen*, Berlin (DDR): Dietz Verlag.

Bonder, S. C., 1979, "Changing the Future of Operations Research", *Operations Research*, 27, No. 2, pp. 209–224.

Caldwell, B., 1982, *Beyond Positivism, economic methodology in the 20th century*, London: Allen and Unwin.

Calvert, M. A., 1967, *The Mechanical Engineer in America, 1830–1900*, Baltimore, MD: John Hopkins University Press.

Carlson, S., 1983, *Studier utan slut ekonomi, företag, människor* (Studies without an End), Stockholm: SNS.

Celsius, A. & Berch, A. 1731, *De felicitate patriæ per oecconomiam promovenda*, Uppsala (diss.).

Celsius, A. & Råfelt, J., 1732, *De felicitate civili per philosophiam comparanda*, Uppsala (diss.).

Chandler, A. D. Jr., 1977, *The Visible Hand, the management revolution in American Business*, Cambridge, MA: Harvard University Press Belknap Press.

— with the assistance of Takashi Hikiono, 1990, *Scale and Scope the dynamics of industrial capitalism*, Cambridge, MA: Harvard University Press Belknap Press.

Cheit, E. F., 1975, *The Useful Arts and the Liberal Tradition*, New York: McGraw-Hill.

— 1985, "Business School and their Critics", *California Management Review*, 27, Spring, pp. 43–62.

Churchman, C. W., 1970, "Operations Research as a Profession", *Management Science*, 17, No. 2, pp. B37-B53.

Cicourel, A., 1986, "The Reproduction of Objective Knowledge: Commonsense Reasoning in Medical Decision-making", In: Böhme, G. & Stehr, N. (eds.), *The Knowledge Society. The Growing Impact of Scientific Knowledge on Social Relations* (Sociology of the Sciences Yearbook 10), Dordrecht: Reidel, pp. 87–122.

Clark, B. R., 1983, *The Higher Education System*, Berkeley, CA: University of California Press.

— 1987, "Introduction" and "9. Conclusions", In: Clark, B. R. (ed.), *The Academic Profession*, Berkeley and Los Angeles, CA: University of California Press, pp. 1–9 and pp. 371–399.

— 1979, *The Japanese Company*, New Haven, CT: Yale University Press.

Collins, R., 1971, "Functional and Conflict Theories of Educational Stratification", *American Sociological Review*, 36, December, pp. 1002–1019.

— with a contrib. by Joan Annett, 1975, *Conflict Sociology, Towards an Explanatory Science*, New York: Academic Press.

Conrad, P. & Pieper, R., 1990, "Human Resource Management in the Federal Republic of Germany", In: Pieper, R. (ed.), *Human Resource Management—An International Comparison*, Berlin & New York: de Gruyter, pp. 109–139.

Constable, J. & McCormack, R., 1987, *The Making of British Managers*, Northants: British Institute of Management.

Corcoran, M., 1979, "Who Gets Ahead: A Summary", In: Jenks, C., et. al., *Who Gets Ahead? The Determinants of Economic Success in America*, New York: Basic Books, pp. 213–230.

Coward, D., 1944, *Kostnadsregning i industribedrifter* (Cost Accounting in Industrial Firms), Oslo: Aschehoug & Co.

— 1953, *Økonomisk risiko og usikkerhet* (Economic Risk and Uncertainty), Bergen: Skrifter fra Norges Handelshøyskole.
— 1980, *Studier i bedriftsøkonomi. Utvalgte artikler av professor dr. philos. Dag Coward* (Studies in Business Administration. Selected Papers by Professor Doctor Dag Coward), Bergen: Norges Handelshøyskole.
Cyert, R. M. & March, J. G., 1963, *A Behavioral Theory of the Firm*, Englewood Cliffs, NJ: Prentice-Hall.
Dael, J. van, 1938, *De geschiedenis der psychotechniek van het bedrijfsleven*, Public Lecture, Nijmegen/Utrecht.
Dam, C. van, 1991, "Vijftig jaar bedrijfskunde, 1965–2015", *Bedrijfskunde*, No. 63, pp. 4–12.
— (ed.),1989, *Bedrijfskunde op Weg naar 1990*, Deventer: Kluwer Bedrijfswetenschapen.
Dam, C. van, Keizer, J. A. & Kempen, P. M., 1990, "Living Apart Together?: Over de spanning tussen theorie en praktijk in de bedrijfskunde", *Bedrijfskunde*, No. 62, pp. 173–187.
Dando, M. R. & Bennett P. G., 1981, "A Kuhnian Crisis in Management Science?", *Journal of the Operational Research Society*, 32, No. 2, pp. 91–103.
Diesing, P., 1982, *Science and Ideology in the Policy Sciences*, New York: Aldine.
Divall, C., 1991, "Fundamental Science versus Design: Employers and Engineering Studies in British Universities, 1935–1976", *Minerva*, 29, No. 2, pp. 167–194.
Doorn, J. A. A. van, 1966, *Organisatie en maatschappij: sociologische opstellen*, Leiden: Stenfert Kroese.
Duncan, O. D., 1961, "A Socioeconomic Index for All Occupations", In: Reiss, A. J. Jr, *Occupations and Social Status*, New York: The Free Press of Glencoe Inc., pp. 109–138.
The Economist, 1991, "Management Education", March 2, p. 2.
Economist Intelligent Unit, 1990, *The Quest for the International Manager, A Survey of Global Human Resource Strategies*. Ashbridge: Ashbridge Management Research Group.
Eichner, A. S., 1983, "Why Economics is not yet a Science", In: Eichner, A. S. (ed.), *Why Economics is not yet a Science*, London: Macmillan, pp. 205–241.
Elteren, M. C. M. van, 1987, "Tussen opvoering van arbeidsproduktiviteit en ethiek; de receptie van de "human relations"-benadering in Nederland (1945–1960)", *Psychologie en Maatschappij*, 41, pp. 339–353.
— 1989, "Arbeidssociatrie en bedrijfsleven in Nederland", *Sociale Wetenschappen*, 30, pp. 239–277.
Engwall, L. (ed.), 1980, *Företagsekonomins rötter. Några bidrag till en företagsekonomisk doktrinhistoria* (The Roots of Business Administration. Some Contributions to a History of the Business Administration Doctrine), Lund: Studentlitteratur.
— 1992, *Mercury Meets Minerva*, Oxford: Pergamon Press.
Eucken, W., 1947, *Grundlagen der Nationalökonomie*, Godesberg: Küpper.
Ewing, D. W., 1990, *Inside the Harvard Business School: Strategies and Lessons of America's Leading School of Business*, New York: Times Books.
Ferrner, B., 1776, *Åminnelse-Tal, öfver [...] Herr Doctor Anders Berch, hållet [...] för Kongl. Vetenskaps-academien den 20 Januari 1776* (Speech in Commemoration of [...] Mr. Dr. Anders Berch, Made [...] to the Royal Academy of Sciences on 20 January 1776), Stockholm: Kungl. Vetenskapsakademien.
Feyter, C. de, 1986, "Amerika en de Nederlandse economische wetenschap", *Grafiet*, 6, pp. 150–167.

Fishgrund, T. (ed.), 1990, *The Insider's Guide to the Top Ten Business Schools*, Boston: Little, Brown (4th ed.).
Fortuyn, W. S. P., 1983, *Kerncijfers 1945–1983 van de Sociaal-Economische Ontwikkeling in Nederland: Expansie en Stagnatie*, Kluwer: Deventer.
Frankfurter Allgemeine Zeitung, October 31, 1991.
Friedrich, G., 1957, "Probleme der staatlichen Leitung unserer Industrie", *Einheit*, 12, No. 9, pp. 1134–1140.
Friedrich, G., & Gerisch, R., 1966, "Die Information als Führungsaufgabe in der sozialistischen Industrie", *Wirtschaftswissenschaft*, 14, No. 1, pp. 44–63.
Friedrich, G., Richter, H., Stein, H. & Wittich, G., (eds.), 1987, *Leitung der sozialistischen Wirtschaft. Lehrbuch*, Berlin (DDR): Die Wirtschaft.
Friedrich, W. & Voβ, P. (eds.), 1988, *Sozialpsychologie für die Praxis*, Berlin (DDR): Deutscher Verlag der Wissenschaften.
Friend, I., 1973, "Mythodology in Finance", *Journal of Finance*, 28, No. 2, pp. 257–282.
— 1977, "Recent Developments in Finance", *Journal of Banking and Finance*, 1, October, pp. 103–117.
Furusten, S., 1992, *Management Books—Guardians of the Myth of Leadership*, Licentiate thesis, Department of Business Studies, Uppsala University.
Gårdlund, T., 1976, *Marcus Wallenberg 1864–1943. Hans liv och gärning* (Marcus Wallenberg 1864–1943. His Life and Work), Stockholm: Norstedts.
Gaston, J., 1973, *Originality and Competition in Sciences*, Chicago, IL: Chicago University Press.
Geddes, B., 1992, "Explaining the Gap? A Sociological Analysis of the Relationship between Research and Practice in Accounting", *Paper Presented to an EIASM Workshop on "The Relationship between Accounting Research and Accounting Practice"*, Manchester, June 1992.
Gils, M. R. van, 1991, "Van Dam en de zin en onzin van de algemene bedrijfskunde", *Bedrijfskunde*, 63, pp. 17–20.
Gordon, R. A. & Howell, J. E., 1959, *Higher Education for Business*, New York: Columbia University Press.
Gosselink, F. J., 1986, *Organisatiekunde in historisch perspectief*, Onderzoeksrapport 8617/0, Rotterdam: Erasmus Universiteit.
— 1988, *Ontwikkelingen in de Organisatiekunde: Organisatiekunde en Maatschappelijke Kontekst*, Rotterdam: Proefschrift.
Goudriaan, J., 1932, "De ontwikkeling van de Bedrijfsleer als Toegepaste Wetenschap", in: de Jongh, J. G. *et al.*, *Bedrijfseconomische Studiën: een verzameling herdrukken van redevoeringen, referaten en artikelen*, Haarlem: De Erven F. Bohn, pp. 534–554.
Graichen, D. & John, F., 1964, "Das neue ökonomische System und die Ausbildung ökonomischer Hoch- und Fachschulkader in der DDR", *Wirtschaftswissenschaft*, 12, No. 11, pp. 1761–1775.
Graduate Management Admission Council, 1990, *Leadership for a Changing World. The Future Role of Graduate Management Education*, Los Angeles, CA: Graduate Management Admission Council.
Grether, E. T., 1959, "Handelsutbildning. American Style" (Business Education. American Style), *Ekonomen*, 35, No. 15, pp. 24–30.
Griffin, M., 1955, "Problems of Liberal Arts Magnified by Disunifying Campus Influences", *The Daily Pennsylvanian*, January 14, p. 3, 7.
Groenman, S. Hasselt, R. van & van Heek, F., 1959, *De Vestiging van Hoger Onderwijs in Oost-Nederland: een nadere uitwerking*, Enschede.

Gunnarsson, E., 1988, *Från Hansa till Handelshögskola. Svensk ekonomundervisning fram till 1909* (From the Hanseatic League to a School of Economics. Swedish Business Education up to 1909), Acta Universitatis Upsaliensis. Studia Oeconomiae Negotiorum 29, Uppsala: Almqvist & Wiksell International (diss.).

Gutenberg, E., 1951, *Grundlagen der Betriebswirtschaftslehre, Band 1: Die Produktion*, Berlin, Göttingen & Heidelberg: Springer.

— 1962, *Unternehmensführung: Organisation und Entscheidungen*, Wiesbaden: Gabler.

Gvisiani, D. M., 1974, *Management. Analyse bürgerlicher Theorien von Organisation und Leitung*, Berlin (DDR:) Die Wirtschaft.

Hagen, K. P., 1990, "Nobelprisen i økonomi for 1990" (The Nobel Prizes for Economics in 1990), *Sosialøkonomen*, 44, No. 11, pp. 10–12

Hager, K., 1971, "Die entwickelte sozialistische Gesellschaft", *Einheit*, 26, No. 11, pp. 1203–1242.

Hales, C. P., 1986, "What Do Managers Do? A Critical Review of the Evidence", *Journal of Management Studies*, 23, January, pp. 88–115.

Hallendorff, C., 1909, "Handelshögskolerörelsen och den svenska handelshögskolan" (The Business School Movement and the Swedish School of Economics), *Föredrag vid Handelskammarföreningens årsmöte den 24 april 1909* (Speach at the Annual Meeting of the Society of the Chambers of Commerce on 24 April 1909).

Halpern, S. A., 1985, "Professional Schools in the American University", *Working Paper # 6*, Comparative Higher Education Group, University of California, Los Angeles, CA (mimeo).

Handelshøjskolen i Århus 50 år (The History of Århus School of Economics), 1989, Århus: Handelshøjskolen i Århus.

Handelshögskolan i Stockholm (Stockholm School of Economics), 1909, Stockholm: HHS.

Handelshögskolan i Stockholm 1909–1959 (Stockholm School of Economics 1909–1959), 1959, Stockholm: HHS.

Harré, R. & Secord, P. F., 1982, *The Explanation of Social Behaviour*, Oxford: Blackwell.

Hartmann, W. D., 1980, *Management. Kapitalistische Führungstechniken im kritischen Vergleich*, Berlin (DDR): Die Wirtschaft.

— 1988, *Handbuch der Managementtechniken*, Berlin (DDR): Akademie-Verlag.

Hayes, R. H. & Abernathy, W. J., 1980, "Managing Our Way to Decline", *Harvard Business Review*, 58, July/August, pp. 67–77.

Haynes, P., 1991, "Management Education", *The Economist*, March 2, p. 2.

Heckscher, E., 1942, "Anders Berch och den ekonomiska vetenskapens första steg i Sverige" (Anders Berch and the First Steps of the Economic Sciences in Sweden), *Lychnos*, 7, pp. 33–64.

— 1951, "Handelshögskoleidéen och Handelshögskolans begynnelse i Sverige" (The Business School Idea and the Beginning of the Business School in Sweden), In: Forsberg, B. (ed.), 1951, *Handelshögskolorna i Sverige* (The Business Schools in Sweden), Stockholm: Forsbergs förlag, pp. 11–23.

Heinen, E., 1966, *Das Zielsystem der Unternehmung*, Wiesbaden: Gabler.

— 1969, "Zum Wissenschaftsprogramm der entscheidungsorientierten Betriebswirtschaftslehre", *Zeitschrift für Betriebswirtschaft*, 39, No. 4, pp. 207–220.

— 1971, "Der entscheidungsorientierte Ansatz der Betriebswirtschaftslehre", In: Kortzfleisch, G. von (ed.), *Wissenschaftsprogramm und Ausbildungsziel der Betriebswirtschaftslehre*, Berlin: Duncker und Humbolt, pp. 21–37.

Heitzer, H., 1984, *DDR:—Geschichtlicher Überblick*, Berlin (DDR): Dietz Verlag.

Hellauer, J., 1910, *System der Welthandelslehre*, Berlin: Puttkammer & Mühlbrecht.
Hensmann, J., 1969, *Die Entwicklung der Betriebswirtschaftslehre in Skandinavien unter besonderer Berücksichtigung Schwedens*, Inaugural Dissertation zur Erlangung des akademischen Grades eines Doktors der Wirtschaftswissenschaft durch die Rechts- und Staatswissenschaftliche Fakultät der Westfälischen Wilhelms-Universität zu Münster. (diss.).
Hertog, J. F. den, 1977, *Werkstructurering: Ervaringen met Alternatieve Werkorganisaties binnen het Philips Bedrijf*, Alphen aan den Rijn: Samsom.
Hiebisch, H. & Vorwerg, M. (eds.), 1965, *Sozialpsychologie im Sozialismus*, Berlin (DDR): Deutscher Verlag der Wissenschaften.
— (eds.), 1968, *Einführung in die marxistisch-leninistische Sozial-psychologie*, Berlin (DDR): Deutscher Verlag der Wissenschaften.
Hijmans, E., 1948, *Hoofdlijnen der Toegepaste Organisatie*. Deventer/Batavia: Kluwer.
— 1950, *De Toekomst van onze Arbeid*. Leiden: Stenfert Kroese.
Hjelt, A., 1900, *Det svenska tabellverkets uppkomst, organisation och tidiga verksamhet* (The Origin of the Swedish Collection of Statistical Tables, Its Organisation and Early Activities), Stockholm: Fennia.
Hofstede, G., 1980, *Culture's Consequences: International Differences in Work-related Values*, Beverly Hills, CA: Sage.
— 1983, "Motivation, Leadership, and Organizations: Do American Theories Apply Abroad?", *Organizational Dynamics*, 9, No. 1, pp. 42–63.
Hogan, M. J., 1987, *The Marshall Plan: America, Britain, and the Reconstruction of Western Europe*, Cambridge/New York: Cambridge University Press.
Hörnig, H., 1972, "Die Aufgabe der Wirtschaftswissenschaften in der Gegenwart", *Einheit*, 27, No. 5, pp. 616–624.
Horringa, D., 1966, *Ondernemingsbestuur in de Moderne Samenleving*, Utrecht/Antwerpen: Het Spectrum.
Hoskin, K. & Macve, R., 1988, "The Genesis of Accountability: The West Point Connection", *Accounting, Organizations and Society*, 13, No. 1, pp. 37–73.
Hugstad, P. S., 1983, *The Business School in the 1980s*, New York: Praeger.
Hundt, S., 1977, *Zur Theoriegeschichte der Betriebswirtschaftslehre*, Köln: Westdeutscher Verlag.
Jenks, C., et. al., 1979, *Who Gets Ahead? The Determinants of Economic Success in America*, New York: Basic Books.
Jensen, O. H., 1980, "Bedriftsøkonomen Dag Coward" (The Business Administration Scholar Dag Coward), In: Coward, D., 1980, *Studier i bedriftsøkonomi. Utvalgte artikler av professor dr. philos. Dag Coward* (Studies in Business Administration. Selected Papers by Professor Doctor Dag Coward), Bergen: Norges Handelshøyskole, pp. 1–10.
Jensen, O. H. & Strømme Svendsen, A., 1986, *Norges Handelshøyskole femti år* (The Norwegian School of Economics Fifty Years), Bergen: Norges Handelshøyskole
Johnson H. T. & Kaplan, R. S., 1987, *Relevance Lost: the Rise and Fall of Management Accounting*, Boston, MA: Harvard Business School Press.
Jonge, J. A. de, 1976, *De industrialisatie in Nederland*. Nijmegen: SUN.
Jönsson, S., 1992, "Editorial: Applying for Research Grants", *Scandinavian Journal of Management*, 8, No. 4, pp. 281–282.
Junker, B., 1951, "Svenska Ekonomföreningen 1938–1950" (The Swedish Association of Economists 1938–1950), In: Forsberg, B., *Handelshögskolorna i Sverige* (The Business Schools in Sweden), Stockholm: Forsbergs förlag, pp. 79–90.

Kagona, T., et al., 1981, "Mechanistic vs. Organic Management Systems: A Comparative Study of Adaptive Patterns of U.S. and Japanese Firms", *Annals of the School of Business Administration*, 25, Kobe University, Kobe, Japan.

Kampfert, K., 1957, "Gegen das Aufkommen revisionistischer Auffassungen in den Wirtschaftswissenschaften", *Wirtschaftswissenschaft*, 5, Sonderheft 3, pp. 1-19.

Kampfert, K. & Krause, W., 1960, "Für einen schnellen Umschwung in Lehre und Forschung an den wirtschaftswissenschaftlichen Fakultäten und Hochschulen", *Wirtschaftswissenschaft*, 8, No. 4, pp. 481-501.

Karnøe, P., 1992, "Approaches to Innovation in Modern Wind Energy Technology: Technological Policies, Science, Engineers and Craft Traditions in United States and Denmark 1974-1990", *Center for Economic Policy Research Publication No. 20, Stanford University*, Stanford, CA.

Karsten, L., 1990, *De achturendag*, Amsterdam: IISG.

Kastelein, T., Bijsterveld, K. & Meulen, H. van der, 1988, *Een eigenzinnige koers,: 40 jaar Faculteit der Economische Wetenschappen in Groningen*, Groningen: Rijksuniversiteit Groningen.

Kataoka, S., 1990, *Nihon Keiegakusi Jyosetsu* (Introduction to the History of Japanese Business Management Studies), Tokyo: Bunshindo.

Key, H., 1900, "Om betydelsen av handelshögskolor" (On the Importance of Business Schools), *Svensk Export*, 6, 149, pp. 73-76.

Kirkland, E. C., 1956, *Dream and Thought in the Business Community, 1860-1900*, New York: Cornell University Press.

Kirsch, W., 1971, *Entscheidungsprozesse*, Wiesbaden: Gabler (3 vols.).

— 1977, *Die Betriebswirtschaftslehre als Führungslehre: Erkenntnisperspektiven, Aussagensysteme, wissenschaftlicher Standort*, München: Institut für Organisation, Universität München.

Kjaer Hanssen, M., 1927, *Almindelig bedriftsokonomi* (General Business Administration), Copenhagen.

Klamer, A. & Colander, D., 1990, *The Making of an Economist*, Boulder: Westview.

Klein, P. W., 1966, *Traditionele ondernemers en economische groei in Nederland 1850-1914*, Public lecture, Rotterdam.

Kleßmann, C., 1984, *Die doppelte Staatsgründung*, Göttingen: Vandenhoeck und Ruprecht.

Koenen, S. & Plantenga, J. (eds.), 1986, *Amerika en de sociale wetenschappen in Nederland*, Utrecht: Grafiet.

Koike, K., 1981, *Nihon no Jyukuren Sugureta Jinzai-Keisei Sisutemu* (Labour Skills in Japan. An Outstanding System for Manpower Development), Tokyo: Yuhikaku.

Kono, T., 1984, *Strategy and Structure of Japanese Enterprise*, London: Macmillan.

Koubek, N., Küller, H. D. & Scheibe-Lange, I., 1980, *Betriebswirtschaftliche Probleme der Mitbestimmung*, Köln: Westdeutscher Verlag.

Koziolek, H., 1960, "Zur Lehre der politischen Ökonomie im Sozialismus", *Wirtschaftswissenschaft*, 8, No. 6, pp. 1030-1045.

Kristensson, R., 1936, *Omkostninger i bedriftsøkonomisk teori og kalkulasjon* (Costs in Business Administration Theory and Calculation), Bergen: Eides.

Kuhn, T. S., 1977, "The Essential Tension: Tradition and Innovation in Scientific Research", In: Kuhn, T. S., *The Essential Tension*, Chicago, IL: University of Chicago Press, pp. 225-239.

Kupfernagel, E. & Polaschewski, E., 1966, "Zur Theorie der Kostenrechnung", *Wirtschaftswissenschaft*, 14, No. 6, pp. 1409-1420.

Kupfernagel, E. *et al.*, 1970, "Über die weitere Entwicklung der sozialistischen Betriebswirtschaft bei der Gestaltung und umfassenden Anwendung des ökonomischen System des Sozialismus in der DDR", *Wirtschaftswissenschaft*, 18, No. 10, pp. 1504–1522.

Ladensack, K. & Weidemeier, A., 1977, *Leitungsentscheidungen—soziale Prozesse im Betrieb*, Berlin (DDR): Die Wirtschaft.

Lambers, H. W., 1959, "De industriële ondernemer in een bewegende economische orde", in: M. Rooy, *Ondernemend Nederland*, Leiden, pp. 96–121.

Lammers, C. J., 1963, *Het Koninklijke Instituut voor de Marine. Een sociologische Analyse van de inlijving van groepen adspirant-officieren in de zeemacht*, Assen: Van Gorcum.

— (ed.), 1965, *Medezeggenschap en Overleg in het Bedrijf*, Utrecht/Antwerpen: Het Spectrum.

Landa, O., 1990, "Human Resource Management in Czechloslovakia—Management Development as the Key Issue", In: Pieper, R. (ed.), *Human Resource Management. An International Comparison*, Berlin-New York: de Gruyter, pp. 155–176.

Lane, C., 1989, *Management and Labour in Europe*, Aldershot: Edward Elgar.

Lane, R. E., 1966, "The Decline of Politics and Ideology in a Knowledgeable Society", *American Sociological Review*, 31, No. 5, pp. 649–662.

Larson, M. S., 1977, *The Rise of Professionalism*, Berkeley, CA: University of California Press.

Ledarskap, 1987, "Ekonomerna styr företagen" (Business Graduates Control the Companies), 6, No. 11, pp. 45–46.

Lemmnitz, A., 1949, "Das Rentabilitätsprinzip in der demokratischen Wirtschaft", *Deutsche Finanzwirtschaft*, 3, No. 10, pp. 268, 275–278.

— 1958, "Einige Fragen der wissenschaftlichen und politisch-ideologischen Arbeit unserer Wirtschaftswissenschaftler", *Einheit*, 13, No. 2, pp. 257–267.

Lendin, W., 1946, "Hallendorff, Carl", In: *Svenska män och kvinnor 3* (Swedish men and women 3), Stockholm: Bonniers, pp. 256–257.

Liedman, S.-E., 1986, *Den synliga handen* (The Visible Hand), Stockholm: Arbetarkultur.

Light, D. W., 1983, "The Development of Professional Schools in America", In: Jarausch, K. H. (ed.), *The Transformation of Higher Learning 1860–1930*, Stuttgart: Klett-Cotta, pp. 345–365.

Lijftogt, S. G., 1966, *De genormaliseerde methode voor werkclassificatie, waardering en kritiek*, Proefschrift, Utrecht.

Limperg, T., 1950, "Het object der bedrijfshuishoudkunde voor de accountant", in: *Vijfentwintig jaar Maandblad voor Accountancy en Bedrijfshuishoudkunde*, Purmerend: Muusses, pp. 24–52.

Lindblom, C., 1990, *Inquiry and Change*, New Haven, CT: Yale University Press.

Lintsen, H., 1980, *Ingenieurs in Nederland in de Negentiende Eeuw*, Den Haag: Martinus Nijhoff.

Locke, R. R., 1984, *The End of the Practical Man: Entrepreneurship and Higher Education in Germany, France, and Great Britain, 1880–1940*, Greenwich CT: JAI Press.

— 1985, "Business Education in Germany: Past Systems and Current Practice", *Business History Review*, 59, Summer, pp. 232–253.

— 1989, *Management and Higher Education since 1940. The Influence of America and Japan on West Germany, Great Britain, and France*, Cambridge: Cambridge University Press

— 1993, "Business Education and Managerial Performance: A Study Comparing Japan and America to France, Germany and England", In: Brown, J. & Rose, M. (eds.), *Entrepreneurship and the Growth of the Firm*, Manchester: Manchester University Press.

Luostarinen, R. & Pulkkinen, T., 1991, *International Business Education in European Universities in 1990*. Helsinki: Helsingin Kauppakorkealuolun julkaisuja.

Maas, A., 1988, *Ongedefinieerde Ruimten: Sociaal-symbolische configuraties*, Delft: Eburon.

Maastrigt, A. J. van & Metzemaekers, L. A. V. M., 1983, *Een eeuw in balans: De wordingsgeschiedenis van Moret en Limperg, 1883–1983*, Nijmegen: Thieme.

Mahlberg, W., 1922, *Bilanztechnik und Bewertung bei schwankender Währung*, Leipzig: Gloeckner (2. ed.).

Malik, F., 1986, *Strategie des Managements komplexer Systeme*, Bern & Stuttgart: Haupt (2. ed.).

Man, H. de, 1988, *Organizational Change in its Context: A Theoretical and Empirical Study of the Linkages between Organizational Change Projects and their Administrative, Strategic and Institutional Environment*, Delft: Eburon.

March, J. G. & Olsen, J. P., 1976, *Ambiguity and Choice in Organizations*, Bergen: Universitetsforlaget.

March, J. G. & Simon, H. A., 1958, *Organizations*, New York: Wiley.

Marshall, R., 1987, *Unheard Voices: Labor and Economic Policy in a Competitive World*, New York: Basic Books.

Maurice, M., Sellier, F. & Silvestre, J.-J., 1986, *The Social Foundations of Industrial Power*, Boston, MA: MIT Press.

Maurice, M., Sorge, A. & Warner, W., 1980, "Societal Differences in Organising Manufacturing Units", *Organization Studies*, 1, pp. 59–86.

Mellerowicz, K., 1947, *Allgemeine Betriebswirtschaftslehre*, Berlin: de Gruyter (5. ed.).

— 1949, "Betriebswirtschaftslehre und politische Ökonomie", *Deutsche Finanzwirtschaft*, 3, No. 15, pp. 519–527.

— 1950, "Wirtschaftsordnung und Betriebsordnung—Das Problem theoretisch betrachtet", *Zeitschrift für Betriebswirtschaft*, 20, No. 8, pp. 497–509.

— 1952, "Eine neue Richtung in der Betriebswirtschaftslehre. Eine Betrachtung zu dem Buch von E. Gutenberg", *Zeitschrift für Betriebswirtschaft*, 22, No. 3, pp. 145–161.

— 1963, *Unternehmenspolitik*, Vol. 1, Freiburg: Haute.

Meulen, R. ter & Hoorn, W. van, 1982, "Psychotechniek en menselijke verhoudingen. Bedrijfspsychologie in Nederland tijdens en kort na het Interbellum", *Grafiet*, No. 1.

Meyer, H., 1990, "Human Resource Management in the German Democratic Republic: Problems of Availability and the Use of Manpower Potential in the High Qualification Spectrum", In: Pieper, R. (ed.), 1990, *Human Resource Management. An International Comparison*, Berlin & New York: de Gruyter, pp. 177–193.

Miller, E., 1990, *Barron's Guide to Graduate Business Schools*, New York: Barron's Educational Series (7th ed.).

Milner, B. S. & Tschishow, J. A., 1980, *Amerikanische bürgerliche Theorien der Leitung*, Berlin (DDR): Die Wirtschaft.

Ministry of Education (ed.), 1988, *Daigaku-Shinsa Youran* (Handbook of University Foundation and Examination), Tokyo: Bukyou-kyoukai.

— 1990, *Gakkou Kihon-Chousa Houkokusho* (Basic Statistics of Education. 2 Volumes), Tokyo: Ookurasho-Insatsukyoku.

Mossin, J., 1966, "Equilibrium in a Capital Asset Market", *Econometrica*, 34, No. 4, pp. 768–783.
Munthe, Å. W:son & Nordfeldt, A., 1907, *Handelshögskola i Stockholm. Redogörelse och förslag* (School of Business in Stockholm. Report and Proposal), Stockholm: Nordstedt & söner.
Mußler, W., 1962, "Die politische Ökonomie des Sozialismus muß ein wirksames Instrument für die Lösung volkswirtschaftlicher Aufgaben werden", *Einheit*, 17, No. 3, pp. 69–81.
"Naar een business school in Nederland", 1966/67, *Doelmatig Bedrijfsbeheer*, 18/19.
Nagaoka, K., 1987, "Business Management Study in Japan. Its Development under the Influence of Germany and the USA", *Paper presented at the Symposium on the Relationship between Academic Business Education and Industrial Performance in Europe and Japan*, Brussels, 21–22 May 1987.
National Economic Development Office, 1987, *The Making of Managers. A Report on Management Education, Training and Development in the USA, West Germany, France, Japan and UK*, London: National Economic Development Office.
Nicklisch, H., 1912, *Allgemeine kaufmännische Betriebslehre als Privatwirtschaftslehre des Handels (und der Industrie)*, Leipzig: Poeschel.
— 1932, *Die Betriebswirtschaft*, Stuttgart: Poeschel.
Nielsen, M. M., 1986, "Erhvervsøkonomiens udvikling i forskning och praksis" (The Development of Business Adminstration in Research and Practice), In: Andersen, H. (ed.), *Videnskabsteori & metodlaere for erhvervsøkonomer* (Theory of Science and Methodology for Business Administration Students), Fredriksberg: Samfundslitteratur, pp. 59–111.
Nordfelt, A., 1943, *Läroverksminnen. Ur Alfred Nordfelts memoarer* (Memories from the Secondary School. From the Memoirs of Alfred Nordfelt), Falun: Föreningen för svensk undervisningshistoria.
Norges Handelshøyskole 1936/37—1953/54, *Beretninger for året* ..... (Annual Reports), Bergen: Norges Handelshøyskole.
Norstrøm, C. J., 1991, "Bedriftsøkonomiens innhold" (The Content of Business Administration), Presentation at the 1991 Norwegian Conference of Business Administration, NHH, Bergen (mimeo).
Nultsch, G., 1955, "Über einige Fragen des ökonomischen Studiums", *Wirtschaftswissenschaft*, 3, No. 5, pp. 755–761.
Oelßner, F., 1952, *Über die wirtschaftliche Rechnungsführung*, Berlin (DDR): Die Wirtschaft.
Onderwijs en Onderzoek inzake Leiding van Bedrijven en Instellingen, 1964, Den Haag: Commissie Opvoering Productiviteit/sociaal-Economische Raad.
Paulson. E. W., 1940, *Norsk regnskapslovgivning. En bedriftsøkonomisk studie* (Norwegian Accounting Laws. A Study in Business Administration), Oslo: Aschehoug.
Penrose, E., 1980, *The Theory of the Growth of the Firm*, Oxford: Basil Blackwell (2. ed., 1. ed. 1959).
Perridon, L., 1967, "Ansätze und Methodik der Vergleichenden Betriebswirtschaftslehre", *Zeitschrift für Betriebswirtschaft*, 37, Heft 11, pp. 677–686.
Perridon, L., 1975, "Betriebswirtschaftslehre, Vergleichende", in: Grochla, E. & Wittmann, N. (eds.), *Handwörterbuch der Betriebswirtschaft*, Stuttgart: Poeschel, pp. 808–816.
Petander, K., 1912, *De nationalekonomiska åskådningarna i Sverige sådana de framträda i litteraturen. Bd I, 1718–1765* (The Economics Way of Thinking in Sweden as they Appear in the Literature. Vol. I, 1718–1765), Stockholm: Norstedts.

Pieper, R., 1988, *The Management of Technological Change in GDR Combines*, Berlin: Freie Universität Berlin.
— 1989a, "Rekonstruktion der Geschichte von Betriebswirtschaftslehre und Leitungswissenschaft in der DDR", *Die Betriebswirtschaft*, 49, No. 5, pp. 577–595.
— (ed.), 1989b, *Westliches Management—östliche Leitung. Ein Vergleich von Managementlehre und DDR-Leitungswissenschaft*, Berlin & New York: de Gruyter.
— 1989c, "The GDR System for Managing Change: The Managerial Instruments", In: Gerber, M. et al. (eds.), *Studies in GDR Culture and Society*, 9, Lanham & New York: University Press, pp. 35–56.
— 1989d, *Business Schools in den USA. Mythen und Fakten*, Berlin & New York: de Gruyter.
— 1990a, "Introduction", In: Pieper, R. (ed.), *Human Resource Management. An International Comparison*, Berlin & New York: de Gruyter.
— 1990b, "Personalmanagement und personalwirtschaftliches Wissen in der DDR—Versuch einer Bestandsaufnahme", In: Pieper, R. (ed.), *Personalmanagement. Von der Plan- zur Marktwirtschaft*, Wiesbaden: Gabler, pp. 7–48.
— 1991, "OD in Germany", *Organization Development Journal*, 8, No. 4, pp. 50–58.
— 1992, "Socialist HRM: An Analysis of HRM Theory and Practice in the Former Socialist Countries in Eastern Europe", *The International Executive*, 34, No. 6, pp. 499–516.
Pieper, R. & Richter, K. (eds.), 1990, *Management. Erfahrungen, Bedingungen, Ansichten*, Berlin (DDR) & Wiesbaden: Die Wirtschaft and de Gruyter.
Pierson, F. C. et. al., 1959, *The Education of American Businessmen*, New York: McGraw-Hill Book Company.
Polak, N. J., 1953, "Het huidige stadium en de naaste taak van de bedrijfsleer", in: H.T. Go en J.P. Kikkert (eds.), *Verspreide Geschriften van prof. dr. N.J. Polak*, Purmerend: Muusses, pp. 1–15.
Porter, J. L., Muller, H. J. & Rehder, R. R., 1989, "The Making of Managers: an American Perspective", *Journal of General Management*, 14, No 4, pp. 62–76.
Porter, L. W. & McKibbin, L. E., 1988, *Management Education and Development: Drift or Thrust into the 21st Century?*, New York: McGraw-Hill.
Projektgruppe im WSI, 1974, *Grundelemente einer Arbeitsorientierten Einzelwirtschaftslehre*, Köln: Westdeutscher Verlag.
Purg, D., 1990, "Human Resource Management in Yugoslavia: Problems and Perspectives", In: Pieper, R. (ed.), *Human Resource Management. An International Comparison*, Berlin & New York: de Gruyter, pp. 143–154.
Rapport van de Commissie Technische Studie en Maatschappijwetenschappen, 1962, november.
Rapport van de Contactcommissie Bedrijfsleven-Hoger Onderwijs, 1957, 17 mei, Den Haag.
Redaktionskollegium, 1957, "Das 30.Plenum und die Wirtschaftswissenschaften", *Wirtschaftswissenschaft*, 5, No. 2, pp. 161–165.
— 1962, "Zu den Aufgaben der Wirtschaftswissenschaften nach der 14. Tagung des Zentralkomitees der Sozialistischen Einheitspartei Deutschlands", *Wirtschaftswissenschaft*, 10, No. 2, pp. 161–168.
Redding, G., 1990, *The Spirit of Chinese Capitalism*, Berlin: de Gruyter.
Redlich, F., 1957, "Academic Education for Business: Its Development and the Contribution of Ignaz Jastrow (1856–1937). In Commemoration of the Hundredth Anniversary of Jastrow's Birth", *Business History Review*, 31, Spring, pp. 35–91.

Regnstrand, O., 1951, "Svenska Ekonomföreningen under dess första kvartssekel 1912–1937" (The Swedish Association of Business Graduates During Its First Twenty-Five Years 1912–1937), In: Forsberg, B. (red.), 1951, *Handelshögskolorna i Sverige* (The Business Schools in Sweden), Stockholm: Forsbergs förlag, pp. 53–78.

Rieger, W., 1928, *Einführung in die Privatwirtschaftslehre*, Nürnberg: Krische und Co.

Ronen, S., 1986, *Comparative and Multinational Management*, New York: Wiley.

Rossum, W. van, 1979, *Wetenschappelijke ontwikkeling als een sociologisch probleem met speciale aandacht voor ontwikkelingen in de Nederlandse bedrijfseconomie*, dissertatie, Amsterdam.

Ruml, F., 1928, "The Formative Period of Higher Commercial Education in American Universities", In: Marshall, L. C. (ed.), *The Collegiate School of Business*, Urbana: University of Illinois.

Saito, T., 1988, *Gendai no Keiei Kyoiku* (Contemporary Management Education), Tokyo: Chuo-Keizaisha.

— 1992, "Education of Management in Japan—Present and Future", In: *Proceedings of the First International Federation of Scholarly Management (IFSAM) Conference*, Tokyo, 7–9 September 1992, pp. 222–225.

Samuelson, R. J., 1990, "What Good Are B-Schools", *Newsweek*, May 14, p. 45.

Sandström, H., 1977, *Handelshögskolan vid Åbo Akademi 1927–1977* (The Business School at Turku Academy 1927–1977), Skriftserie utgiven av Handelshögskolan vid Åbo akademi, serie A:18, Turku.

Sankei-Shinbun, S. (ed.), *Daigaku o tou. Kouhaisuru Genba karano Houkoko* (Report on University Problems), Tokyo: Sinchousha.

Sayer, A., 1984, *Method in Social Science*, London: Hutchinson.

Schanz, G., 1977, *Grundlagen der verhaltensorientierten Betriebswirtschaftslehre*, Tübingen: Mohr.

— 1978, *Verhalten in Wirtschaftsorganisationen*, München: Vahlen.

Schär, J. F., 1911, *Allgemeine Handelsbetriebslehre*, Leipzig: Gloeckner.

Schieb, P.-A., 1990, "Des modèles nationaux ou un modèle européen?" (National Models or a European Model?), *Revue française de gestion*, 15, Mars-avril-mai, pp. 105–110.

Schlossman, S., Sedlak, M. & Wechsler, H., 1987, *The "New Look": The Ford Foundation and the Revolution in Business Education*, Los Angeles, CA: Graduate Management Admission Council.

Schmalenbach, E., 1911, "Die Privatwirtschaftslehre als Kunstlehre", *Zeitschrift für handelswissenschaftliche Forschung* 1911/1912, 6, pp.304–316.

— 1919, *Grundlagen dynamischer Bilanzlehre*, Leipzig: Gloeckner.

— 1922, *Goldmarkbilanz*, Berlin: Springer.

— 1947, *Die dynamische Bilanz*, Leipzig: Meiner (9. ed.).

Schmidt, F., 1921, *Die organische Bilanz im Rahmen der Wirtschaft*, Leipzig: Gloeckner.

Schneider, D., 1987, *Allgemeine Betriebswirtschaftslehre*, München: Vahlen (3. ed.).

Schneider, E., 1947, *Einführung in die Wirtschaftstheorie*, Tübingen: Mohr.

Schreber, D. (ed.), 1755–62, *Sammlung verschiedener Schriften, welche in die Ökonomischen, Policey- und Cameral auch andere Schriften einschliessen*, Halle: Henselmann.

Schück, H., (ed.), 1918, *Bokwetts gillet*, Uppsala: Uppsala universitet.

Seely, B. E., 1984, "The Scientific Mystique in Engineering. Highway Research at the Bureau of Public Roads", *Technology and Culture*, 25, No.4, pp. 798–831.

Seyffert, R., 1926, "Betriebswirtschaftslehre, ihre Geschichte", In: Nicklisch, H. (ed.), *Handwörterbuch der Betriebswirtschaft*, Stuttgart: Poeschel Verlag, Vol. 1, cc. 1198–1220.
Simon, H. A., 1947, *Administrative Behavior*, New York: MacMillan.
— 1991, *Models of My Life*, New York: Basic Books.
Smiddy, H. F. & Naum, L., 1954, "Evolution of a 'Science of Managing' in America", *Management Science*, 1, No. 1, pp. 1–31.
Smith, A., 1776, *An Inquiry into the Nature and Causes of the Wealth of Nations*, London.
Smith, K. V. & Goudzwaard, M. B., 1970, "Survey of Investment Management: Teaching versus Practice", *Journal of Finance*, 25, No. 2, pp. 329–47.
Söderlund, E., 1946, "Eli Heckscher", In: *Svenska män och kvinnor 3* (Swedish men and women 3), Stockholm: Bonniers, pp. 336–338.
Solomon, E., 1966, "What Should We Teach in a Course in Business Finance?", *Journal of Finance*, 21, No. 2, pp. 411–415.
Spender, J. C., 1989, *Industrial Recipes*, Oxford: Blackwell.
Staehle, W. H., 1989, "Entwicklung der Managementlehre in Deutschland", in: Pieper, R. (ed.) *Westliches Management—Östliche Leitung*, Berlin & New York: de Gruyter, pp. 13–36.
— 1991, *Management*, München: Vahlen (6. ed., 1. ed. 1983).
Staf, N. (ed.), 1972, "Borgarståndets protokoll från frihetstidens början" (The Records of the Burghers from the Beginning of the Gustavian Era), I: *Borgarståndet*, Stockholm: Almqvist & Wiksell.
Staritz, D., 1985, *Geschichte der DDR 1949–1985*, Frankfurt am Main: Suhrkamp.
Stieda, W., 1906, *Die Nationalökonomie als Univärsitätswissenschaft*, Leipzig: Königl. sächsischen
Stiglitz, J. E., 1975, "The Theory of 'Screening', Education and the Distribution of Income", *American Economic Review*, 65, June, pp. 283–300.
Strategie BBW 1992–2000, 1991, Heerlen: Open universiteit.
Stuart, B. S., 1990, *Top Business Schools: the Ultimate Guide*, New York: Arco: Prentice Hall Press.
Stuyvenberg, J. H. van, 1963, *De Nederlandsche Economische Hoogeschool 1913–1963*, Rotterdam: Nijgh van Ditmar.
Subocz, V., 1984, "Management Education in Japan: Extent, Directions and Problems", *Journal of Management Development*, 3, No. 4, pp. 23–46.
The Sunday Times, 1991, "Schools of Failure", 21 April, pp. 2–4.
Symposium Bedrijfskunde, 1984, 29–30 november, Noordwijk, 's-Gravenhage: Ministerie van Onderwijs en Wetenschasppen.
Taussig, F. W., 1967, *The Tariff History of the United States. Including a Consideration of the Tariff of 1930*, New York: A. M. Kelley.
Taylor, F. W., 1911, *Shop Management -Presented at the Saratoga meeting June 1903*, New York: McGraw-Hill Book Co.
Thompson, J. D., 1967, *Organizations in Action*, New York: Harper.
Thurow, L. T., 1972, "Education and Economic Equality", *Public Interest*, 28, Summer, pp. 66–81.
ter Vehn, A., 1959, *Kompendium. Inledning till företagsekonomien* (Compendium. Introduction to Business Administration), Gothenburg School of Economics (mimeo).
Teulings A. W. M. (ed.), 1978, *Herstructurering van de Industrie: Praktijk, beleid en perspectief*, Alphen aan den Rijn: Samsom.
Thamm, J., 1958, "Wie kann die Leitung unserer sozialistischen Betriebe verbessert werden?", *Einheit*, 13, No. 2, pp. 268–271.

Thompson, J. D., 1967, *Organizations in Action*, New York: McGraw-Hill.
Tichomirov, J. A., 1975, *Die Leitungsentscheidung*, Berlin (DDR): Staatsverlag der DDR.
Ulbricht, W., 1959, *Das Gesetz über den Siebenjahrplan und die Aufgaben der Partei bei der Durchführung des Planes in der Industrie*, Berlin (DDR): Dietz.
Ulrich, H., 1969, *Die Unternehmung als produktives soziales System*, Bern & Stuttgart: Haupt.
— 1984, "Skizze eines allgemeinen Bezugsrahmens für die Managementlehre", In: Ulrich, H. et al. (eds.), *Grundlegung einer allgemeinen Theorie der Gestaltung, Lenkung und Entwicklung zweckorientierter sozialer Systeme*, St. Gallen: Hochschule St. Gallen, Institut für Betriebswirtschaft, pp. 1–30.
Veblen, T., 1918, *The Higher Learning in America*, New York: B. W. Huebsch.
Vibaek, J. & Kobbernagel, J., 1980, *Foreningen til Unge Handelsmaends Uddannnelse 1880–1980* (The Association for the Education of Young Merchants 1880–1980), København: Nyt Nordisk Forlag Arnold Busck.
Vidmer, R. F., 1981, "The Management Theory 'Jungle' in the USSR", *ISMO*, 11, No. 3/4, pp. 3–22.
Vijfentachtig jaren statistiek in tijdreeksen, 1984. Den Haag: Centraal Bureau voor de Statistiek.
Vincenti, W., 1984, "Technological Knowledge without Science. The Innovation of Flush Riveting in American Airplanes", *Technology and Culture*, 25, No. 3, pp. 540–576.
Visitatiecommissie Open universiteit, 1990, *De Open universiteit: een tussenbalans*. Den Haag.
Vorwerg, G., 1971, *Führungsfunktion in sozialpsychologischer Sicht*, Berlin (GDR): Deutscher Verlag der Wissenschaften.
Vries, J. de, 1985, *Geschiedenis der Accountancy in Nederland*, Assen: Van Gorcum.
Wächter, H., 1980, *Praxisbezug des Wirtschaftswissenschaftlichen Studiums*, Expertise für die Studienreformkommission: Wirtschaftswissenschaften.
Waddington, C. H., 1940, *Science in War*, London: Allen & Unwin.
Walb, E., 1927, *Kameralwissenschaften und vergleichende Betriebswirtschaftslehre*, Köln: Oskar Müller Verlag.
Wallerstedt, E., 1988, *Oscar Sillén, Professor och praktiker. Några drag i företagsekonomiämnets tidiga utveckling vid Handelshögskolan i Stockholm* (Oscar Sillén. Professor and Practician. Some Features of the Early Development of Business Administration at the Stockholm School of Economics), Uppsala: Acta Universitatis Upsaliensis, Studia Oeconomiae Negotiorum 30, Stockholm: Almqvist & Wiksell.
Wanous, S. J., 1969, "A Chronology of Business Education in the United States", *Business Education Forum*, 23, No. 7, pp. 36–43.
Wattel, A., 1956, *The Teaching of Organization and Management of an Enterprise at Universities and in Industry in the United States: Report of Personal Experiences*, Philadelphia: Wharton School of Finance and Commerce, University of Pennsylvania.
— 1962, *Vorming voor Leidinggevende Arbeid in de Onderneming: het economisch-organisatorische vraagstuk van management-development*, Leiden: Stenfert Kroese.
Weingart, P., 1978, "The Relation between Science and Technology—A Sociological Explanation", In: Krohn, W. et al. (eds.), *The Dynamics of Science and Technology*, Dordrecht: Reidel, pp. 251–286.
Westney, D. E., 1987, *Imitation and Innovation. The Transfer of Western Organizational Patterns to Meiji Japan*, Cambridge, MA: Harvard University Press.

Weyermann, M. & Schönitz, H., 1912, *Grundlegung und Systematik einer wissenschaftlichen Privatwirtschaftslehre und ihre Pflege an Universitäten und Fachhochschulen*, Karlsruhe: Braun.
Whalley, P., 1986, *The Social Production of Technical Work*, London: Macmillan.
Whitehead, A. N., 1929, *The Aims of Education and Other Essays*, New York: MacMillan.
Whitley, R., 1984, *The Intellectual and Social Organisation of the Sciences*, Oxford: Oxford University Press.
— 1986a, "The Transformation of Business Finance into Financial Economics: The Roles of Academic Expansion and Changes in U. S. Capital Markets", *Accounting, Organizations and Society*, 11, No. 2, pp. 171–192.
— 1986b, "The Structure and Context of Economics as a Scientific Field", *Research in the History of Economic Thought and Methodology*, 4, Greenwich, CT: JAI Press, pp. 179–209.
— 1987, "Taking Firms Seriously as Economic Actors: Towards a Sociology of Firm Behaviour", *Organization Studies*, 8, No. 2, pp. 125–147.
— 1988a, "The Transformation of Expertise by New Knowledge: Contingencies and Limits to Skill Scientification", *Social Science Information*, 27, No. 3, pp. 391–420.
— 1988b, "The Management Sciences and Managerial Skills", *Organization Studies*, 9, No. 1, pp. 47–68.
— 1989, "On The Nature of Managerial Tasks and Skills. Their Distinguishing Characteristics and Organization", *Journal of Management Studies*, 26, No. 3, pp. 209–224.
Whitley, R., 1992, *Business Systems in East Asia*, London: Sage.
Whitley, R., Thomas, A. & Marceau, J., 1981, *Masters of Business. Business Schools and Business Graduates in Britain and France*, London: Tavistock.
Whyte, W. H. Jr, 1956, *The Organization Man*, New York: Simon and Schuster.
Wie Volgt Ons Op?: Rapport betreffende de Management Development in het Amerikaanse Bedrijfsleven uitgebracht door de Studiegroep Industrie, 1952, Den Haag: Contactgroep Opvoering Productiviteit.
Willmott, H., 1987, "Studying Managerial Work: A Critique and a Proposal", *Journal of Management Studies*, 24, No. 3, pp. 249–270.
Windmuller, J. P., 1969, *Labor Relations in the Netherlands*, Ithaca, NY: Cornell University Press.
Winternitz, J., 1950, "Zur Kritik der betriebswirtschaftlichen Metaphysik", *Deutsche Finanzwirtschaft*, 4, No. 2, pp. 52–57.
Wintgen, G., 1962, "Churchman, C. W., Ackoff R. C. & Arnoff, E. L.: Operations Research. (Buchbesprechung)": *Wirtschaftswissenschaft*, 10, No. 12, pp. 1895–1898.
Wöhe, G., 1975, "Betriebswirtschaftslehre, Entwicklungstendenzen der Gegenwart", In: Grochla, E. & Wittmann, W. (eds.), *Handwörterbuch der Betriebswirtschaft*, Stuttgart: Poeschel, pp. 710–747.
— 1990, "Business Administration: Present Theoretical Approaches", In: Grochla, E. et al., *Handbook of German Business Management*, Stuttgart: Poeschel, pp. 270–291.
Wren, D. A., 1987, *The Evolution of Management Thought*, New York: Wiley.
Wunderer, R. (ed.), 1988, *Betriebswirtschaftslehre als Management- und Führungslehre*, Stuttgart: Poeschl (2. ed.).

Yasumuro, K., 1993, "Organised Entrepreneurship and the Reconstruction of Japan's Export-Oriented Economy", In: Brown, J. & Rose, M. (eds.), *Entrepreneurship and the Growth of the Firm*, Manchester: Manchester University Press.

Young, M. D., 1958, *The Rise of the Meritocracy 1870–2033*, London: Thames and Hudson.

Zakboek onderwijsstatistieken, 1989, Den Haag: Centraal Bureau voor de Statistiek.

Zanden J. L. van & Griffith, R. T., 1989, *Economische geschiedenis van Nederland in de 20e eeuw*, Utrecht: Het Spectrum.

Zuthem, H. J. van, 1961 *De Integratie van de Onderneming als Sociologisch Vraagstuk*, Assen: Van Gorcum.

Name Index

Abbott, A. 167, 172, 174–175
Abernathy, W. J. 26
Ackoff, R. L. 175
af Trolle, U. 56
Afanasjew, V. G. 128
Albach, H. 116
Amdam, R. P. 11, 14, 73, 77, 80
Andersson, G. 48
Annerstedt, C. 37
Aoki, M. 163
Arndt, J. 73
Arnold, H. 122
Atkinson, P. A. 171
Auerbach, J. S. 174
Auras, H. H. 122, 124
Autorenkollektiv, 128

Bakke, E. W. 79
Barnevik, P. 45
Bartlett, C. A. 163
Becker, H. A. 103–104
Behrens, F. 121–122, 124
Behrman, J. N. 26
Beinum, H. J. van, 98, 102
Benary, A. 124
Bennet, P. G. 186
Berch, A. 13–14, 20, 33, 35–43, 45
Berch, C. 40, 46
Berch, C. R. 36
Berenschot, B. W. 95–96, 100, 103
Berg, I. 28
Berger, P. L. 23
Berger, W. 121–122, 124
Berglund, H. 49
Bertels, K. 92
Bhaskar, R. 175
Bierens de Haan, J. 88
Bijsterveld, K. 98
Blaug, M. 28
Bloemen, E. S. A. 88–90
Bohlin, E. 62
Böhme, G. 168–169
Böhren, Ø. 59
Böhring, G. 129
Bonder, S. C. 175
Boone, P. C. 97

Borch, K. H. 72, 75
Borchert, H. 122
Brandt, E. 78
Braß, H. 122, 124
Brevoord, C. 103
Byrt, W. 47

Cadwell, B. 169
Cals, J. M. L. Th. 103
Calvert, M. A. 172
Carlsson, S. 50, 56
Carrand, A. 97
Celsius, A. 33–34, 36
Chandler, A. D. Jr. 157
Charles, H. 163
Cheit, E. F. 24–26
Christernin, N. P. 43
Churchman, C. W. 184
Cicourel, A. 171
Clark, B. R. 18, 19
Clark, R. 181
Colander, D. 184
Collins, R. 25, 181, 185
Constable, J 19–20
Corcoran, M. 26
Coward, D. 69–71
Cyert, R. M. 22, 58, 102

Daele, W. van den, 169
Dahlberg, L. 62
Dam, C. van, 110
Dando, M. R. 186
Danzig, G. 128
Davenant, C. 38
Diesing, P. 169
Divall, C. 168
Doorn, J. A. A. van, 100
Duncan, O. D. 26

Economist Intelligent Unit, 163–164
Eichner, A. S. 169
Elteren, M. C. M. van, 97
Elvius, P. 38
Engwall, L. 11, 14, 20–23, 45, 49–50, 66, 73, 75
Eucken, W. 121

209

Ewing, D. W. 51

Fallon, I. 155–156, 159–160, 162, 164–165
Ferrner, B. 33, 36
Filseth, T. 70–71, 73
Fishgrund, T. 24
Fostvedt, A. 70–71
Frankfurter Allgemeine Zeitung, 131
Friedrich, G 124, 128–129
Friend, I. 183
Fromm, E. 119

Gårdlund, T. 46
Gaston, J. 185
Geddes, B. 173, 177, 186
Gerisch, R. 128
Ghosal, S. 163
Gils, M. R. van, 98, 102
Ginneken, J. van, 92
Gondzowaard, M. B. 171
Gordon, R. A. 22, 24, 26
Gosselink, F. J. 96–97
Goudriaan, J. 91–92
Graichen, D. 125
Grant, J. 38
Grether, E. T. 53
Griffin, M. 23
Groenman, S. 100
Grönfors, K. 49
Gunnarsson, E. 11, 19, 21, 45, 49, 51
Gutenberg, E. 15, 120–123, 126, 128
Gvisiani, D. M. 123, 128

Hagen, K. P. 72, 125
Håland, G. 70
Hales, C. 178
Hales, C. P. 26
Hallendorff, C. 21, 47–48, 52, 55
Halpern, S. A. 24
Hansen, M. K. 70, 73
Harré, R. 169
Hartmann, W. D. 128
Hasselt, R. van, 100
Hayes, R. H. 26
Haynes, P. 164
Heckscher, E. 21, 46, 48, 52, 55, 61
Heek, F. van, 100
Heinen, E. 126, 128
Heitzer, H. 119
Hellauer, J. 117
Hensmann, J. 47

Hertog, J. F. den, 102
Hiebisch, H. 125–126
Hijmans, E. 89, 96
Hjelt, A. 38
Hogan, M. J. 95
Holbaek-Hansen, L. 73
Hörnig, H. 125
Horringa, D. 105
Hoskin, K. 157
Howell, J. E. 22, 24, 26
Hugstad, P. S. 47
Hume, D. 43
Hundt, S. 120

Jangård, R. 72
Jastrow, I. 21
Jenks, C., *et al* 26
Jensen, O. H. 67, 69–71, 75
John, F. 125
Jonge, J. A. de, 86
Julinsköldd, P. 43
Junker, B. 53, 61

Kagona, T. 163
Kamp, J. J. 103
Kampfert, K. 122, 124
Karnøe, P. 29
Karsten, L. 11, 15
Kastelein, T. 98
Kataoka, S, 151
Keizer, J. A. 110
Kempen, P. M. 110
Key, H. 46
Kile, S. M. 72
King, G. 38
Kirkland, E. C. 21, 25
Kirsch, W. 126–127
Klamer, A. 184
Klein, P. 86
Kleßmann, C. 119
Knight, F. H. 69
Kobbernagel, J. 66
Koenen, S. 95
Koike, K. 146
Komissar, G. 75
Kono, T. 181
Koubeck, N. 121
Koziolek, H. 124–125
Krause, W. 122
Kristensen, R. 68
Kristensson, R. 68–70
Krohn, W. 169

Kuhn, T. S. 62, 175
Kupfernagel, E. *et al* 125, 127
Küller, H. D. 121

Ladensack, K. 128–129
Lambers, H. W. 86
Lammers, 102
Landa, O. 129
Lane, C. 181
Lane, R. E. 168,
Lemmnitz, A. 121, 124
Lendin, W. 21
Lewin, K. 22, 119
Lewin, R. I. 26
Liedman, S.-E. 11, 13, 20
Light, D. W. 21
Limperg, T. Jr, 86, 90–91, 93
Lindblom, C. 169
Linnaeus, C. 37, 41
Locke, R. R. 11, 16–18, 25, 46, 53, 62, 77, 84–85, 156–157, 167–168, 175
Louwerse, J. M. 90, 96
Luckmann, T. 23
Luostarinen, P. 155

Macve, R. 157
Mahlberg, W. 117
Major, J. 155
Malik, F. 126
Man, H. de, 12, 15
Marceau, J. 20–21, 47
March, J. G. 22, 25, 58, 102
Marken, J. C. van, 87–88
Marshall, R. 165
Maurice, M. 179, 181
McCormack, R. 19–20
McKibbin, L. E. 19, 22, 26, 28
Mellerowicz, K. 120–123
Mertens, 162
Meulen, H. van der, 98
Meyer, H. 129
Miller, E. 24
Mordt, G. 80,
Moss Kanter, R. 163
Mossin, J. 72, 75
Mulder, M. 98
Munthe, Å. W:son 46
Mußler, W. 124
Münsterberg, G. H. 92, 118
Myrvoll, O. 75

Nagaoka, K. 12, 16, 21, 151

National Economic Development Office, 19–20
Naum, L. 175
Nicklisch, H. 117–119
Nielsen, M. M. 53
Nordfeldt, A. 46
Norstrøm, C. J. 11, 14, 59
Nultsch, G. 122

Oelßner, F. 122
Øien, F. 73–74, 76
Olsen, J. P. 25

Paulson, E. W. 68–71
Penrose, E. 178
Petander, K. 33
Petty, W. 38
Pieper, R. 11, 15, 122–123, 127, 129–130, 132
Pierson, F. C. *et al*, 22, 24, 26
Plantenga, J. 95
Polack, N. J. 91
Polaschewski, E. 125
Porter, L. W. 19, 22, 26, 28
Pulkkinen, T. 155
Purg, D. 129

Quanjer, J. F. 89

Råfelt, 36
Rapport van de Commissie Technische Studie en Maatschappijwetenschappen, 104
Redaktionskollegium, 124
Redding, G. 187
Redlich, F. 19–21, 47, 167
Regnstrand, O. 61
Reuterskiöld, C.-A. 46
Rieger, W. 117
Roels, F. 92
Rosum, W. van, 91
Ruml, F. 47

Samuelson, R. J. 164
Sandström, H. 53
Sankei-Shinbun-Shakaibu, 150
Satio, T. 146, 151
Sayer, A. 175
Schanz, G. 127
Scheib, P.-A. 20, 155
Scheibe-Lange, I. 121
Schlossman, S. 24

Schmalenbach, E. 53, 69, 117, 120
Schmidt, F. 69, 117
Schmidt, J. 122
Schneider, D. 116, 121, 127, 129
Schneider, E. 69
Schreber, D. 41
Schück, H. 34
Schär, J. F. 117
Schönitz, H. 117
Secord, P. F. 169
Sedlak, M. 24
Seely, B. E. 168
Sellier, F. 179, 181
Seyffert, R. 47
Sillén, O. 48–49, 51, 55–56, 68
Simon, H. 99, 102
Simon, H. A. 22, 58
Smiddy, H. F. 175
Smith, A. 34–35, 40
Smith, K. V. 171
Snoep, P. P. 89
Söderlund, E. 21
Solomon, E. 171
Spender, J. C. 179
Staehle, W. H. 118, 123, 127, 129
Staf, N. 37
Staritz, D. 124
Stehr, N. 168
Stieda, W. 35
Stiglitz, J. E. 28
Strømme Svendsen, A. 67, 75
Stuart, B. S. 24
Stuyvenberg, J. H. van, 90
Subocz, V. 25

Taussig, F. W. 21
ter Vehn, A. 19, 47, 49, 55–56, 61, 68–70
Thamm, J. 124
Thomas, A. 20–21, 47
Thompson, J. D. 58
Thurow, L. T. 28
Tichomirov, J. A. 128
Törnqvist, G. 52, 56

Ulbricht, W. 124
Ulrich, H. 126

Västhagen, N. 49
Veblen, T. 23

Verhagen, E. J. 102
Vibaek, J. 66
Vidmer, R. F. 128
Vijfentachtig jaren statistiek in tijdreeksen, 106
Vincenti, W. 168
Volmer, J. G. C. 86, 88
Vorwerg, M. 125–126
Voß, P. 129
Vries, J. de, 86, 89

Waaler, R. 72
Wächter, H. 160–161
Waddington, C. H. 158
Walb, E. 48, 51, 55
Wallerstedt, E. 45, 48, 55, 69
Wanous, S. J. 47
Warner, W 179, 181
Waterink, J. 92
Wattel, A. 100–101, 104
Weber, M. 118
Wechsler, H. 24
Wedervang, F. 71
Wedervang, I. 69
Weidermeier, A. 128
Weingart, P. 169
Westbeck, G. 40
Westney, D. E. 21
Weyermann, M. 117
Whalley, P. 171
Whitehead, A. N. 28
Whitley, R. 12, 17, 20–21, 25, 47, 69, 174–175, 178–179, 181–182, 184–185, 187
Whyte, Jr, W. H. 25
Willmott, H. 178
Windmuller, J. P. 94
Winternitz, J. 121
Wintgen, G. 125
Wöhe, G. 116, 120
Wolff, C. 33
Wren, D. A. 116, 118
Wunderer, R. 129

Yasumuro, K. 159
Young, M. D. 26

Zuthem, H. J. van, 102

Subject Index

Aachen 116, 118
academic professional skills 173
academically certified skills 180
academization 178
accountants 15, 86, 89–91, 93
accounting 22, 68–71, 74, 88, 90, 94, 99, 102, 109, 111, 117, 119–120, 122–123, 125,143, 152–153, 160, 172
Administratieve Arbeid (Administrative Labour) 92
Administrative Research Foundation (ARF) 72, 79
administrative 91, 122
advertising 70
advertisment 71
Advisory Bureau for Organization and Metalworking 89
american 138, 150, 153, 156, 165, 167, 172
American Assembly of Collegiate Schools of Business 19
American business 153
American business schools 160, 164–165
American management 123, 126–127, 129, 132
American tradition 157
American counterparts 139
American dominance 14
American impact 21
American influence 15, 73, 81
Amsterdam 91, 93
Amsterdam university 90
Anglo-Saxon 180–181
Arbeiter- und Bauernfakultäten 119
Arnhem 101
athletics 23
auditing 70–71, 86, 143
autopoiesis 126
Bachelor of Business Administration (BBA) 19, 81, 105, 144
bachelor degree 155
balance sheets 28
banking 71, 153
barriers to entry 23
Bedriftskunde 84
Bedriftsøkonomen 67, 70

Bedriftsøkonomisk Institutt (BI) 73, 74
bedrijfsleer 90, 91
behaviour 127
behavioural 84, 100, 110,1 18, 129
behavioural approach 73
behavioural aspects 14, 22, 128
behavioural science 119, 126–128, 158
behavioural theories 53, 56–59
behaviourist psychology 169
Bergen 21, 73–80
Berlin 21, 118–119, 125, 130
Berlin wall 123
berufsfertig 17, 162
berufsfähig 17, 162
Betriebsgemeinschaft 119
Betriebswirtschaftslehre (BWL) 91, 116–118, 120, 122–123, 127–129, 132
Betriebswissenschaft 118
Betriebsökonomik 122
Bodø 66, 81
Bodø Graduate School of Business 78, 80, 82
bookkeepers 86
bookkeeping 70–71, 88, 90, 143, 152
Borgströmianska professuren 37
Breda 87
British Open university 108
British Tavistock Institute of Human Relations 98, 102
British 159, 163
British standard 86
business 80
business administration 22–23, 27, 66–72, 74, 79–80, 116–123, 127–128, 130–132, 146, 148, 150–153
business administration department 14, 79
business economics 90, 93, 94, 98, 101, 102, 106, 108–109, 112, 143
business economists 99, 103, 105, 111
business environment 143
business games 102
business history 153
business management 139–140, 143
business schools 14–6, 19, 21, 23–24, 46–56, 66–82, 84, 94, 99, 101, 105,107,

213

109–111, 117–118, 120, 122, 127–132
business schools 144, 148, 156, 158–159, 160, 162–163, 168, 181
business studies 104, 107–108, 110–112
capital asset pricing model (CAPM) 72
capitalism 121, 124
capitalist 122, 128, 178
career paths in Japanese firms 15
Carnegie Tech 158
Case Western 158
Central Normalization Bureau 89
Central Psychologicall Professional Office 92
CEO 147
certification 171, 177, 181
Christian Psychological Centre 92
civil school (HBS) 87
civil servants 35
civilekonom 19
civilekonom title 60–61
Cologne 19, 21, 70, 120
commerce 139–140, 152–153
commercial 91
commercial geography 67–68
commercial history 67–68
Commissie Opvoering Productiviteit 95
Committee on Technical Education and Social Sciences 103
competence standars 177
competing research based skills 173–174
computer 142
computing 125
Contact committee for Industry and Higher Education 103
Contactcommissie Opvoering Productiviteit 95
COP 95, 103
Copenhagen 21, 70, 73, 78
Cornell 101
corporate planning 102
cost accounting 68, 143
credentialization 186
credentialize 174
credentials 180
curricula 51–54
cybernetics 124–125, 128
data processing 76, 77, 143, 152
De felicitate patrioe per oeconomiam promovenda 33, 36
decision 160
decision science 158
decision-making 126–127

degree of control over skill definition and certification 173
Delft 87–88, 90, 92–93, 95, 99–100, 105, 111
Delft School of Management 107,
democratic 26,
Denkschulung 162
Department of Insurance 72
Department of Marketing 73
dependence on formal research based knowledge 173
Diplomkaufmann 81
dispositiver Faktor 120
distribution 71, 153
distribution and trade 70
distribution system 152
doctoral dissertations 57–59
Doelmatig Bedrijfsbeheer 105
dominant research based skills 173–174, 177
Drammen 79
Dutch academic degree 20
Dutch Accountants Association 86
Dutch Centre for Managers (NCD) 105
Dutch Institute for Efficiency (NIVE) 90, 101
Dutch Institute of Accountants 86
Dutch Institute of Preventive Medicine (NIPG) 102
École Polytechnique 87
Econometrica 72
Economic Cooperation Administration 95
economic science 13–4, 20, 33–36, 43
economic theory 72
economics 14–15, 21–23, 27, 52–53, 67, 69–70, 72, 74, 89–91, 93, 98, 104, 106, 109–110, 117, 119, 121, 127–128, 131, 139, 146, 151–152, 169
education 102
Eindhoven 100, 104, 108–109, 111
employer control 179
employers 17
engineer 15, 68, 72, 87, 89–91, 93, 98, 100, 103–104, 111, 177
engineering 25, 84, 94, 109–110, 112, 118, 159, 167–168, 170–172
engineering schools 158
English accountancy 173
English accountancy associations 177
English accounting departments 186
entrepreneurship 159

entscheidungsorientierte 126
European business 153
express trains 147
extent of control over work jurisdictions by academically certified skills 173
Fachhochschulen 27
finance 22, 70–71, 74, 77, 109, 117, 130, 143, 153, 158, 160
financial 14, 91
financial economies 184–185
financial mathematics 70
foreign inspiration 51–53
foreign languages 117
formal knowledge 17, 170–172, 187
formal research based knowledge 175
Foundation of Normalization in the Netherlands 89
Frankfurt 120
Frankfurt School 119
functional management 153
Führungslehre 129
German 156, 172
German background 99
German influence 14, 20–21, 81
German invasion 68
German tradition 66
German type 81, 138
Germany 69, 91, 94, 155, 160, 167, 169, 179, 181
Global Human Rescource Management 163
Gothenburg 21
Gothenburg School of Economics 14, 49, 56
graduated diffusion 59–62
Grandes Écoles 21
Groningen 98, 108, 111
Groningen School of Management 100
Groningen University 105
group 163
Grundlagen in die Betriebswirtschaftslehre 120
Handelshochschule 19, 67, 74, 91, 116 , 119
Handelshögskola 19
Handelshøjskolen i Århus 66
Handelshøyskole 19
Handelswissenschaft 117
Hannover 118
Harvard 69, 73, 93, 101, 155, 167
Harvard Advanced Management Course 79

Harvard University 118
Hembrug 89
Henley Administrative Staff College 79
Hesse (Rinteln) 35–36
history 21, 23, 131
history of business and entreprise 143
history of management 143
history of management ideas 153
Hochschule für Ökonmie 130
Hogere school 88
Hoogeschool 88, 91
Human Relations 15, 98, 118
human resource management 129–130
humanities 25–26
Humbolt University 119, 121
individual 163
industrial administration 158
industrial consultants 90
industrial economics 68
industrial engineering 84, 118
industrial organisation 70
industrial psychology 72, 93, 102
industrial relations 143
information 142
Inledning till Allmänna Hushållningen (Introduction to General Economic Science) 39
Institut für Sozialistische Wirtschaftsführung 125
Institute of Sales and Advertizing 69
Institute of Technology in Trondheim 68
institutions 45–51
insurance 70, 72
intellectual standards 183
Interacademic Foundation for Oranization Studies (SIOO) 101
International University Contact for Management Education 100, 103
international business 143
international business management 153
international management 142
Introduction to General Economic Science 40
Japan 117, 160, 169, 181
Japanese 163
Japanese business history 143
Japanese education system 138
job reassignments 147
Kaufmann/Diplom Ökonom 20
kaufmännischer Direktor 118
key qualifications 160
Kristiansand/Agder 66, 81–82

kunstleer 90
kunstlehre 91, 117
language 67–68, 92
law 25, 67–68, 99, 104, 109, 117, 143, 146, 172, 174
lawyers 103
lay control 186
Leipzig 116, 119, 121
Leipzig University 118
Leitungswissenschaft *15*, 123–124, *127–128, 130*
Leyden 102
lifetime employment 145–146
linear programming 102, 158
Linnaeus 41
local trains 147
Lunds University 50, 56–57
Lutheran countries 35
M.B.A. 19, 21, 108, 132, 144, 148, 152, 159, 162–163, 173, 178, 180–181
maîtrise 20,
Management and Higher Education Since 1940 156
management accounting 28
management information 139
management information system 152–153
management science 123, 153, 167
management theory 142
managerial economics 22
managers 17
Mannheim 120
marketing 22, 70, 102, 109, 127, 130, 158, 160
Marxism 127
Marxist-Leninist Organization Theory 125
Master of Arts
Master of Business Administration 19, 21, 108, 132, 148, 152, 159, 162–163, 173, 178, 180–181
master's degree 155
mathematical 27–28, 98–99, 101, 169
mathematical model 160, 162
mathematical model building 158
mathematics 16, 33, 74, 76–77, 84, 101, 110, 121, 125, 143
Max-Planck-Institut 131
medicine 172
mercantilism 34, 40
meritocratic 26
microeconomics 120–121

military 17
Ministry of Foreign Affairs 88
MIT 101, 158
money 153
Munich 126
natural science 109
Nederlandse Maatschappij voor Nijverheid en Handel (Dutch Society for Industy and Commerce) 101
neo-classical economies 183
Neuchâtel 78
New Economic System (NÖS) 124–125
new paradigm 17, 22, 24, 77, 84, 94, 99, 110–111, 156–157, 167–170, 187
new science paradigm 158
Nijenrode 101, 105, 108
Nijmegen Catholic University 108
NIPG 98, 100
Nobel Prize 72
Norges Handelshöyskole 67, 69, 78
North American influences 99
Norwegian Association of Master of Science in Business 78
Norwegian Parliament (Stortinget) 75
Norwegian School of Economics and Business Administration in Bergen (NSEBA) 14, 19, 66–69, 71–73, 75–80, 82
Norwegian School of Management (NSM) 14, 66–67, 73–82
Norwegian School of Management in Oslo 79
Norwegian School of Marketing 81–82
Norwegian State Educational Loan Found 78
Nuremberg 161
Nürnberg 120
oeconomia principum 34
oeconomia privata 34
oeconomia publica 34
off-the-job-training 148
Open university of the Netherlands 108
operations research 22–23, 76–77, 99, 123–124, 126, 158, 175, 184–185
Order of Consulting Engineers 89
organization 71, 118, 122, 127
organization people 17
organization psychology 72
organization theory 104, 127, 142–143
organizational behaviour 130
organizational sociology 102
Oslo 73, 79–80

Oslo Business School 81, 82
Oslo Institute of Business Administration 67
perestroika 128
performance criteria 173
Personalwirtschsaftslehre 127
personnel 99, 109
personnel management 71, 72, 118, 127
personnel recruitment 22
personnel selection 118
Ph. D. 72–73, 75, 144, 148–149
philosophy 104
physics 74
planning 122, 128
political arithmetic (statistics) 13, 38, 40
political economy 15, 37, 120–123
political science 131
polytechnic 93
Polytechnique 87–88
practical man 25
practical philosophy 34
practical skills 170
practioner elites 17
private donation 41
private universities 140
Privatwirtschaftslehre 117–118
problem selection 171
problem solving activities 171, 173, 177
professional craft skills 173
professions 172
professorial evaluations 55–57
professorship 13
profit-and-loss statements 28
protestant Free University of Amsterdam 92, 102
Prussia (Halle and Frankfurt an der Oder) 35, 36
Psychologie und Wirtschaftsleben 92
psychologists 15, 93
psychology 102, 104, 118, 143
psychotechnicians 92
PTT 104
Public Business Organization (PBO) 95
RAND Corporation 158
regional (including municipal) 139
regional colleges 66
Reichswirtschaftsrat 117
reputational control 183, 186
research based knowledge 171
research methods 184
research orientation 54–59
research-based knowledge 17–18, 187

Retrenchment and Efficiency Congress 90
retrenchment inspectors 90
risk and insurance 70
rites of incorporation 23
Rockefeller scholarship 69
Rotterdam 91, 94, 103, 105–105, 107–109, 111
Rotterdam School of Economics 98, 105
Royal Academy 87
Royal Decree 87
Royal Institute of Engineers 89
Royal Institute of Technology in Stockholm 68
Russian 122
sales 70–71
Scale and Scope: The Dynamcis of Industrial Capitalism 157
Scandinavia 117
Schlüsselqualifikationen 17, 160
School of Economics and Commercial Law (Gothenburg) 19
School of Management 105
scientific management 22, 27, 90, 92, 95, 118
scientific method 17
scientification 178
screening 23
seniority 145
Shop Management 88
sivilökonom 14, 19, 66, 74–77, 78–82
skill definition 171
skill development 171–172
social psychology 98, 102, 119, 126
social science 104, 106, 138–140, 142, 144, 146, 150, 160
socialism 121, 123–124
socialist 122, 125, 129–131
socialist economy 128
Society for Commerce and Industry 88–89
socioeconomic 91
sociological 125
sociology 98, 102, 119, 125–126, 131, 143, 163–164, 187
solving problems 171
Soviet Union 123–124, 128
Sowjetwissenschaft 122
Sozialistische Wirtschaftsführung 125–126
St. Gallen 78, 116
St. Louis 88

217

state 17, 139
statistical analysis 158
statistics 38, 76–77, 143, 158
Stichting Studiecentrun Bedrijfsbeleid 101
Stockholm 1, 21
Stockholm School of Economics 14, 19, 21, 46–56, 68
Stockholm University 50, 56–58
strategic management 130
strategic management research 184
Study Centre for Business Policy 101
Superior School of Commerce 90, 98
Superior School of Commerce in Rotterdam 91
Superior School of Economics in Rotterdam 91
Swiss 126
systems approach 128
systems theory 15, 84, 102, 124, 126
Sätt, att igenom Politisk Arithmetica utröna länders och rikens Hushållning 38
tacit knowledge 168
task definition 177
Taylorism 88, 89
technical 91
Technische Hogeschool Delft 105
Technische Hogeschool Eindhoven 104
technischer Direktor 118
terminology 18
The Visible Hand: The Managerial Revolution in American Business 157
The wealth of Nations 40
Theatrum Oeconomico-Mechanicum 13, 41
Theoretical physics 76
Tillburg School of Economics 98
time-and-motion study 22

trade 70
Traning institute for Foreign Countries 101
Treuhand 130
Twente 100, 108–109, 111
U.C.L.A. 155
U.K. 159
U.S. Air Force 158
U.S. economy 169
U.S.A. 168, 172, 181
United Kingdom 155
United States 68, 119
University of Chicago 69
University of Oslo 69, 72, 76
Uppsala 35
Uppsala University 45–46, 50
utilitarians 35
Utrecht university 92
Vienna 116
Vulgärökonomie 121
Werturteilsstreit 118
Wharton School 19, 21, 23, 101
Wirtschaftliche Rechnungsführung 122
Wirtschaftswissenschaften 127
Wissenschaft 21, 27
work jurisdictions 17, 171–172
work organization 179
World Exhibition 88
Yeast and Methylated Spirit Works in Delft 87
Zeitschrift für betriebswirtschaftliche Forschung 117
Zeitschrift für Handelswissenschaft und Handelspraxis (DBW) 117
Zeitschrift für Handelswissenschaftliche Forschung (ZfbF) 117
Zentralinstitut für sozialistische Wirtschaftsführung 130
Zweigökonomien 128

ACTA UNIVERSITATIS UPSALIENSIS
Studia Oeconomiae Negotiorum
Editors: Lars Engwall & Jan Johanson

1. Sune Carlson: International Business Research. 1966.
2. Mats Forsgren & Nils Kinch: Företagets anpassning till förändringar i omgivande system. En studie av massa- och pappersindustrin. 1970.
3. John Skår: Produksjon og produktivitet i detaljhandelen. En studie i teori, problem og metode. 1971.
4. Anders Mattsson: Dumping och antidumpingåtgärder. 1972.
5. Anders Mattsson: The Effects of Trade Barriers on the Export Firm. 1972.
6. Erik Hörnell & Jan-Erik Vahlne: The Deciding Factors in the Choice of a Subsidiary Sales Company as the Channel for Exports. 1972.
7. Finn Wiedersheim-Paul: Uncertainty and Economic Distance. Studies in International Business. 1972.
8. Björn Wootz: Studies in Industrial Purchasing with Special Reference to Variations in External Communication. 1975.
9. Håkan Håkansson: Studies in Industrial Purchasing with Special Reference to Determinants of Communication Patterns. 1975.
10. Hans Christer Olson: Studies in Export Promotion: Attempts to Evaluate Export Stimulation Measures for the Swedish Textile and Clothing Industries. 1975.
11. Sune Carlson: How Foreign is Foreign Trade? A Problem in International Business Research. 1975.
12. Lars Engwall & Jan Johanson (eds.): Some Aspects of Control in International Business. 1980.
13. Lars Hallén: International Industrial Purchasing: Channels, Interaction, and Governance Structures. 1982.
14. Hans Jansson: Interfirm Linkages in a Developing Economy. The Case of Swedish Firms in India. 1982.
15. Björn Axelsson: Wikmanshyttans uppgång och fall. En kommentar till angreppssättet i en företagshistorisk studie. 1982.
16. D. Deo Sharma: Swedish Firms and Management Contracts. 1983.
17. Pervez N. Chauri: Negotiating International Package Deals. Swedish Firms and Developing Countries. 1983.
18. Lars Engwall (ed.): Uppsala Contributions to Business Research. 1984.
19. Jannis Kallinikos: Control and Influence Relationships in Multinational Corporations. The Subsidiary's Viewpoint. Application of the Resource Dependence Perspective for Studying Power Relationships in Multinational Corporations. 1984.
20. Edith Penrose: The Theory of the Growth of the Firm Twenty-Five Years After. 1985.

ACTA UNIVERSITATIS UPSALIENSIS
Studia Oeconomiae Negotiorum
Editors: Lars Engwall & Jan Johanson

21. Amjad Hadjikhani: Organization of Manpower Training in International Package Deals. Temporary Organizations for Transfer of Technology. 1985.
22. Lars Engwall: Från vag vision till komplex organisation. En studie av Värmlands Folkblads ekonomiska och organisatoriska utveckling. 1985.
23. Anders Larsson: Structure and Change. Power in the Transnational Enterprise. 1985.
24. Bengt Lorendahl: Regionalutvecklings- och lokaliseringsprocesser. Beslut och handling i kommunal näringspolitik och industriell lokalisering. 1986.
25. Howard Aldrich, Ellen R. Auster, Udo H. Staber & Catherine Zimmer: Population Perspectives on Organizations. 1986.
26. Peter J. Buckley: The Theory of the Multinational Enterprise. 1987.
27. Malcolm Borg: International Transfers of Managers in Multinational Corporations — Transfer Patterns and Organizational Control. 1988.
28. Carl G. Thunman: Technology Licensing to Distant Markets — Interaction Between Swedish and Indian Firms. 1988.
29. Elving Gunnarsson: Från Hansa till Handelshögskola. Svensk ekonomundervisning fram till 1909. 1988.
30. Eva Wallerstedt: Oskar Sillén — Professor och praktiker. Några drag i företagsekonomiämnets tidiga utveckling vid Handelshögskolan i Stockholm. 1988.
31. Alexandra Waluszewski: Framväxten av en ny mekanisk massateknik — en utvecklingshistoria. 1990.
32. Sune Carlson: Executive Behaviour. Reprinted with contributions by Henry Mintzberg and Rosemary Stewart. 1991.
33. Harold Demsetz: The Emerging Theory of the Firm. 1992.
34. Horst Albach: The Transformation of Firms and Markets. A Network Approach to Economic Transformation Processes in East Germany. 1994.
35. Lars Engwall & Elving Gunnarsson (eds.): Management Studies in an Academic Context. 1994.

Distributed by
Almqvist & Wiksell International, Box 4627,
S-116 91 Stockholm, Sweden

ISSN 0586-884X
ISBN 91-554-3238-7

1
MC